Meat Matters

Changing Perspectives on Early Modern Europe

James B. Collins, Professor of History, Georgetown University
Mack P. Holt, Professor of History, George Mason University

(ISSN 1542-3905)

Changing Perspectives on Early Modern Europe brings forward the latest research on Europe during the transformation from the medieval to the modern world. The series publishes innovative scholarship on the full range of topical and geographic fields and includes works on cultural, economic, intellectual, political, religious, and social history.

Private Ambition and Political Alliances:
The Phélypeaux de Pontchartrain Family
and Louis XIV's Government, 1650–1715
Sara E. Chapman

The Politics of Piety: Franciscan Preachers
During the Wars of Religion, 1560–1600
Megan C. Armstrong

"By My Absolute Royal Authority":
Justice and the Castilian Commonwealth
at the Beginning of the First Global Age
J. B. Owens

Meat Matters: Butchers, Politics, and Market
Culture in Eighteenth-Century Paris
Sydney Watts

Meat Matters

Butchers, Politics, and Market Culture in Eighteenth-Century Paris

Sydney Watts

University of Rochester Press

First published 2016
Transferred to digital printing 2019

University of Rochester Press
668 Mt. Hope Avenue, Rochester, NY 14620, USA
www.urpress.com
and Boydell & Brewer Limited
PO Box 9, Woodbridge, Suffolk IP12 3DF, UK
www.boydellandbrewer.com

ISSN: 1542-3905
ISBN: 978-1-58046-211-2

Library of Congress Cataloging-in-Publication Data

Watts, Sydney, 1965–
Meat matters : butchers, politics, and market culture in eighteenth-century Paris / Sydney Watts.
p. cm.—(Changing perspectives on early modern Europe, ISSN 1542-3905)
Includes bibliographical references and index.
ISBN 1-58046-211-1 (hardcover : alk. paper)
1. Meat industry and trade—France—Paris—History—18th century. 2. Meat industry and trade—Government policy—France—Paris—History—18th century. 3. Butchers—France—Paris—History—18th century. I. Title. II. Changing perspectives in early modern Europe
HD9422.8P2 W38 2006
338.1'760094436109033—dc22

2005032884

A catalogue record for this title is available from the British Library.

For Sarah

CONTENTS

Illustrations

Acknowledgments

In the many years spent researching and writing this book, I have benefited from the support of numerous people and institutions. My studies at Cornell, where this work began, were made possible through the support of the Andrew W. Mellon Foundation (Sage Fellowship), the Institute for European Studies (Einaudi Fellowship and Sicca Grant), and the History Department (Gilmore Fellowship). My advisor, Steven Kaplan, provided invaluable direction in the conception, research, and writing of the dissertation, *Meat Matters*. This project also profited from the knowledge and wisdom of many other university professors: Jane Fajans, Isabel Hull, Dominick LaCapra, Rachel Weil, John Borneman, David Sabean, and Govind Sreenivasan. I am deeply indebted to members of the European History Colloquium, including Cynthia Koepp, Ben Brower, Eileen Crosby, Mary Gayne, Kelly Grotke, John Lee, Tracy Matysik, and Judith Surkis who read early versions of chapters. My special thanks to Sara Beam, Daniella Kostroun, Clare Crowston, Janine Lanza, and Vu Pham for their encouragement and camaraderie over the past decade.

As this project progressed I benefited from the critiques and comments of many historians in France, especially Daniel Roche, Jean-Michel Roy, Yves-Marie Bercé, Giles Postel-Vinay, Martin Bruegel, and Jean-Michel Chevet. During my research years, the Ecole des Hautes Etudes provided a stimulating and warm environment where I profited from many seminars and discussions with Jacques Revel, Simona Cerutti, Arlette Farge, Jean-Yves Grenier, Maurice Aymard, and Jean-Louis Flandrin.

The transformation of this dissertation into a publishable work took place in another supportive academic home, the University of Richmond, which provided travel grants, three summers of funding, and one semester's leave to complete this project. David Routt, Joan Bak, Woody Holton, Teri Halperin, Ed Larkin, and Erik Craft read drafts and made helpful suggestions. Hugh West, my department chair, not only provided support and guidance through my first years as a professor, but also read the entire manuscript at an early stage and offered perhaps some of the most salient comments that helped put the conceptual framework in place. I have also been extremely fortunate in working with a group of productive scholars (Laura Browder, Abigail Cheever, Dorothy Holland, Carol Summers, and Janet Winston) who read virtually every word as this project moved toward completion. Kathy Fugett and Debbie Govoruhk provided invaluable departmental support and countless blessings. Student assistants David Schilling, Marty Manor, and Vanessa Giles aided me and cheered me on to the finish line. My dear friend and colleague, Joanna Drell, ministered me selflessly through the trials and tribulations of academic publishing; for this, I cannot thank her enough.

I have been fortunate to draw on the expertise of a vibrant circle of Old Regime scholars in Washington, DC. I am deeply indebted to James Collins not only for his mentorship; but his careful reading and suggestions that helped me distill the arguments and synthesize a great deal of research. My thanks to Mack Holt, Thomas Brennan, and Donald Sutherland for their comments that made me think afresh about the topic while keeping me grounded in early modern French history. The Economic History group at the University of Pennsylvania challenged, in the best collegial spirit, my rather unorthodox approach to markets and credit for which I am grateful. Bill Sewell, Donna Gabaccia, Phil Scranton, and Haim Burstin also offered critical remarks at various conferences that improved the work. This book is much richer thanks to a serendipitous encounter that evolved into a three-year collaboration with fellow meat historians Jeffrey Pilcher and Roger Horowitz, the results of which were published in *The American Historical Review*. My thanks to the anonymous readers who carefully read and critiqued the manuscript, and to Suzanne Guiod and her editorial staff at University of Rochester Press, whose professionalism, assiduousness, and timeliness were greatly appreciated.

Finally, this work could not have been completed without the support of my family. I am blessed by the generosity and encouragement of Sarah, Valerie, Jeff, Miles, Michelle, Tom, and most dearly, Lila. Blair's love, most of all, has provided me with strength, perspective, and constancy. The joy in my heart is Seth. The inspiration and lifelong example of scholarship I take from my mother to whom this book is dedicated.

S. W.
January 2006

Figure 1: *Le Boucher* (The Butcher), a late seventeenth-century engraving by François Guérard, shows an artisan butcher serving a female client. The large dog "guarding" the butcher stall exemplifies the important role that domestic animals played in the workplace. Used with permission of the Bibliothèque Nationale de France.

Introduction

In September 1774, former Minister Léonard-Jean-Baptiste Bertin (1719–1792) wrote to then Controller General Anne-Robert-Jacques Turgot (1727–1781), remarking how the attitude of Parisians toward food provisions had shifted. As he explained it, butcher's meat (that is, beef, veal, and mutton) represented "a commodity in some sort of first necessity, as is white bread."[1] In that same year, a burgeoning demand for red meat–a demand that defied Lenten rules of fasting and fueled an expansive black market–dictated a royal edict to end state-enforced fasting. In October of 1790, the popular consumption of red meat had become a major political issue for Parisian revolutionaries addressing the newly constituted National Assembly.[2] At the height of the revolution, the Jacobins designated meat as one of the primary goods to fall under the 1793 Law of the General Maximum. A fixed price and rationing were instituted to ensure that every Parisian enjoyed a continuous supply of meat as a dietary staple.

The importance of red meat–the primary good of the butcher trade–grew for Parisians as the city itself expanded. Over 40,000 steer and over twice that number of sheep were needed to provision Paris in 1637 (pop. 412,000). As the city's population surpassed a half-million by the beginning of the eighteenth century, cattle traders and farmers supplied anywhere from 150,000 to 200,000 head of cattle (including cows and veal) and 300,000 to 400,000 sheep.[3] Paris rivaled London not only in its size and in its concentration of urban elites, merchants, and artisans, but also as the land of beef eaters, consuming on average 60 kilograms (132 pounds) of beef and mutton per year.[4] Paris, like London, was the country's center for consumption, a magnet that drew skilled and unskilled labor and raw and finished goods. A network of local and regional markets developed to make the capital relatively rich in fresh meat.

Most French people living outside of Paris considered meat a luxury; Parisians, however, did not live by bread alone. This robust consumption compelled the governing class to acknowledge not only the economic significance of meat, but also its political and social importance for Parisians. The leadership recognized its responsibility for provisioning the burgeoning capital and understood the connection between the food supply and the city's political and social stability.

This large-scale demand for meat underscored its power as a consumable, a power both material and symbolic. Although the decision to consume meat was governed by its quality, availability, and affordability, its consumption carried more subtle and sometimes contradictory meanings. A meat-centered diet was viewed as the epitome of good living and a guarantee of good health, whereas the violent slaughter of livestock and the gluttonous impulse behind its consumption made it synonymous with carnality and sexual excess. Both the upsurge in the desire to eat meat and the efforts of political leaders to ensure its consistent supply occurred against the backdrop of a transformation in Parisian society and politics, especially the Parisians' changing expectations regarding political leadership, as the onetime subjects became citizens in the 1790s.

This book examines why meat mattered to a growing number of Parisians and explores the political, economic, and cultural matters of the meat trade in order to understand more fully the changing world of Old Regime Paris. Hundreds of guild butchers, along with numerous merchants and street vendors, played a vital role in Parisian life, but we know little about their working lives or about how these victualers responded to rising demand and to the changing expectations of consumers.[5] The variegated historical landscape of meat consumption and production endowed it with economic, social, and political peaks and valleys. Hence, this study goes beyond the mechanics of production, distribution, and marketing of meat to include the social institutions such as the guild and family firm, the political environment, as well as popular attitudes toward flesh, blood, and violence that shaped the role of butchers in Parisian life.

Master butchers and their journeymen sold not only meat but also by-products such as hides, tallow, and tripe in over three hundred locations throughout the city. Their shops and butcheries lay mostly along the capital's two axes: the boulevard Saint Michel from the south to the boulevard Saint Denis to the north, and the boulevard Saint Honoré from the west to the boulevard Saint Antoine to the east. Proximity to these major thoroughfares allowed butchers to move herds from rural cattle markets to urban butcheries where they were slaughtered as needed. Merchants then transported sides of beef, veal, and mutton to individual shops and the households of major clients. The marketplaces and residential neighborhoods where butchers worked provided easy access for consumers to purchase their daily provisions. Several hundred country butchers and tripe sellers operated small ambulatory businesses by selling meat out of carts and wagons that doubled as makeshift stalls. An equal number of retail meat peddlers carried baskets of goods throughout the city and noisily hawked them. Ministers, the king's officers, and police commissioners oversaw this diverse population engaged in the meat trade–guild members as well as untitled merchants and workers–to ensure that their interests intersected with those of the state. The contradictory policies and competing interests in this world of meat production and consumption demonstrated meat's complex role as a measure of social worth and a source of political power.

This history centers on the meanings of meat, revealing a series of paradoxes inherent in the social life and political economy of this consumable. Primary among the paradoxes is that the government claimed meat as a basic food for all, knowing that, in reality, the bulk of fresh red meat filled the tables of elites. As a tool of distinction, meat's symbolic appropriation worked against the politics of subsistence. In theory, this policy ensured that a certain portion of fresh meat was available and affordable to all. Yet, in practice, production was limited by the state-sanctioned monopoly held by the butcher guild and the few powerful families who dominated the trade. Held by the police to standards of fair commerce and hygiene, butchers annually pledged to provide Parisians meat that was "good, trustworthy, and marketable," while they systematically contributed to a skewed distribution of the meat supply and threatened the public health by their refusal to relocate sites of slaughter from the urban center. The discourse of royal administrators claimed meat was "a good of first necessity, second only to bread." Yet unlike the grain trade, the crown imposed fiscal burdens on the sale of cattle while putting limits on the market price of fresh meat.

An examination of the chasm between the meaning of subsistence in word and subsistence in deed is essential as these seemingly contradictory attitudes and patterns of behavior reveal the complexity of Parisian market culture, especially in the ways in which consumers, producers, and the third parties who regulated and policed the market employed a wide array of social and political symbols and meanings in the course of day-to-day economic exchanges. In this case, what characterized the market culture of eighteenth-century Paris was its overlapping ideologies that, at times, worked at cross-purposes. These countercurrents pitted traditional, paternalistic behavior against modern, individualistic behavior and market practices that were bound by moral and just notions against ones that argued for rational and liberal innovations.

The first four chapters describe the paradoxical circumstances regarding meat. The notions of meat that are at once associated with high status and subsistence needs are discussed in a political context in Chapter 1. The importance of meat as a food staple for the elites of urban society may in fact have artificially elevated it to what royal officials posited as "a good of first necessity," whatever the reality. Few food commodities–namely bread, salt, and wine–were regulated as tightly as meat. A close examination of word and deed is crucial to the resolution of this conundrum. Chapter 2 pursues this historical problem at the level of exchanges in the market. Butchers–the decisive intermediaries in the meat market–shaped the distribution of meat to satisfy a hierarchy of consumers. The resulting hierarchical pattern of consumption competed with the demands of the individual in the marketplace. Chapter 3 explores the policy paradox within the regulation of Paris's provisioning markets. The complex interplay between regulatory and laissez-faire impulses becomes apparent upon close examination of the livestock trade at Poissy and Sceaux. Cattle traders and merchant butchers engaged in a variety of formal and informal commercial dealings, and royal officers tried to bring greater consistency and transparency to these market transactions through market reforms. Chapter 4 traces the movement of meat to the urban butcher stalls and considers how urban merchants altered the scale of this enterprise to conform to the standards enforced by the Parisian police and the demands of an increasingly carnivorous populace.

The final chapters delve deeper into this market culture by investigating how the guild of master and merchant butchers contributed to the paradoxes inherent to the meat trade. In many ways, the guild monopoly over production and distribution clashed with royal policies promoting abundance and cheapness. At the same time, the government maintained a symbiotic relationship with a guild from which it drew revenue and with which it negotiated commercial regulation. Guild butchers inhabited a privileged, protected space that allowed them to endure difficult times. Their commercial practices must be understood within the scheme of social ranking that characterized the trade and its cultural assumptions of privilege and reputation. The distinctions among apprentices and journeymen, young masters and senior guild officers, butcher widows and independent meat sellers were unambiguous. At the same time, butchers developed strategies to overcome professional limitations and seek out new commercial possibilities that defied the corporate (guild) system. Chapter 5 discusses the formation and governance of the guild, social processes characterized by contention and diversity as much as by solidarity and uniformity. Although the ethics of the corporate system held to a collective notion of mastership as defined by the guild, in fact, the guild's history is replete with discord and competition, inclusion and exclusion. Similarly, Chapter 6 discusses the various life-trajectories of those who entered the trade that further explain the sources of contention and competition, experiences that ranged from becoming a master to exclusion from the guild. Chapter 7 focuses on the family-owned butchery that built its wealth through marriage and lifelong strategies of capital accumulation and preserved its integrity across generations. As social relations were imbricated in commercial relations, the solidarity of the family firm could be equally threatened at moments of marriage and death when property was transmitted. Chapter 8 completes this social study, assessing the ways in which guild butchers acquired property and other forms of capital, namely credit and reputation, assets that influenced a butcher's success or failure with his or her clients and suppliers. Butchers had to negotiate credit relations carefully that at best, cemented the bonds of exchange between butcher and client and, at worst, put butcher businesses at risk of failure.

In the uncertainty that characterized early modern agriculture and food markets, when dearth, disease, and fears of shortage spurred hoarding, malfeasance, and rumors of famine plots, the everyday dealings of butchers and their clients relied upon the strength and stability of kinship and clientage that cemented their commercial relations. As the market for meat continued to grow throughout the eighteenth century, tradesmen circumvented these good faith agreements and sought more formal commercial relationships that followed state-enforced legal codes. One example, addressed in Chapter 3 is the Caisse de Poissy, a lending institution that joined the interests of financiers and state regulators to instill stricter banking methods to provide greater reliability to market transactions and therefore abundance. Market reforms–encouraged by a growing number of nonguild entrepreneurs and meat vendors–challenged traditional merchant practices and the privileged social standing of guild merchants. By the end of the century, the corporate structure could no longer contain individual pursuits to produce and trade in a wide variety of luxury and "populux" goods. An examination of the cleavages both within the guild community and among the workers and merchants at the guild's periphery brings into focus how butchers negotiated their rapidly changing commercial world.

Following the path of meat and its rise as a consumable reveals the beliefs and practices that structured the meat trade and were, in turn, structured by it. All those involved in the provisioning of meat to this metropolis encountered a variety of individual strategies, as well as conflicting moral obligations about the necessity of meat for the people of Paris. Such a holistic look at the meat trade takes a perspective that is grounded in relationships and institutions, yet at the same time influenced by a world of expanding possibilities and perpetual constraints by market forces, regulatory policies, merchant practices, and social expectations about the food Parisians ate. Taking the vantage point of butchers and viewing their world of work, this study aims to provide a comprehensive response to the question of meat's importance in Parisian life as it was socially reproduced and culturally constituted.

Conversely, the meat trade offers a unique perspective on how Parisians redefined needs and wants over the eighteenth century. Bringing meat to this metropolis was fraught with contradictory economic policies and market inefficiencies as a result of the transition to a market economy. Previously, economic life was grounded in long-held traditions and paternalistic practices, where individuals held the expectation that each person consume and produce within his or her rank, and the obligation to provide for the commonweal rested on the king. The market economy, akin to modernization, altered how individuals determined their material needs, how they chose what goods to buy, and how they purchased them through cash transactions. The spread of markets and market-mediated consumption both required and intensively promoted the breakdown of the old status order, resulting in the corrosive (or liberating) effect of monetary relations on traditional society. However, before the triumph of the market economy could take place, a new understanding of resources and consumer needs had to develop: the limiting mindset of the world of scarcity had to be replaced by the mindset of the world of consumption, a world in which the limits of what was possible could be explored.

Chapter 1

The Political Economy of Meat

On October 5, 1789, the women of the central Parisian marketplace, Les Halles, marched all night to Versailles to "bring home the baker." These self-elected representatives of the working poor took action to remedy what to them was a political crisis: The price of bread and meat had risen beyond what was just, and their king had neglected one of his primary duties to ensure the subsistence of his people. This popular initiative pointed to the political necessity of food staples, an urgent need that required direct confrontation with the head of state. Once in Versailles, they made their demands clear to Louis XVI (r. 1774–1792) and subsequently the National Assembly. The assembly responded with decrees prohibiting the export of grain, setting the price of wheat at 24 *livres* a *muid* and the price of meat at no more than 8 *sous* a pound. A flower seller in the Palais Royal district, who claimed to be the head of the band of women, said that she had a private audience with the king, who, having sanctioned the assembly's decrees, embraced her and sought that she and her fatigued and hungry compatriots return to Paris by royal coach. Interestingly enough, these women were satisfied only when their monarch (known to Parisians as the great provisioner) agreed to return with them to liberate Paris from the future designs of the aristocracy and, most importantly, to feed them. Faced with these demands, the king responded by accommodating the crowd, which included male volunteers of the Bastille, Lafayette, and the National Guard, with "all the bread and meat that could be had." Far more than simply giving them bread, "the staff of life," Louis furnished them with meat, what most Parisians understood to be an absolute necessity as it was "one of the most common foodstuffs after bread."[1]

The Paradox of Meat: Luxury or Necessity?

Historians of early modern France have long considered meat an object of status and luxury rather than a subsistence good. Long-term studies of French agricultural production, prices, and population have pointed to a period rich in meat followed by general decline beginning in 1550 with little change until the nineteenth century.[2] The seventeenth and eighteenth centuries were marked by popular revolts and political crises sparked, in large part, by grain shortages and sudden rises in the price of bread. Most scholars would agree that the "grain-dependent French" fixated upon their ability to purchase bread not meat, as it was the basic measure of popular budgets in the Old Regime.[3] The predominant historical thesis that explains popular action among the Paris crowds has focused on the cries for bread that clearly dominated any common craving for meat.[4]

How much meat did people eat in Old Regime France? Consider the peasant population, whose resources were limited by obligations to the lord of the manor, the church's tithe, and the royal tax collector who, even in the best of circumstances, may have poached small game from the lord's lands and raised their own chickens (for eggs) and swine (which they cured and smoked). The vast majority subsisted on barley, oats, chestnuts, and root vegetables. Meat was not a centerpiece of the peasant's meal, but remained a condiment with which they flavored their soups and a feast-day supplement to what was a meager diet.

By comparison, the people living in towns and small cities with larger markets and more developed economies had greater resources. Nearly every major town throughout France supported a legally sworn butcher trade and an urban population that depended upon victualers of all sorts to furnish them with their basic needs. The Venetian ambassador to the court of Henry III observed that shopkeepers and artisans, even small-scale ones, wanted to eat leg of mutton, capon, and partridge. Jean-Jacques Hémardinquer posits that Paris, like other early modern cities, was as much a center of independent animal raising as it was a consumer center. His scattered evidence on the family pig suggests that artisans and workers, even in dense urban areas of Paris, raised small numbers of farm animals for their own consumption.[5]

Butcher's meat, on the other hand, was unique as an urban commodity and, compared with other urban locales, Paris was its privileged city. Recent studies on food provisioning underscore the capital's preeminence as a central market, showing the rise of annual per capita consumption for Parisians from 52 kilograms at the mid-seventeenth century to 62 kilograms at the end of the eighteenth century. Where in smaller cities, such as Caen whose surrounding Normandy region boasted a growing livestock trade, the level remained only 20 to 30 kilograms.[6] This Parisian exceptionalism is demonstrated not only by the scope and scale of this great marketplace, but by the expansion of commercial life that came in conflict with a powerful group of guild merchants. As later chapters will show, the butcher trade's multilayered regulatory apparatus focused on maintaining the dominance of a powerful core of guild merchants and fending off competition from unlicensed butchers.

Royal policymakers understood the need both to supply and to regulate the meat trade for the well being of all Parisians. Its aim was to ensure meat was plentiful, healthful, and affordable. According to a 1719 royal declaration concerning the regulation of Parisian butcher stalls, the crown announced "a singular attention to procure for their subjects and principal inhabitants of our good city of Paris the abundance and cheapness of goods [butcher's meat] necessary for their subsistence."[7] As stalls and shops opened throughout the city and meat became more readily available by the end of the eighteenth century, ministers were more apt to see this normative vision of meat for the masses in regard to popular expectations. Bertin's acknowledgment that butcher's meat represented, "for the people of Paris, a commodity in some sort of first necessity, as is white bread" put into words the Parisian idea of subsistence that went beyond the people's needs to the more refined tastes for white bread and butcher's meat. Those who held the greatest influence over the meat trade–the royal administrators and officers who regulated commerce as well as the influential urban elites who consumed the greatest proportion of the meat supply–were the ones who ultimately determined whether or not meat was a good of first necessity.

One explanation for why elites assumed the ubiquity of meat can be linked to its historical meaning as what stands for all that is edible, if not the elemental ingredient that made up a meal. Until the seventeenth century, dictionaries defined "*la viande*" as the general term for solid food. In Jean Nicot's *Thresor de la langue francoyse* (1606), la viande corresponded to all forms of nourishment, not simply meat, as Nicot cites the common usage, "all viande other than bread and wine."[8] The meaning of viande evolved from this basic nutrient to a meaning that was further defined by its constitutive matter (flesh), an essential part of the meal; more commonly, it referred to what is served as the centerpiece of the dining experience.[9] What finished the meal (dessert) and what negated a normal meal of meat (literally, a day of fish, *un jour de poisson*) had to be made explicit. In this sense, viande operated as the fundamental ingredient as well as the common term for meal.[10]

The significance of meat as the meal *par excellence* extended to other idiomatic expressions used at the court of Louis XIV (r. 1661–1715) where the royal meal became "the king's meat" (*la viande du Roi)*. When bringing forth the numerous platters of roasts and terrines that made up the French service, the palace's kitchen staff paraded through the halls of Versailles, shouting, "*La viande du Roi est servie! C'est la viande du Roi!*" The announcement rang out to all the courtiers to come eat; the service of the king's meal (or meat) would soon begin.[11] This call to feast was a call for meat in the broadest sense–a majestic presentation of the essential prepared food–a food that embraced the idea of the meal.

Elites claimed meat was as much a necessity as bread most likely because for them it was. This staple food had long been the centerpiece of every meal. Feasts that featured overflowing platters of roasted meat and game stood as one of the avatars of the nobility. The act of eating and drinking with another held an important place in fulfilling the expectations of hospitality and confirming the fellowship of noble rank. Even wealthy commoners could at least live nobly through the conspicuous consumption of this elite food. The politically influential became arguably the trade's most demanding overseers even as the extent of popular consumption of fresh meat varied enormously. Although the privileged were unlikely to emulate bread riots by going out into the streets, through their own more inconspicuous connections they made clear the value of regulation to ensure a constant, healthy supply.

The need to provision Paris with butcher's meat, even as a good of first necessity, did not translate into a unified policy. Throughout the eighteenth century, the fiscal needs of the government often conflicted with the provisioning obligations of royal officials in determining the priority of meat as a foodstuff and its place in the economy. At one level, government leaders and intellectual elites regarded a plentiful and healthful meat supply as part of the obligations of city leaders, even though they knew its unregulated circulation made it particularly susceptible to corruption. These aspects encouraged ministers to intervene on the behalf of consumers, capitalizing on the value of meat that made it an important measure of social standing for Parisians. Simultaneously, this rhetoric masked policies that sought to extract as much wealth from an agricultural surplus with burdensome tax policies and strict market rules. By demarcating and controlling the traffic in cattle, tax farmers (as royal officers) gained a significant source of revenue for the crown. Going against this line of action was the paternalistic manner in which the government put forth provisioning policies: dictating meat be fresh, healthful, and sold at a just price. In many ways, the political economy of meat demonstrated the contradictions of Old Regime food policy caught between a tradition of kingship that served the public good, and the reaches of the state that sought greater sources of national wealth and centralized power.

Meat and the Public Good

Since the king first imposed his will on the Parisian butcher guild in the twelfth century,[12] the importance of meat coincided with the paternalistic obligations of government to feed its people. Magistrates and royal officers, following the king's lead, expressed their moral responsibility in overseeing the food supply for the common good. According to Steven Kaplan, more than the service of a monarchical leader to his common subjects, "provisioning acted as the social contract that bound the king to his people."[13] The failure to ensure an adequate food supply could jeopardize the public trust, or at worst, the crown's legitimacy. These obligations went beyond notions of Christian charity to the essentials of public service. The lieutenant general of police and his neighborhood *commissaires* as officers of the crown performed an important role in serving the basic needs of the public.[14] They intervened when the trade threatened the safety of Parisians, policing the markets and stalls to ensure the quality, quantity, and price of butcher's meat. Their regulations followed the rules of early modern kingship that centered on providing for "the public good" (*le bien public*),[15] a responsibility that included the basic necessities of life. The monarch (who embodies the state) serves for the good of *his* state, putting his particular interest beneath the public interest. The state's jurisdiction over the public interest is no better defined than in the *Traité de la police.*

Nicolas Delamare (1639–1723) compiled four volumes on urban policing that included centuries of legal precedents along with the author's own commentary. Delamare meant for his work to be read as a source of jurisprudence, "entirely devoted to the common good, and for a number of reasons merits a singular attention."[16] In the introduction to his treatise, he attempts to outline the code of law that unifies the public weal. He emphasizes what is just for "the good order upon which depends the fortunes of state,"[17] in particular, "the conduct of man in regards to his spirit and in his heart–to procure for himself the goods of substance . . . [that among these are] health, food provisions, clothing, housing, the ease of travel, and the protection against attacks, that could threaten one's life, or disturb one's peace. . . ."[18] Thus, he establishes the minimum requirements that must be guaranteed by the police. Such a platitude soars far above the hard realities Delamare would have experienced as a Paris commissaire. As he noted later in the treatise, "one would have trouble imagining that there are sources capable of filling this vast pit."[19]

In Delamare's high theoretical vision of the public good, the concerns for meat differed from bread; more specifically, they bypassed issues of subsistence, to focus on the quality of urban life where large populations depended upon public servants to ensure a level of health and safety. A significant part of his attention centered on the surveillance of food trades that fulfilled basic needs for a large urban community like Paris. The commerce in meat appears throughout the treatise as meat touched on almost every police concern. For instance "Religion," in Book 2, outlines the rules that regulated meat eating during fast days. The following book, "Customs," devoted to a discussion of manners and customs, explains the evolution of sumptuary laws surrounding meat consumption. In Book 4, "Health," Delamare focuses on the regulation of the slaughterhouses and butcheries as a source of pollution and contagion, as well as for the establishment of standards of quality for fresh meat. The final book, "Transport," touches upon the traffic on public streets and highways and maintenance of order in the commerce of livestock. Perhaps the place where butchers and their trade figured most prominently is in Book 5, "Victuals," where Delamare outlines the policing of food that begins with grains and follows with meat, primarily butcher's meat. Throughout his work, Delamare consistently places meat as "still one of the most important matters of police."[20] How this plays out in this text reveals not only legal norms that surround these primary food trades, but also the close relationship between maintaining a healthy food supply and performing a public service. Delamare carefully outlines these policing imperatives within the spirit of the law, a spirit bound by the centrality of a healthy and plentiful meat trade for all Parisians.

The police of Paris who were familiar with Delamare's treatise relied upon an array of regulations to either enable or compel commerce to perform its victualing service. This had to be accomplished under a careful eye to maintain standards of health and hygiene and to avoid fraud and malfeasance. As much as they possibly could, police took measures against the illegal sale of meat during Lent, the black market in cattle, and the rogue butchers who peddled illegal meat. Later in the eighteenth century, policing the trade became a bigger issue with the greater scale of the Parisian market and the growing number of private slaughterhouses located throughout the dense, urban landscape. The following chapters detail these primary concerns of the police that centered on the well being of Parisians who depended upon the meat trade for their provisions, or at the very least, who lived in the midst of urban butcheries who confronted this polluting and hazardous trade.

The *Encyclopédie méthodique,* another eighteenth-century text more common in the libraries of Parisian elites, echoed these civic obligations in its "butcher" entry. In this vast compendium of practical knowledge that glorified many of the mechanical arts and promoted Enlightenment ideas of economic liberalization,[21] meat appears as a common food that represents a risk for the unsuspecting consumer and therefore demanded the careful eye of inspectors and other officials:

> Butcher's meat is the most ordinary of foods after bread, and by consequence, one of those that must be a further and more constant health concern. That is why the police attentively watch over this object and take all the necessary precautions such that the livestock destined for the butchery be healthful, so that those [livestock] be slaughtered and not dead from sickness or suffocation, so that the preparation/dressing of meat be done properly, and that the meat be sold in an expedient time.[22]

According to this statement, the stakes of heavy regulation rested upon grave health concerns unique to meat, concerns that touched the vast majority of the population. In both the *Encyclopédie méthodique* and *Traité de la police,* the rationale that structured the social value of meat drew on the assumption that meat was readily available to all in the Parisian markets. Presupposing its popular status, political elites made meat a central focus of regulation and subscribed this food to a single, political directive that spoke to subsistence needs. Meat may well have followed bread in this rhetoric of subsistence, yet to what extent was the crown able to fulfill these promises given the rest of the country's limited agricultural resources and grain-dependency? A closer look at the wholesale end of the meat trade (in livestock) reveals the constraints under which the meat supply operated, as well as the limits of the paternalist state that sought to fulfill the public good.

The Practice of Agricultural Policy

Typically, early modern royal policy aimed to extract as much wealth as possible from the agrarian economy with little concern for cycles of production or for the most efficient and productive use of resources. The presumption was that supply was always sufficient to ensure a surplus for the needs of Parisians. Problems only occurred with the transportation, hoarding, and speculation of these essential commodities. In terms of the livestock trade, at least one of these problems was lessened by the fact that cattle and sheep transported themselves and, by their very nature, made for an ideal vehicle of investment as "moveable capital." But the primary purpose of raising livestock was not for human consumption, but for use as draught animals and sources of fertilizer.

Until the nineteenth-century revolution in agricultural production, most farmers regarded animal husbandry as secondary to the cultivation of grains and the survival of the farm. Jean Jacquart has argued that early modern agriculture was plagued by 'a necessary evil' which was the contradictory demands of man, plants, and animals, in which an unstable equilibrium existed to the detriment of all.[23] The rapid growth and development of husbandry, dependent upon a surplus of cultivated fodder to feed farm animals, would not take place until the introduction of new agricultural systems and advancements in veterinary medicine that gave new impetus to agricultural productivity in the nineteenth and twentieth centuries.[24]

Despite these ecological pressures, the cattle trade attracted drovers, itinerant (*forain*) merchants, and farmers, both locally and regionally, who supplied Paris with an exceptional quantity of red meat. Normandy, a nearby region that specialized in the cattle trade late in the seventeenth century, led the way in providing the Paris market with a steady supply of butcher's meat.[25] At the end of the seventeenth century, the provisioning markets in the villages of Sceaux and Poissy just outside Paris were well established as much by royal directive as by long-held merchant practices. During the latter part of the eighteenth century, cattle traders and farmers supplied anywhere from 150,000 to 200,000 head of cattle (including cows and veal) and 300,000 to 400,000 sheep to these provisioning markets, some of their herds originating from 400 kilometers away.[26] Butchers themselves publicly professed in 1768 that production had grown by a fifth in the past several years.[27] Nevertheless, the livestock trade faced enormous constraints; at best, the privileged community of guild merchants limited its ability to grow and meet the demands of Parisians throughout the year, and at worst, its large investment combined with high risk often left successful cattle and sheep farmers with devastating losses.

Nevertheless, to say that political leaders ignored the issues of livestock production would be wrong. In some cases, ministers acted swiftly and effectively to relieve the pressures producers felt at certain moments of crisis by supplementing provisions with imported supplies, particularly cattle. In 1713, a blight of livestock that devastated nearly four-fifths of all herds in certain districts of Champagne, Burgundy, and the Franche-Compté spurred the king to import over 100,000 head from Augsburg, Hesse, the Palatinate, and Württemburg to Paris. Rumors of cattle blight in March 1724 propelled the controller general to take preventative measures.[28] The government, already well versed in such rescue operations, drew on a number of entrepreneurs and bankers ready to act in the interest of the state–as well as for the legal interest of 6 percent. Memos to the controller general list contact names in Geneva, Lyon, Strasbourg, and Belgrade whose banking practices flowed through a wide international network. These contacts provided the needed sources of funding in the form of *lettres de change* that circulated like currency from one end of Europe to another. The treasury also advanced relatively moderate sums for purchases (200,000–500,000 livres) and wrote out passports for livestock brought from abroad. Royal provisioners proposed elaborate itineraries where they could cover as many territories from April through August to furnish the marketplace in Paris with several thousand head of cattle before its opening at the end of Lent.[29]

In other ways, the crown actively pursued policies that benefited cattle production. In its most liberal endeavors, the government attempted to stimulate commerce by eliminating the barriers to circulation and exchange left by feudalism. It worked to abolish the fiscal privileges of particular individuals, expand the field of trade, and foster abundance in the livestock markets.

A more active provisioning policy took form in the seventeenth century under Jean Baptiste Colbert (1619–83). The finance minister took decisive measures to stimulate trade by creating an alternate cattle market to the longstanding one at Poissy (northwest of Paris) in Sceaux (south of the city). In other ways, he aimed to protect and even increase the cattle population. In 1667, he promulgated royal orders that prohibited the seizure of cattle for the payment of debts for four years. These laws to protect livestock as a valuable investment continued throughout most of the eighteenth century.[30] Colbert also pushed to allow poor farmers and sharecroppers to lease herds of cattle from large proprietors that would allow both parties to share in the fertilizer and the profits from sales. He suspended tariffs on cattle that came from twenty leagues around Paris, as well as the entry and exit duties on cattle that moved from one province to another, or came from abroad.[31] According to historian Henri Martin, the effect of these measures produced a rapid multiplication of livestock that far exceeded the demand, so much so that in 1669, farmers sold cattle for export. By 1670, the provincial reports indicated that this sudden increase in the livestock population was even causing problems for farmers.[32]

More than these large-scale initiatives it was the police of Paris who, as royal officers responsible for provisioning Paris, had the greatest influence over the daily workings of the meat trade. In the vast world of merchant butchers and meat cutters, suppliers and cattlemen, police monitored (as much as they possibly could) the activities at stalls and cattle markets to maintain scrupulous commercial standards and to ensure honesty and efficiency. Police took measures against forestallers who tried to prevent supplies from reaching the market and against engrossers and regraters who tried to inflate the values of goods through hoarding or resale or to form cartels to drive up prices.

Colbert, like other ministers who succeeded him, realized that a healthy commerce in meat contributed to a robust government. The crown financed its military ambitions and its state apparatus by taxing the meat trade both indirectly and directly. Tariffs and duties associated with the traffic in livestock generated significant revenue for the king and his chronically overdrawn war chest.[33] These same fiscal pressures also drew the attention of city administrators. Municipal officials had a keen interest to keep the cattle trade within their purview because the trade generated funds for their local wants.

Indirect taxes on comestibles entering Paris called *droits d'entrées* (also called the *octrois*) provided additional revenue for the Paris government. These taxed items comprised nearly every food item: wine, poultry, fish, red meats, fruits, and vegetables. While many well fed Parisians paid these added costs, there were those unfortunate city dwellers who, as working poor with meager diets, contributed little to this revenue.[34] The octrois taxes concerned both finished goods and wholesale items. Merchants and consumers entering the city with butchered mutton and beef, either raw or cooked, paid 1 livre 1 *sol* per pound in entry duties. Those with veal, always the more expensive meat, paid 2 sous 3 *deniers* per pound. The trade in smoked or salted meats faced additional taxes called the *droits de domaine, poids-le-roi, plancheyeurs, gardes de nuit, vingtièmes,* and *sous pour livre,* amounting to 2 livres 6 sols every hundred pounds. Butchers who drove livestock into the city on hoof paid taxes per head no matter what size or weight, thereby inflicting a greater share of the burden on the smaller purchases of underweight cattle. In addition were tariffs called the *droits de pied fourché,* a category of customary taxes on bovine and ovine animals in addition to swine, separate from levies on animals with *pieds ronds* such as horses. These royal and municipal impositions that date back to 1360 corresponded to the resale of domesticated animals whether for human consumption or not.[35]

The levies that evoked the greatest negative response from butchers were the tariffs and duties at the cattle markets (*droits de marché*). The most infamous of these tariffs served to inflate the purchases of livestock by 1 sol per livre (or 5 percent) of the sale price. In times of war, these taxes increased and changed from a proportional tax to a fixed tax like the octrois. For example in 1639, the *juré-vendeurs* who managed tax collection at the market replaced the 5 percent with a tax per head: 40 sous per steer, 20 sous per cow, 5 sous per veal and sheep.[36] The same year, a new levy grouped under the *pied fourché* tax added another 3 livres 4 sous per steer, 1 livre 12 sous per cow, and 7 sous 6 deniers per sheep to the butchers' cost at market.

As the needs of the state and city grew, so did the number and amount of taxes on the trade in meat. In 1680, the overlapping fiscal jurisdictions ushered in an era of reform under Colbert. Through the *Ordonnance des Fermes,* the entry duties once administered by officers of the *Cour des Aides* were now under jurisdiction of the general farms (*fermes unies*). These united tax farms, also under the title *Cinq Grosses Fermes,* encompassed a large region where trade circulated freely. Guild inspectors as royal officers, along with tax farmers, administered the collection of the sol pour livre that supplied the crown with steady revenue. In 1692, according to the accounts of the king, the old and new tariffs on bovine and ovine species brought in 700,000 and 500,000 livres respectively.[37] Many of the entry duties on cattle that began in the early sixteenth century grew steadily over the course of the next two centuries amounting to roughly 7 percent of the current price by 1760.[38]

Beyond the tariffs on the purchase price of cattle that butchers and cattle merchants faced were other tariffs related to the traffic in livestock such as the *droit de barrage* and *de domain.* Butchery inspectors and guild officers (*jurés*) visited guild members in the city and suburbs once a week to collect their levies on butcher stalls. At the cattle markets, butchers paid *droits de parcage* and *de rateliers* to those who managed the stockyards at the marketplace.[39]

The policies the royal government followed in provisioning Paris with meat were perplexing. Although the importance of this elite food was second to bread, the livestock trade was subject to tariffs and multiple indirect taxes, but the grain trade was not. In reality, the fiscal impositions on the meat trade came closer to another vital good for Parisians–wine.[40] Yet the levies on wine more than doubled its cost, but the levies on meat only increased it by 20 percent. In essence, the monarchy's food policy worked at cross-purposes: it aimed to provide an abundant supply of meat at a price that fell within even some of the more modest budgets, while it sought every possible way to raise small sums of money through indirect taxation. Clearly, these concurrent aims can be credited to a double standard that regarded the trade in livestock and the market for fresh meat as two separate economies. For once within the city, the police focused their attention on the needs of the public and their notion of subsistence. Here, the concern went beyond supply to the cost of meat in the market stalls. This skewed policy that taxed on one end while controlling prices on the other demonstrates the extent to which the political economy of meat held to social constraints, particularly the perceived needs of consumers that demanded a just price.

The Just Price of Meat

A common precept, unique to food staples like bread, dictated that the price of goods was determined by a kind of commutative or contractual justice. It required a strict equivalence between what was offered and what was given, otherwise the price was deemed unfair. The just value given to any commodity depended upon the fair and open actions of every market participant. Prices that were unjust reflected a kind of covetousness or greed. Like the notion of usury, the just price originated in medieval scholasticism, when religious ethics governed the temporal world of commerce. At one level, the just price was similar to the modern notion of the market price, in that its value was determined by supply and demand. But whenever the market failed to function and the price became unfair, the public authorities had a duty to step in and correct it through market regulation. This scholastic doctrine of fairness, which gave officials the right to place items under legal price ceilings, dates from the fourteenth century and according to Raymond de Roover, "usually embraced goods of necessity such as bread, meat, wheat, wine, and beer."[41]

The tenets of the just price appear in Delamare's police treatise. When referring to the price of butcher's meat, the *Traité de la police* speaks directly to the ethical obligations of the city police: "It is not enough that merchandise displayed for sale be of good quality; it is even more necessary to make commerce legitimate and beneficial to the public, that it be given a price proportional to its just value."[42] Unlike other luxury goods characterized by their flexible demand, the price of fresh meat was held within legal limits.

Although never being published as the official *prix taxé* or fixed price, butcher's meat maintained a more or less constant price of 8 sous per pound until the height of the French Revolution, when the Committee of Public Safety included meat as part of the "general maximum" (1793) and capped the price at 9 sous a pound.[43] The Jacobin's dictatorial system of price making, which extended to other "necessary goods" and wages, was a temporary measure, based upon actual prices in 1790 plus a certain percentage for inflation. But which "just" determinants set the price of meat throughout the Old Regime even as the price of cattle varied widely? And for whom was that price just–the butcher, the cattle trader, the market-goer?

Sir William Mildmay, an Englishman writing in 1763 about the police of Paris, offered his observations on the process of price-making. According to his definition, magistrates determined the price of an object based on its supply, rather than through the proper balance sheet of costs and returns, as well as profits and losses,

> . . . magistrates have a power to settle the price of provisions proportionally to the natural plenty, and the duty imposed; and to this purpose officers are appointed, such as measurers of corn, inspectors of meat, &c. whose distinct duties consist in examining and certifying that several provisions offered to sale are just and conformable in goodness and measure to the price which is fixed upon them, which being settled according to the quantity exposed to sale, and the duty that is levied is from thence called *le prix taxé* to which all sellers are bound to conform.[44]

In the case of the Paris market, price making fell directly under the power of the magistrates whose municipal offices and city courts were housed at the Châtelet. Mildmay's understanding of the just price gives us no better answer as to whom this justice served beyond that of city leaders. Moreover, the determination of just relies upon "goodness and measure," an equally perplexing and slippery control. Such a determinant seems anachronistic when applied to the liberal notion of market price where competition influences exchange value. According to Mildmay, the just price, particularly for subsistence goods, rested upon the good judgment of disinterested third parties who attempted to impose order and reliability onto a precarious market. Because of the vagaries of the provisioning system, the police could not relinquish its role in seeing that prices kept within certain limits and that commercial practices abide by certain rules and regulations. In many ways, the police understood the necessity of regulating the market when competition was not in play. Without such regulation, they knew the butchers would put their own interests before those of the public. The potential for fraud and malfeasance in the sale and distribution of fresh meat was great and was even more criminal as it concerned a necessary food for the public. Thus, the limits on the price of certain cuts of meat abided by the police's own market rules, rather than the commercial concerns of butchers themselves.

These market rules, such as the price limits on fresh meat, demonstrate a mandate from several royal and judicial authorities. The royal procurator, one of the many Parisian justices who oversaw legal guidelines on provisioning, relayed instructions to the police of Paris to limit the price of poor quality meats in an effort to provide for a broad section of the people of Paris. In response, a police ordinance set limits on the highest quality meat at 7 sous a pound and 6 sous a pound for lesser cuts.[45] Only occasionally did the police impose a prix taxé or fixed price on the lesser cuts, typically during Lent. Nonetheless, the enforcement of these regulations could be fierce. A police sentence, dated January 18, 1788, convicted a merchant butcher 50 livres for selling over the "*prix fixé*." Any butcher who sold meat above the price set by the police could potentially face a 200 livre fine and possible imprisonment.[46]

More often government allowed the price of meat to fluctuate according to demand without going beyond what it deemed reasonable. The efforts of the lieutenant general of police and his commissaires closely monitored the price of the cheaper cuts of red meat that remained distinct from meat destined for elite consumption. In a letter that complained of the pride and fierce independence of the butcher guild leaders, the Lieutenant General of Police, Antoine-Raymond-Jean-Guilbert de Sartine (1729–1801), pointed out several of their "abuses," which included going over the psychological limit of 8 sous per pound of fresh meat. Breaking this imaginary barrier raised immediate concerns as it affected "Parisians from all walks of life, commoner as well as nobleman."[47] Police also set the price on several popular organ meats and the lowest cuts called the *basse boucherie* in keeping with this policy of provisions for the poor at a just and reasonable cost.[48] The lieutenant general of police set these prices under the belief that "the offal of steer and sheep having always been regarded by the magistrates as the food for the poorest sector of the populace, we have carefully worked without fail to fully retain this food for them."[49]

Given the fact that the price of basse boucherie and other organ meats were set at a level that met the needs of the many, one is hard pressed to consider at least this portion of the meat supply a luxury or a food staple for the few. Furthermore, in terms of its price history, butcher's meat as a whole maintained a more or less constant price throughout the eighteenth century–even outside of this protected market for lesser cuts and organ meats. Seen across the long term, the price of meat rose and fell less rapidly throughout this period than the price of bread.[50] If we limit our regard to the logic of prices and consumer behavior, this may begin to explain the different public reactions to market conditions. Although the sudden increase in the price of bread could anger a crowd of women at market, the constant supply of meat at a steady price brought on a kind of consumer confidence. Even toward the end of the eighteenth century when meat prices rose over 8 sous a pound, contemporaries such as Louis-Sebastien Mercier (1740–1814) noted with surprise:

> that the price of meat has kept up at a level that is not excessive; it costs nine to ten sous a pound. When one bears in mind the enormous consumption and cattle diseases [and losses], one is even more astonished that it [meat] is regularly provisioned at any time at this invariable price.[51]

The royal government aimed to appease the most modest of Parisian consumers with a policy that categorized meat as a subsistence issue, second only to bread. Knowing how the people sought retribution when prices became unjust and the extent to which food riots undermined social order, the king and his officers went to great lengths to guarantee an affordable and regular meat supply. As with bread, the regulatory policy toward meat worked within a paternalist framework; its intentions were to ensure peace and stability among Parisians, however unlikely meat riots may have been.

When entering the cattle market, however, these rules changed. Here, price-making gave way to an open market in which prices fluctuated with supply and demand. Butchers negotiated the price of livestock with traders without governmental controls. From the police's perspective, greater supply fostered freer competition and this was more likely to positively influence the value of goods, hence making the price just without any state-imposed price ceilings. Police intervened only to guarantee the free movement of goods and an abundance of supply in the marketplace so that no one person or group of merchants could fix prices. The timing and location of cattle auctions were closely monitored so as to bring regularity and confidence to the market. As Thomas Brennan has argued for the eighteenth-century French wine trade, the regulation of markets sought "pure" competition by emphasizing "transparency," defined as "the direct access of sellers to buyers and their general access to information about the market."[52] Throughout *Traité de la police,* Nicolas Delamare delineated the role of the police ensuring that the exchange of livestock took place within clear legal guidelines that fostered a healthy and abundant supply that would indirectly bring about a just price.[53] So why not follow the same logic for the retail sale of butcher's meat?

One could argue that the police control over transactions at the butcher stalls was a prejudicial response to a powerful and independent group of guild merchants who drove up the cost of meat, or the unqualified and rogue meat sellers who sold defective or ersatz meat. The guild often buckled at these intense regulations as much as the police suspected the loyalties of guild merchants. Part of this conflict stems from misunderstanding of the actual market pressures under which butchers operated. Delamare, himself, posits that merchant butchers could easily profit from selling meat at a lower price. More significantly, his evaluation (put forth below) reveals a great deal about the early modern conceptions of market realities when operating under economic principles that were morally bound.

Butcher's Margin on Meat

Merchant butchers who bought livestock and from it sold the meat, hides, and tallow operated under extensive cost limitations. The fact that many bought wholesale and sold retail meant that certain merchant butchers could maneuver within these margins. The costs of running a butcher shop more often affected their sale of by-products than the price of meat at market. Butchers, some more successfully than others, held to the price ceiling on fresh meat through business strategies that relied on economies of scope and scale. Even though butchers may have pursued their own self-interests within the rational choice of more or less atomized individuals, their actions nonetheless are heavily embedded in social relations.[54] Butchers bargained, negotiated, remonstrated, contracted, and adjusted their individual needs to meet the needs of family, fellow merchants, and the state. Even more, they displayed business strategies born of mentalities particular to the early modern period: fear and uncertainty. Often their decisions came out of limited information about clients and creditors, as well as limited views of future earnings or payments.

But what kind of margins did butchers work within? Was the 8 sous price ceiling profitable as much as it was deemed just? The question of the butcher's profit confronted many Parisian administrators, as butchers complained of the excessive taxes they faced and as consumers accused butchers of inflating prices. From what we can glean in his treatise, Delamare constituted legitimate commerce as one that allowed for a 10 percent gain. In his analysis of the price of butcher's meat, Delamare contends, "butchers have no place complaining." Taking into account the sale of meat by-products and the variable price of cuts of meat, he concludes that butchers could easily lower the price of meat. He tallies this wide margin based upon the cost of one steer (at 120 livres), plus tariffs (12 livres) and transport costs (20 livres), totaling 152 livres, minus the revenue from its hide, tallow, and tripe (60 livres). In a move curious to contemporary accounting, Delamare adds 10 percent to this total of 92 livres as the legitimate profit on the butcher's cost of meat, rounded to 110 livres to account for differences in cuts of meat. He then figures the retail price per pound based upon this total for 800 pounds of butcher's meat from this one steer. This retail price comes to just under 3 sols a pound.[55] By stating that meat could be sold at a lower price (less than half of the market price), Delamare implies that butchers grossly overcharge the public and the price should come within the price of an essential food staple: a 4-pound loaf of bread. Yet the assessment he makes of butchers' profit margins must be viewed critically. His analysis, like those of tax farmers who supported increased duties on the cattle trade, clearly made all butchers out to be wealthy merchants. Some master butchers who operated large businesses succeeded in acquiring multiple residences, large landholdings in the countryside, and other marks of distinction (jewels, gold coins and plates, silver), but most operated on thin margins. Delamare's balance sheet belongs to those butchers who had the capital to make big purchases in large livestock and sell off the by-products as well as the fresh meat. The vast majority of butchers did not benefit from this lucrative wholesale to retail trade but operated solely in the urban meat markets that offered Parisians various cuts from sides of beef, mutton, and occasionally veal. They sold meat literally "by the ankles" (*à la cheville*) that they acquired from wholesale merchant butchers and, on occasion, country butchers. Furthermore, Delamare puts forth grossly underestimated operating costs that neglect the cost of labor and a myriad of other overhead costs such as housing, heat, food, equipment, etc.

In an unpublished legal brief (*mémoire*),[56] guild leaders took issue with claims that butchers raked in big profits. Their public defense rested on the limits of the market that drove prices up for cattle, drew a meager lot of animals, and curtailed levels of production. According to their estimates given in the 1730s, the price of a steer comparable to Delamare's in weight (800 pounds) was more than double–that is, if one could find a steer of such proportions. Most cattle came from Normandy and were known for their large stature, weighing anywhere from 600 to 800 pounds.[57] Yet, butchers' records typically show small animals well under 600 pounds that sold, on average, from 150 to 160 livres. Limousin cattle, the stoutest breeds furnishing 800 pounds of meat, could command a price of 180 to 220 livres. The accounts of butcher Poupet gathered for the 1746 season give the unit price for steer from 80 to 135 livres, cows from 54 to 80 livres, and sheep from 4 livres 5 sous to 7 livres. Forty years later the accounts from the papers of butcher Danet give the unit price for steer that range from 270 to 425 livres, calves from 58 to 78 livres, sheep from 13 to 24 livres. Clearly many of these price variables depended upon the weight and race of the animals (never specified), as well as the market demand.[58]

Following the same guild appraisal, butchers claimed that they could not expect to extract more than 60 pounds of fat from a steer. The price of 40 sous for tallow corresponded to the common weight (*la mésure*) of 5.5 pounds each, which comes to less than 8 sous a pound (far above Delamare's 5 sous). Yet, even with this price increase, the total revenue is less than what the police treatise puts forth (20 livres). Similarly, Delamare's price for skins far exceeds what butchers paid. "A single hide may be worth

20 livres, even so, that is if it is sold by the hundred [the customary practice of a tannery] . . . otherwise it is worth only half."[59]

The guild mémoire offers a second interpretation of operating costs that divides expenses from income in two neat summations. One cannot, however, compare the two side by side as the comparison between what one could gain from a large steer as opposed to a small one is different. Yet, the second assessment of costs is arguably the more realistic one. The price and weight of the steer fall within ranges noted in other sources.[60] The two prices of meat that correspond to the better cuts *(haute boucherie)* at 7 sous a pound and the lesser cuts *(basse viande)* at 4 sous a pound are also within contemporary levels. The second account adds an additional cost of 10 livres for "butchery costs." The authors of the document leave the category deliberately vague. These costs could correspond to a plethora of charges levied by the guild or the city, or they may simply refer to the cost of food or rent. Even without this cost, what a butcher could draw as profit from the difference falls to about half what Delamare deems as "legitimate profit."

When looking at the accounts of butcher businesses, the range of costs incurred and revenue generated become clear. In this last example, a steer's variable costs and levels of output (heavier or lighter weight affects yields) could make or break the margin of profit for a butcher. As the retail price of meat remained within certain limits, the wholesale merchant butcher was left with a number of choices. One choice was to evade the fixed costs of sales taxes and entry duties through the illegal traffic of cattle. A butcher's second choice was to play with his returns by either selling his hides and tallow at a higher price or increasing the yield on animal flesh through stocking and rearing. Most merchant butchers took advantage of their right to graze animals freely throughout the vacant lands, roadways, and fallow fields surrounding Paris. During the winter months, the cost of feed and shelter for livestock (a figure that could range from 20 to 40 livres per head)[61] could be played to a merchant's advantage. Butchers with means and know-how could also choose to increase their margins by lowering their production costs through increased efficiency to meet demand. Rather than hire a high-paying journeyman, a butcher would increase the number of workers with low-paid day laborers or unpaid family members. Rather than add another stall (the number per master was limited by law), a butcher would expand his trade through a greater wholesale business, selling sides of beef to large households and other master butchers. The most prominent merchant butchers and entrepreneurs who worked within large-scale economies succeeded in generating greater output, bringing higher returns for their additional investment on equipment, livestock, property, or labor, thus containing the variable costs of production more efficiently.

In the end, the success of a butcher's business depended upon his or her own ability to work within the legal boundaries that limited the sale price of meat. Butchers also sought solutions that circumvented the public control over the marketplace. Although legal codes may have represented a standard that many butchers did not always follow, they held to their obligations as food providers as a matter of reputation. Most often, police regulations answered to an idea of justice borne from consumer dissatisfaction. Many Parisians complained to city police about butchers' commercial practices, contributing to the slander against butchers as aggressive merchants, hungry rascals, and frauds. As we shall see in the following chapters, butchers' market practices were often put under scrutiny as they engaged in a polluting trade, selling a highly perishable good that was susceptible to corruption, a food whose real or imagined necessity carried great social value.[62]

Conclusion

The political value of meat, regarded as an essential provision as well as a staple of the people's sustenance, dominated the discourse of its regulation. The king and his finance ministers followed the rules of good governance that obliged the monarch to feed his people, claiming meat as a subsistence good. These men turned their attention to regulating the marketplace and placed the price of meat under strict control for moral, not purely economic reasons. Their political directives that fixed the price of certain meats (organ meats and lesser cuts) within the reaches of the general populace operated within the paternalistic obligations of the public good. The distribution and sale of fresh meat faced strict regulation because of its primary importance as a foodstuff and its perishable nature. Meat had to be plentiful and wholesome as well as affordable. Although the price of butcher's meat did not fall completely outside the range of market forces, its fairly consistent 8-sous ceiling suggests that the pressures of a moral economy had some affect on market prices.

Once outside the urban meat markets, however, the state's regulatory role shifted as the price of cattle varied widely according to supply and demand. The same guardians of the public good allowed the free market to have sway at the margins of the meat trade, where the survival of society itself was not at stake. In this case, the monarchy looked to the cattle trade as it sought every possible way to raise small sums of money. Their various taxes and tariffs on the cost of livestock and its commercial trade, though not oppressive, aimed to keep the king's coffers full.

When analyzing the political economy of meat, the normative vision of a meat-eating populace–too easily read as the conceit of elites that allowed them to tax with one hand and make noble gestures of charity with another–has to be considered within the overlapping goals of meat provisioning. Supplying meat to Paris occurred at multiple levels whereby officials understood the sale and distribution of this food as a valuable commodity and a basic necessity of life. Regulation offered certain assurances of quality and consistent supply; the assurance of a healthy commercial life fed the needs of the state as much as the people of Paris. As the following chapters will show, this paternalistic imperative increasingly came into conflict with demands for greater liberalization from above as well as demands from below for less intervention in the merchant practices of butchers and cattle traders. Such impositions aggravated the competing interests between a self-governing corps of guild butchers and individuals who operated outside the corporate system. To be sure, these theoretical prescriptions on the importance of meat, a good of first necessity, had a limited hold on the actual experience of Parisians as they entered the butcher shop. As we shall see in the following chapter, the rhetoric ignored meat's range of social value (from luxury to necessity) that corresponded to its many forms (from tenderloin to tripe). Only in the economic process of exchange does the meaning of social value become visible. In this case, the cuts a shopper acquired and the clients' butcher served became the social and political markers of distinction.

Chapter 2

Meat and the Social Hierarchy

On a busy Christmas Eve, one of the great feasting days of the year, a young governess named Jeanne Marseille sent the housemaid to shop for meat at Master Butcher Drieux's stall. The governess worked for the Non family in the Saint Eustache parish, a bourgeois household that had been a regular client of butcher Drieux over a year-and-a-half. Upon the maid's return from the Quinze-Vingt butchery, Jeanne discovered that the meat Drieux supplied was not only rotten, but of the poorest cut. In her report to the police, she claimed the quality of the food "did not at all agree with the house of Monsieur Non."[1] As the most senior servant responsible for the household provisions, Jeanne took it upon herself to return to butcher Drieux's stall and to demand a better portion. Drieux met her pleas for better service with fierce indignation as her rejection of his goods threatened the butcher's honor and reputation as a guild master. Drieux let his temper fly, calling Jeanne a slut and a whore, finally accusing her of "serving her master" in a less than respectable way. His diatribe struck at the notion of civility that a domestic of elevated stature such as Jeanne would expect. Seeking to restore her honor, she left the butchery immediately and filed a formal complaint with the local police commissaire.

Jeanne's encounter at the meat market remains an isolated case with no further evidence of whether or not the police pursued this complaint against Drieux. While ordinances forbade butchers from accosting shoppers at market,[2] and on occasion, even fined unruly merchants who "publicly insulted their clients,"[3] one can only imagine how many other less respectable (and less influential) shoppers succumbed to the caprices of master butchers and their journeymen. The Parisians who shopped at the meat markets negotiated for the upper and lower cuts that followed a taxonomy of prestige. In contrast to the previous chapter's view of how the market for meat was regulated and idealized, this chapter examines the workings of the market for meat in terms of merchant strategies and consumer preferences. How were the particular needs and desires of Parisians met in a market culture where the quantity and quality of consumption demonstrated one's social position?

Contrary to what we might think about the "bazaar economy" of early modern market exchange,[4] butchers held a great degree of sway over the distribution of meat, acting as powerful mediators between a limited supply and a carnivorous public. Guild members pledged yearly to provide meat that was "good, trustworthy, and marketable," an oath that held to the dictates of the public good. Yet these same food-providers, with their independently run shops, depended upon a loyal clientele to keep their businesses solvent. Their job consisted of transforming livestock into a number of marketable goods consistently and reliably. As merchants, they worked to build relationships with customers that would sustain their businesses throughout the season and from year to year. Many butchers did this quite successfully. Merchant Butcher Pierre Barré (perhaps one of the most prominent butchers in Paris) managed a business that at the time of his death in 1738 distributed more than 6,700 pounds of meat a week from two locations on the rue Saint-Honoré and the rue Saint-Martin.[5] Barré reserved the majority of their business for wealthy clients who contracted with him seasonally. From his own stockyards outside of Paris, he supplied beef, mutton, and veal to large households and other retail butchers (as well as hides, tallow, and tripe to other dealers) and sold the remainders in stalls run by lesser master butchers or journeymen. Hence, this division of labor contributed to a segmented market, much of which was contracted outside the public markets, which precluded some shoppers from finding what they wanted at the market stalls. Moreover, the differentiation in the meat market corresponded not only to price and availability, but also to socially distinct food regimes, where a status-conscious servant would know enough not to serve a lesser grade meat as it was not in keeping with the dignity of her master. Not only the quantity of meat consumed, but the quality of meat from noble game to bourgeois beef corresponded to the social hierarchy.

Many varieties and types of meat fed all levels of urban society, a fact that made Paris exceptionally well provisioned. Visitors to eighteenth-century Paris remarked on the richness of Parisians' diet. The countryman fresh to the town could only point out with disdain the stark differences: "If you saw how indulgent and gluttonous they are at their master's table, in comparison to our own! Everyone there consumes as much meat as three of us; it is as if the city lives only for eating. . . ."[6] Although newcomers to Paris saw abundance, these ways of eating were by no means uniform nor democratic. Even though elites claimed that meat was ubiquitous and a subsistence good, it would be facile to assume a populist notion of meat eating, or that beef (butcher's meat par excellence) became the standard of living for all Parisians. Likewise, the historian's claim of 'miserabilism,' that all underprivileged Parisians lived on bread and water simply because the vast majority of the meat supply served elite households, misses the variable aspects of meat as a consumable and the power it held as a marker of social identity. For in as much as the meat trade operated under rules of a moral economy where regulations aimed to hold butchers to a just price and to serve the public good, the distribution of meat followed implicit rules and cultural norms that structured exchange as well as were structured by it. As we shall see, the attitudes and values toward meat eating directed the circuit in which meat came to both wealthy and poor, both noble and common, households in varying degrees to one another.

Historians of gastronomy have shown how increasing numbers of preparations that included beef, veal, and mutton in the culinary literature suggest a growing preference for the more readily available butcher's meat over the more noble (and rare) game. Likewise, the demand for refinement in cuisine encouraged diversity in meat preparation along with more efficient modes of meat distribution for a wide population of meat eaters. The greatest consumers of meat, the wealthy and powerful of Paris, favored smaller servings of select cuts of beef and veal leaving a great number of lesser cuts and variety meats (such as kidney, liver, and tripe) for popular consumption. By the eighteenth-century, the burgeoning Paris population included the magistrates of the Paris Parlement and other important dignitaries in the royal courts and municipal offices along with the thousands of transients, all of whom depended upon the city's provisions to feed them. Meat met the demands of a large number of consumers, not only with rich appetites, but also those with a taste for opulence and power. In this way, both royal policies of provisioning and changing tastes for "bourgeois beef" brought regular supplies at a more or less consistent price to meat eaters throughout the year.[7]

Until recently, our knowledge of eighteenth-century food habits have focused on the elite, because the details of their private lives exist in diaries and letters. Such intimate information is almost impossible to locate for the majority of the illiterate populous of Old Regime Paris. Few sources exist that would allow a historian access to such details on consumption. The one exception is Daniel Roche, who through a serial study of the probate records of eighteenth-century Parisian artisans and domestics, has come forward with a powerful argument for changing food habits and increasing meat consumption among laborers based upon material evidence (frying pans) left behind in urban households. Roche concludes the growing popularity of such equipment in over 80 percent of the inventories suggests a change from infrequent to more frequent meat eating. In this case, the working poor chose quick-fried trimmings called cracklings and tripe to replace the slow, simmering stews known as *pot au feu*.[8] This evidence suggests not only a shift in tastes, but also in the demand for cheap, fresh meats that could be prepared simply. The fact that such modest households would invest in a basic piece of kitchen equipment to fry meats and prepare quick sautés also suggests this cuisine's importance in everyday food preparation. Most importantly, it undermines the claim that the people of Paris did not eat meat.

The Noble Carnivore

While the working poor of Paris may have "indulged" in variety meats, it was the privileged and the wealthy who tipped the scales of meat eating. Their appetite for luxury fostered heavy consumption of roasted joints and sides of beef, which was guaranteed to impress their guests. This extravagant lifestyle formed the ideology of nobility and structured the hierarchies of Old Regime society. As George Duby remarks, "To be noble is to be profligate, it is an obligation to show–to be condemned under threat of *déchéance*–to luxury and to spending."[9] From the cattle cults of the first Germanic tribes, meat provided an essential ingredient for celebratory feasts. Livestock and game remained part of the seignorial dues that the well-landed nobility collected to fill their tables throughout the early modern period. At court, nobles gathered at tables to feast on five courses, each with ten to twenty dishes of various fish, fowl, red meats, and other game set before them, beef being the reserve meat of everyday fare. Many of these foods also took center stage in the extravagant displays of largesse in which the rich, merchant classes engaged. Parisian elites who regularly feasted on large roasts represented a highly skewed cross-section of the population. The corpulent bon vivants who proudly sported their "bellies of gold" set out to prove their stature through physical means, proudly porting their paunch with a gold watch chain.[10] Conspicuous consumption illustrated the capacity of elites to maintain their political status as much as it became a form of self-expression.

The appetite of gourmands did not simply reside in excess but also in a developed appreciation of the culinary arts that included the finer cuts of meat. Nowhere were social skills more important than at the dinner table. What a host served his guests at meals was a political choice that could potentially confer great esteem. As Veblen affirms: "In order to gain and to hold the esteem of men it is not sufficient merely to possess wealth or power. The power and wealth must be put in evidence, for esteem is awarded only on evidence."[11] His or her offerings denoted a place in the social order as much as they entailed the reciprocal obligations from others. Similarly, table manners came to be the expression of the cultivated man and could be used to impress and influence others.

In well-staffed households, domestic servants skilled in carving and light butchering prepared pieces of meat for each meal. The best-laid tables stopped serving large joints that sat prodigiously as the meal's centerpiece. Instead, cooks prepared meats in smaller servings cooked rare, aiming for a kind of delicacy and restraint. As Louis-Sebastien Mercier remarked in 1783:

> In the last century, they used to serve huge pieces of meat, and pile them up in pyramids. These little dishes, costing ten times as much as one of

> those big ones, were not yet known. Delicate eating has been known for only a half a century. The delicious cuisine of the reign of Louis XV was unknown even to Louis XIV.[12]

Roasts continued to remain popular and though less impressive in size still provided an opportunity to demonstrate the social graces of a good carver. Even as late as 1808, Grimod de la Reyniere (1758–1837) author of the eight-volume *Almanach des gourmands,* continued to publish handbooks on table-side meat cutting techniques. Grimod's early nineteenth-century publication, *Manuel des Amphytryons,* contains "a treatise on the dissection of meats at the table, the nomenclature of the latest menus for every season, and the elements of a polite gourmand."[13] In it, Grimod extols the virtues of what he sees as an important, although recently forgotten, social skill (something he calls an art) that is "indispensable for every master of the house jealous to prove that he was not born yesterday." The author adds "the elements having been lost in the revolutionary torment, we have tried to bring them back to life."[14] His desire to see society return to pleasures and indulgences of the noble feast hearkened to an earlier civilization (the Old Regime) where one cultivated the rules of social etiquette as a way of life. Grimod, in his nostalgia for a bygone era, desired to restore an element of French heritage he recognized as the essential instruction for any man of taste. Indeed, he promoted the social transformation that cast the nineteenth-century bourgeoisie into the forefront of culinary consumption.

The art of carving, once a display of a noble stature, became for Grimod a way for a man to show his knowledge of good manners and, as the head of the household, to exercise a masculine form of conviviality. Grimod's motive was to revive the practice of noble manners after nearly twenty years of warfare that radically changed the social structure of France. While making the skill of meat carving one of the social graces for men of all households to learn, he perpetuates a broadly conceived social value.

A Person of Taste

Early modern court cuisine led the way in shaping fashion and taste that persisted beyond the French Revolution. Yet court culture throughout the Old Regime lived by a different standard from what most Parisians, even the elite households, valued (and ate) on a day-to-day basis. Parisian gastronomes extolled taste as refinement; they distinguished themselves through individual expressions of civility that included grand gestures of hospitality and physical comportment.

In the seventeenth and eighteenth centuries, an educated palate signaled a person's sensibility and refinement as much as it demonstrated a certain cosmopolitanism. Meat-eating Parisians with a desire (and means) to distinguish themselves sought various preparations with a variety of beef, veal, and mutton. The increased consumption of fresh meat brought out levels of distinction that clearly fell along social lines. More than a marker between the privileged and the disadvantaged, these social divisions became increasingly important among a broad number of urban elites whose social standing remained ambiguous to observers. This ambiguity was especially true for the wealthy commoner, who with some success, could be mistaken for a noble. Taste was one of the avatars of nobility. Maintaining these standards of taste meant subscribing to a pattern of consumption that promoted the indulgence of delicacies and the enjoyment of life's fineries.

More specifically, "a person of taste" *(un homme de goût)* in the eighteenth-century referred to someone who held certain alimentary preferences for refined cuisine along with an appreciation for literature and the arts. Such a title referred to a cultivated man whose social world included the Parisian salons of philosophes, statesmen, and worldly merchants, as well as the courtly circles of nobles, bishops, and high, royal officials. Elites as hommes de goût distinguished themselves through individual expressions of civility, namely in social etiquette and eating habits. These rules of behavior formed the constellations that guided men and women through the shifting currents of civilized society.

The transformation of French cooking mirrored the cult of the natural in French rococo. One deemed cuisine that relied on heavily spiced preparations (and those who ate it) as baroque, impure, and of bad taste. Voltaire, whose many contributions to the *Encyclopédie* included an entry entitled "Goût," explicated this critical notion of taste in terms of the culinary arts:

> As bad taste in its natural composition consists in being pleased only with high seasoning and curious dishes, so a bad taste in the arts is pleased only with studied ornament, and feels not the pure beauty of nature.[15]

The cultivation of good taste resided in the refinements in the culinary arts that shunned the heavily seasoned and advocated the natural taste of foods. Hence, a person of good taste demonstrated qualities that corresponded to delicate sensibilities and an appreciation for purity and simplicity. Voltaire believed that taste tended naturally toward things of better quality. The operation of taste was less a marker than a capability of both the intellectual and physical modes of discernment. Here, the mind-body connection resides in the physiology of taste. More than seeing how food affects the body, Voltaire regards dietary regimes in terms of a social pathology of aesthetic principles (i.e., the burlesque and the ornamental versus the simple and the natural); it is an organic sensibility that determines basse from haute cuisine.

Butchers and Their Clients

Parisians who craved the *grosses viandes* and could afford to purchase them regularly, avoided haggling over small cuts by buying larger cuts. Unlike the governess who entered Butcher Drieux's stall, they did not have to convince the butcher to sell them the best morsels of meat. Instead, wealthy clients contracted with butchers on a seasonal basis. These large households ordered sides of lamb and veal, hindquarters and forequarters of beef and mutton that were regularly supplied from Easter to the beginning of Lent.[16] These large carcasses, which hung in the cellar or "*chambres à chair*,"[17] away from the light and flying pests, could be dry-aged, smoked, or salted for later consumption. In well-staffed households, domestic servants skilled in carving and light butchering prepared pieces of meat for each meal.

Pierre Louis Vollée, perhaps one of the largest suppliers of butchered meat to the city, afforded the expense of drawing up a notarized contract with his royal client, Madame la Dauphine, and her entourage of noble escorts and servants. In addition to the Merchant Butcher Vollée, the document names master *traiteur/rôtisseur,* Antoine Crespy, who supplied prepared meats and pork, and Pierre Berthelin Deneuville, another Parisian merchant who dealt in fish and game. The three signed on for a six-year term

> to furnish the house of Madame la Dauphine as much for the ordinary outlay for meals, as for the feasts receiving ambassadors, foreign nobility, or Frenchmen ordered by Madame la Dauphine, or for other extraordinary outlays whatever they may be, and for whatever reason or occasion that may come to be, and to those locations that Madame la Dauphine may go.[18]

These locations included royal residences in Paris, Versailles, Fontainebleau, Saint Germain-en-laye, and Meudon. In the contract, the two parties agreed to a list of prices for each food item. Red meat, catalogued under grosse viande, listed at 8 sous 3 deniers a pound and included mutton and veal. Other special meats such as tongue (raw, stuffed, pork, and beef), marrow, and sweetbreads demanded a greater price (1 to 2 livres a piece). The contract made the expectations of the client explicit: fresh meat in season; if any product is not satisfactory, suppliers would receive one-fourth the noted price.[19] These suppliers agreed to meet the princess's demands and could not ask for any price supplements due to extraordinary circumstances such as seasonal shortages, wartime losses, or epidemics.[20] Clearly, this contract held Vollée to strict standards that did not allow room for any negotiations when faced with difficult circumstances. Moreover, Vollée, eager for the favor of such an important client (and the prestige it would confer), would be more likely to submit to these provisos.

In contrast to notarized provisioning contracts, account books serve as a less formalized record of credit transactions from a range of clientele. Despite their frequent omissions and rudimentary accounting (no double entry, no running tallies, no itemized sales), these sources provide the best evidence of consumption patterns. These account books rarely include the addresses of the butcher's clientele; however, the few that do suggest that most Parisians frequented their local butcher.[21] Each page of the bound registers lists every client week by week with the biggest customers (usually noblemen) heading the column, followed by names of the head of households with lesser, nonnoble titles such as monsieur, madame, or marchand. Butchers noted the amount (in pounds) of meat regularly supplied to individuals or religious houses two to three times a week.

To be sure, not all transactions were noted in the butchers' ledgers, as many merchants were apt to engage in forms of barter. Guides to household management advised stewards of wealthy and noble houses to cultivate good relations with their butcher for the maintenance of a well-run kitchen. According to Audiger, the author of *La Maison reglée* (1692), himself a *maître d'hôtel* for the *grandes maisons* of Paris, the head servant's responsibility consisted of "being familiar with meat and to make an agreement with the butcher, to oblige him in doing this by giving him two deliveries of offal a week."[22] Such exchange in kind existed among other butchers who kept account of meat sold to anonymous artisans such as "the tailor," "the washing woman," and "the leather worker" without any payment due on the account.[23] Likewise, a large number of butchers in this sampling noted the names of fellow butchers and amounts of meat "loaned" to them to store, butcher, or eventually sell. These were usually sides of beef, but could also include basse boucherie. Such practices point to the division of labor in meat production, contributing to a wide distribution of meat throughout the capital.[24] Indeed, the evidence of barter agreements suggests a lively trade never recorded in butchers' account books.

The number of nonnoble clients that filled the account books of butchers (including merchants, artisans, and men and women identified as *"Bourgeois de Paris"*) attests to the social diversity of meat eaters. Their weekly purchases, made 2 or 3 times a week of 3 to 5 pounds of meat on average, point to a regular consumption of a household staple. Not surprisingly, butchers increased their sales in the winter months, with the biggest amounts in late December and January, in time for Christmas feasting. A good example of this pattern of consumption resides in the weekly accounts of Master Butcher Gabriel Sagot who lived on rue au Maire in the parish of Saint Nicolas des Champs. According to his 1756–57 account book,[25] we see a typical mix of titles, both noble and bourgeois, as well as merchants and artisans. Sagot begins the season with 23 clients in his book. The number steadily increases to 35 by the middle of the season and finishes strongly at 32. The average number is 31 clients a week. The amount of meat sold each week also grows steadily throughout the season from a low of 372 pounds in week 6 to a high of 1,064 pounds in week 32. The average amount of meat sold is 700 pounds a week; the average amount per customer is 22.5 pounds per week. The data come from accounts of separate households and do not provide the number of people within each household. Hence, these figures may be offset by a moment of feasting when a single client would make a large purchase of 40–50 pounds of meat, presumably to feed his household and guests. Yet the data do suggest a certain regularity (about three to four visits a week) pointing to consistent demand among a wide range of urban dwellers.

Yet social hierarchies existed (and were often perpetuated) within a butcher's clientele by virtue of his or her business practices. For example, Widow Bouchère Lemoine, who operated an extensive business that supplied the château at Versailles, kept separate books, one for the *"seigneurs"* and another for "bourgeois." Among the 52 accounts of noblemen and women that she carefully catalogued appear, "The Small Apartments of the King" with anywhere from 11 to 39 deliveries a month totaling 589 to 13,655 pounds of meat consumed monthly. The second book of over 100 bourgeois clients includes names of untitled men and women who lived in Versailles as well as royal musicians, royal wet nurses, the château's kitchen staff, and low-ranking officers. For widow Lemoine, the social distinctions among clientele went beyond accounting to pricing where the king paid 10 sous a pound, the lesser nobles paid 9 sous, and the commoners 8 sous. Her method of dividing her customers categorically further illustrates how hierarchies in the market for meat were inscribed in merchant practices.[26]

The consumption of goods as a means of social distinction relied upon a differentiation of offerings that were clearly distinguishable to the public. Meat as a social marker could not exist without a wide selection of edibles for interested shoppers with discriminating palates. The system of ranking the taste for particular meats developed alongside the taxonomy of cuts and organ meats (also known as offal). The classification of meat became more specialized and refined with the greater sophistication in French cuisine. Likewise, the regulation of meat increasingly differentiated between these various cuts for the benefit of Parisian shoppers.

Shopping for Butcher's Meat

Even though the general notion of *viande* allowed for a wide conception of what was edible, by law, butcher's meat corresponded to veal (at least six weeks of age), mutton, and beef; the latter included the meat from both steer (castrated males) and cows, while mutton came from mature, castrated sheep. Yet guild butchers often found themselves turning to substitutes in times of scarcity. The police of Paris recognized that butchers passed off goat for veal and whenever possible punished butchers for the deception. Yet consumers' accusations of fraud were hard to prove, especially when identifying smaller cuts and trimmings. As members of a corporate community that pledged to supply the city with healthy meat, butchers held to standards of quality as well as levels of expertise befitting the character of a guild master. Any violation risked not only a butcher's corporate standing, but also his personal reputation as a food provider.

At the public stalls, Parisian butchers sold generic butcher's meat by the piece, a practice that continued into the eighteenth century. In many ways, by virtue of the animal's various parts and their rapid deterioration once broken down, practical considerations forced butchers to sell off lower-end portions quickly at prices that drew shoppers. Foreign travelers to Paris, such as the Italian Francesco d'Ierni, noted the local custom as it differed from many other cities in Europe. On a visit in 1596, he remarked with surprise how butchers cut meat, "not by weight but by piece."[27] Beginning in the mid-seventeenth century, city administrators enacted legislation to change this practice and required butchers to sell meat by the pound. By the mid-eighteenth century, the vast majority of account books and records of accounts receivable grossed their sales of meat in pounds. These totals did not specify the type of meat sold nor its cut as butchers offered their product as is. Without the commercial controls that held butcher's meat to standards of identification such as today's cuts and grades, butchers could sell any fleshy part of a variety of hoofed quadrupeds by weight or piece. This practice put butchers and their clients into a relationship of trust, where limited information about the product forced both parties into negotiations for the proper meat at a just price.

The common practice of butchers such as widow Lemoine and others who followed the practice of multiple pricing for meat suggests that the quality-to-price ratio corresponded to the social segmentation of the market. Unfortunately, most butcher accounts do not specify the nature of the meat they sold at different prices. Whether these differences correspond to meat varieties (i.e., mutton, lamb, cow, steer, or veal) or differences in cuts of meat (the top loin versus the shank and brisket) remains vague. Without better evidence of the product, without knowing what type or cut of meat butchers actually sold at what price, a clear picture of the price structuring cannot be wholly reconstituted.

The lack of item pricing frustrated contemporary consumers as well and contributed to the reputation of butchers as frauds. Parisians, who complained to the commissaire about butchers' practices, made clear their demand for quality and selection, while they rejected certain meat not fit for human consumption. But no regulation required butchers to itemize their one-price-fits-all butcher's meat, a category that could include cow, steer, veal, mutton, and even goat. Mercier observed the problems Parisians faced when purchasing meat without knowing from which animal it came. He accused butchers of passing cow's meat for steer, which is all that is left to the *"petit bourgeois"* who buy by the piece. Mercier understood how pricing discriminated against the poorest consumers.

> Everywhere else there is a difference in the price of meats; here the cow sells at the same price as steer at market: excessive surcharge for the poor, genuine offense to the public food supply. A new price would be completely equitable; for why is it that I pay the same price for cow's meat as for steer's? And why does one give me cow when I ask for steer? It is only in Paris that such an evil usage is, as it were, consecrated, despite the daily complaints of the people.[28]

Purchasing meat at the butcher stall required knowledge of the product as well as confidence in one's butcher. Certain pieces of beef or mutton were often indistinguishable from that which consumers considered inedible such as goat or horse meat. Lesser cuts full of bone or gristle, some tough, others tender could be added on to other purchases. Butchers could take advantage of their poorer customers by giving them the poorer quality meats as a *surpoid* or supplement,[29] secure in the knowledge that should they complain, they were unlikely to get a sympathetic hearing from police officials. Other butchers could rely upon the intimidation factor of their physical presence. Those savvy customers who filed a complaint to the local police commissaire did so with the backing of their social standing.

The police of Paris imposed rules on butchers and other meat sellers to offer a healthy supply of meat at a range of prices. What politicized consumers, however, was not the quantity or price but the *quality* of meat sold to them. In the butcher stalls where merchants sold the most common meats (beef, mutton, and veal), Parisians selected and haggled for their purchases based upon the freshness, variety, and increasingly the cut of the product. Here, the tactics that surrounded these market exchanges rested on the maintenance of the social structure that (like meat itself) was inherently hierarchical. Within the category of meat came the lesser and better cuts that fed the social and political stability of the kingdom. Essential to this notion, was the supply of several cheap cuts from the underbelly, neck, and limbs of the animal (called basse boucherie) whose price fell within the purchasing power of most commoners in good times.

Cuts and Their Social Value

The classification of butcher's meat lacked any official standard of grading and processing that we know of today. Of course, these absent standards for cuts of meat did not preclude the common understanding of preferred sections and joints or butchers' knowledge of anatomy and their artisanal skill in breaking down an animal. In their account books, butchers would occasionally specify the names of cuts along with their weight, most often as a record of their own inventory,[30] but these appellations were not part of standardized selection, apportionment, and pricing in the marketplace. At best, police and guild regulations delineated a commercial differentiation of meat that consisted of three grades: the high- and low-end meats (haute and basse boucherie) and the offal *(abbatis de viande)*. These three categories conformed to strict price controls ensuring the lesser cuts would remain within reach of the largest population (usually around 8 sous a pound). Yet nowhere in the butcher guild statutes or other prescriptive literature of the period do we find any standard definition of what distinguished the high from the low.[31]

It was in the interest of butchers to sell off the entire animal: meat, skins, organs, bones, and tallow (rendered fat) at the highest price. Given this, butchers often tried to pass off these lesser cuts as high-end meat, prompting a 1779 police ordinance for the bailliage of Versailles that set the standards for basse boucherie.[32] In this document, put forward by the royal procurator in conjunction with the butchers of Versailles, police regulations specified the cuts of basse boucherie for beef, veal, and mutton. These cuts basically corresponded to what we know as the chuck and shoulder clod of the carcass up to the cheek,[33] the first rib of the sirloin, along with the shank, brisket, skirt meat, and "other little cuts"–by far the portions of an animal that contained the most bone and gristle and the least amount of tender flesh.[34] The same ordinance distinguished the head of veal and cow (seen as a kind of delicacy) as separate from these lesser cuts. Likewise, the sale of feet, liver, tripe, and other organ meats remained in a separate category of meat that butchers sold by the piece. A later police regulation, published in 1788, required Parisian butchers to sell meat with a certain portion of the basse boucherie or alternatively the trimmings (known as *réjouissances*)[35] at a designated price. The police's definition of these lesser cuts included the head of veal but not beef, veal feet, beef tongue, the upper end of the shoulder clod or its loin, which could be either the skirt or brisket, and the sirloin.[36] These regulations, despite their internal inconsistencies, moved the meat trade toward better meat apportionment and item pricing. The definitions of basse viande differed greatly as taste and culinary preparations changed,[37] yet these official attempts at regulation began a process of rationalization that placed universal standards upon what had been negotiated between butcher and client.

Police ordinances codified the hierarchical value of meat to ensure that meat distribution met the needs of even the poorest Parisians. Documentation, dated as early as 1725, relays instructions from the royal procurator to the police of Paris at the Châtelet to limit the price of poor quality meats in an effort to provide for a broad section of the people of Paris.[38] In 1717, the price ceiling of basse boucherie stood at 6 sous a pound, by the mid-eighteenth century this price rose to 8 sous a pound.[39] The enforcement of these regulations could be fierce. A police sentence, dated January 18, 1788, fined a merchant butcher 50 livres for selling over the *prix fixé.* Any butcher who sold meat above the price set by the police could potentially face a 200 livre fine and possible imprisonment.[40]

The categorical distinctions between better and lesser cuts of butcher's meat that followed a clear pricing strategy also served a broad base of consumers. According to a police ordinance dated January 1788, all butchers and stall butchers were prohibited, "to sell meat more than 17 sols 6 deniers a pound, without meat commonly known as réjouissances, or 9 sols 6 deniers with one-seventh of lesser cuts [basse viande]." This two-tiered system divided the haute from the basse boucherie, putting the latter under stricter price controls that more or less ensured it fell within the purchasing power of the populace. The municipal government also controlled the price of tripe and other offal, as these were meats "destined for the poor." In the mid-eighteenth century, a shopper paid 2 sous for each beef's liver, 5 sous for the heart, 9 sous a pound for prepared tripe.[41] The lieutenant general of police set these prices under the belief that "the offal of steer and sheep having always been regarded by the magistrates as the food for the poorest sector of the populace, we have carefully worked without fail to fully retain this food for them."[42]

How realistic were these efforts to maintain the price of meat within the budgets of Parisians? Clearly, a fairly well-paid journeyman or water carrier making 15 to 20 sous a day might afford some kind of meat to supplement his diet of bread and soup during the week, and a skilled worker making 30 sous a day could possibly eat some form of animal protein daily.[43] Bringing home enough meat for a wife and children would be another matter. Yet by making prices for offal (meats considered by many as common or nearly throwaway foods) and other lesser cuts relatively affordable, the royal government demonstrated its commitment to include a wide variety of meats for the city's less fortunate.

The police only occasionally imposed a prix taxé or fixed price on basse boucherie. More often government allowed the price of meat to fluctuate according to demand without going beyond what it deemed reasonable. The efforts of the lieutenant general of police and his commissaires closely monitored the price of the cheaper cuts of red meat that remained distinct from meat destined for elite consumption. In a letter dated May 1766 Lieutenant General of Police Sartine reprimanded the butcher guild leaders for not keeping the public good in mind. The most egregious offense was exceeding the 8 sous limit that affected "most particularly the citizens of all orders and especially the poor."[44] Breaching the price that most Parisians held as the accepted limit brought an immediate cry of malfeasance by regulators who sought ways to ensure a level of subsistence for all Parisians.

Popular Consumption

Subsistence policy, while subscribing to the public good, followed closely the Christian tradition of charity. Civic and religious institutions such as city hospitals and churches fed the poor and less fortunate on a regular basis. At these centers, many hungry Parisians could find a bed and a hot meal. The city's commitment to meat provisioning extended to these havens for the hungry year-round, even during Lent when all other commercial stalls closed. In keeping with the logic of subsistence policy, meat provisioning during this holy period of fasting did not preclude the nutritional needs of the sick and nursing mothers.

Bouillon had long been the prescription for good health and the mainstay of hospitals.[45] The meat broth's restorative powers made it the most popular treatment for a number of conditions including malnourishment. For this reason, it became the most common "food therapy,"[46] and especially in the late-eighteenth century, a restorative that gave rise to famous restaurateurs who prepared these popular dishes for virtuous creatures with sensitive constitutions.[47] Understanding the powers within food allowed readers to construct their own regimes as a way of maintaining this particular equilibrium, and as a method "to live until an extreme old age."

At a basic level, the city's charity hospitals run by religious communities supplied bouillon, the liquid essence of meat juices, to many in need. According to the accounts of ten parishes throughout Paris, they provided meat broth to their communities throughout the year. Ten hospitals distributed over 20,000 pounds of fresh meat in the first week of January 1718.[48] The charity of the parish societies, however, did not always reach the most indigent. Its particular purpose was to help towndwellers who had been stricken with poverty, that is, the paupers who were ashamed of their fallen state on the condition that they fulfill their religious vows.[49]

At the central hospital of Paris, L'Hôtel-Dieu, the brothers and sisters served two meals a day at eleven and six. These meals (outside of fast days) included butcher's meat; they fed the sick and the handicapped, as well as over a hundred orphans who lodged there. Records of the meat provisions from 1698 to 1703 reveal that for a population of 1,950 (1,500 patients and 450 ecclesiastics, nuns, and surgeons) the hospital furnished, on average, 168,000 pounds of beef yearly, as well as 66,150 pounds of veal and 237,380 pounds of mutton. If we limit our scope to the hospital's patient population, then the total daily per capita consumption comes to 10.5 ounces of meat.[50]

Conclusion

Hierarchies of consumption within the city of Paris brought stark differences of plenty and want into clear focus. Yet, one too easily assumes that the rich indulged and threw away, and the poor were left to feed on the scraps. This stark contrast, however, misses many aspects of what the poorer classes of Paris ate that cannot simply be classified in residual categories of popular consumption. Just as Pierre Bourdieu has argued for the differential tastes among social groups whose contingency lies less with economic conditions than with habitus, so we must reevaluate the dietary habits of Parisian populace with this complexity in mind.[51] We cannot assume that the taste of the Parisian elite dominated and the urban poor only "made due" with throw-away meats. The fried cracklings, *rejouissance,* liver, and other organ meats, made up a kind of "soul food" for the popular classes of Paris, a poor cuisine that, as African Americans have shown, has its own merits.[52]

As in the confrontation between Butcher Drieux and the servant of Monsieur Non, shopping for meat became a practice of measuring one's social identity. The cut of meat that the housemaid brought to the table had to correspond to the house of Monsieur Non. This man of means faced dishonor when given a poorer cut, as his governess well understood. By being "forced to eat humble pie," a consumer suffered the impudence of a merchant who disregarded his moral obligations as a food provider and dared to test the limits of social rank. As butchers dispensed the appropriate cuts to clients who they felt were worthy, they acted as cultural mediators. The conflict over what one could obtain from one's butcher reveals the purchasing power inherent in the social position of an individual. Moreover, such an acquisition demonstrates the instability of social rank as wealthy commoners acquired a noble diet. In this way, the interaction at the butcher stall became an exercise in the politics of the everyday as much as it was an expression of social position.

Hierarchies existed in Paris, but they were by no means fixed in a social caste. Throughout the eighteenth century, the world of goods proliferated and consumers found themselves confronted with choices. This period saw a promotion of change in dietary habits and the importance of meat, as well as a promotion of the values of the individual whose self-regard came from a lifestyle that was as much private as public. This transition took place through extremely varied and elaborate interactions that were part of the process of constituting new relations between need for meat, the possibility of eating meat, and its far-reaching necessity.

Figure 2: Nineteenth-century rendition of the cattle market at Poissy. As one of the oldest provisioning markets, Poissy (a few miles west of Paris) drew many cattle traders from nearby Normandy. Used with permission of the Municipal Archives of Poissy, France.

Chapter 3

Liberty and Regulation in the Cattle Markets

Every Thursday a deafening cacophony awoke the villagers of Poissy in the early morning hours. Some of these sounds came from the nearby taverns where cattle merchants were carousing after their long journeys from regional fairs. The greatest noise came from the hundreds of cattle and thousands of sheep that had been driven to Poissy, a town dominated by its central square that looked over the river Seine and the Saint Germain forest, beyond which lay the western gates of Paris. The first cattle showing started at 4:00 A.M. in the summer months, 6:00 A.M. in the winter months; a second showing of sheep began at 8:30 A.M. in the summer, 9:30 A.M. in the winter. As the morning continued, market inspectors and tax collectors observed cattlemen and merchants marking their purchases and exchanging money (typically credit slips) for goods until the traders departed for the nearby taverns and country inns before leaving town in the early afternoon.

On the first market day after Lent in 1707, traffic leaving Poissy had suddenly come to a halt. All eyes pointed to the appearance of newly formed company of tax farmers at market, called "Treasurers of the Stock Market." The crown recently awarded them a lease on the sol pour livre or 5 percent tax that they were to collect on the purchase price of all livestock. The tax farm had also imposed a new glitch in this carefully choreographed movement of livestock and merchants, a system whereby all purchases from now on had to be carefully recorded and transactions completed in cash not credit. As on each market day, the clerks of the tax farm, who sat behind their long tables at the exit of the market square, carefully noted the price and quantity of each transaction, ensuring that the tax farmers receive their proper levy in a timely fashion. In addition, these officials made their own terms of credit available for those butchers unable (or unwilling) to complete the transaction in cash–a short-term loan, so to speak, that compounded interest weekly. These cash loans, while keeping the cattle merchants' own finances fluid and the tax farmers' coffers full, did little to help keep butchers' businesses afloat as their terms were stricter than most "good faith" agreements. Moreover, this system, later known as the Caisse de Poissy, provoked the ire of Parisian butchers who preferred the old system of promissory notes and IOUs (called *billets*) that kept the wheels of commerce turning and allowed merchants and their drovers to speed ahead on the road back to Paris.

Needless to say, the new system created more disorder and delay than ease and flow in this commercial world. As the impatient crowd of butchers and cattle merchants grew heated, a fight broke out, and finally, someone broke down the barriers and set herds stampeding toward the river. Lieutenant General of Police d'Argenson, in a memo to the royal controller general, suggested that perhaps the "*bagarre*" or riot was a bit overblown, reasoning that "the wine and the innate brutality had risen to their heads," for it was a single incident. City officials were more concerned about the level of collusion between merchant butchers and cattlemen who resisted the market reforms. By the next week, market inspectors assured these officials that there were no "factions" or "intrigues" to speak of. The police reports announced that things had calmed down and the market had once again "found its tranquility."[1]

Ideally, the weekly activities at the marketplace followed a specific set of market rules that appear in royal proclamations, legislating where, when, and how trade would take place, enforcing a visible, public, and open exchange of goods, so that each actor followed his script unfailingly. In reality, the effort of creating consistency and order each market day provoked conflicts between civic and merchant rationale, between good faith and formalized credit agreements, between Paris and the provinces. These conflicts remained more or less the concern of cattle traders and merchant butchers whose own set of ideas and practices about the livestock trade differed radically from what officials envisioned for meeting the demands of provisioning. Rather than the sale of fresh meat to Parisians, it was this wholesale commerce that mobilized merchants and guild masters against authorities. The main contention of players on both sides resided in whose interests should govern the marketplace.

The control over the marketplace, particularly cattle markets, stemmed from a fear of markets as potentially explosive. Meat, because of its political importance, operated under specific market rules that focused on moral obligations of cattle traders and merchant butchers who offered a good of necessity at a just price. As principal actors in the marketplace, merchant butchers and cattle merchants sought to set the rules that best served their commercial needs. Opposing them were royal tax farmers who made loans to the state in exchange for the right to manage fiscal operations, such as the entry tariffs collected at the twenty gates surrounding the city. In between the two were the Paris police who played the role of overseer, an intermittent watchdog who sought formalized procedures to ensure consistency and reliability in the marketplace and counter the potentially corrosive effects of an unregulated market. By farming out its revenue-collecting role to royal tax farmers, the state also increased the policing of market transactions. The crown also dictated that all trade occurred in a single locale on a weekly basis: Thursdays at Poissy and Mondays at Sceaux.

By the early eighteenth century, the royal government had built a bureaucracy that relied on a system of policing for more efficient communication and control. Long before the cattle arrived at the provisioning markets, the procurator general along with the butcher guild were communicating with feeder and satellite markets via royal *intendants* posted in the provinces. Ministers also sought out independent financiers to buy shares in tax farms, increasing the state's revenue. As a result, tax farmers, who held an interest in every livestock sale, guaranteed that all commercial goods passed through their fiscal gateways. Thus, these royal intermediaries concentrated and centralized the cattle markets making them more efficient. Despite this clear division of labor, by no means did the Old Regime government represent a sweeping, rigorous bureaucracy. Yet, it made great efforts to accomplish the dual task of drawing as much wealth from the agricultural and financial resources that the country had to offer.

Finance ministers and controllers general who managed the royal treasury without a central bank depended upon the private resources of wealthy financiers to keep their public credit solvent and to aid them in collecting as much revenue from as many sources as possible. In Sceaux and Poissy, tax farmers who leased the "privilege" to manage the marketplace and administer its levies, hired an array of men to collect sales taxes, entry and exit tariffs, and duties on sheep stocking (*parcage*). To maximize this system of revenue collecting, they had to direct the traffic in livestock toward these central markets and force merchants to comply with their new market rules. While all parties in this complex interplay understood that "liberty is the soul of commerce" each group had different ideas about how trade should occur. We turn first to the traditional workings of the cattle trade, the beliefs upon which commercial relations between merchants were built, and then turn to the tax farmers whose presence in the marketplace challenged their notion of market exchange.

The Geography of the Cattle Trade

At the end of the seventeenth century, the provisioning markets in the villages of Sceaux and Poissy were well established. Together they commanded a wide supply zone surrounding the capital that extended over as much as 400 kilometers from Paris. Unlike the grain trade, cattle could be conveyed over long distances, traveling 20 to 40 kilometers a day. The ancient network of drove roads spanned continental Europe. Some minor shipments did take place by sea, but for the most part this trade held a distinctly landward character, ranging over distances that gave it international stature by the standards of the early modern period.

Forain merchants, who numbered over three hundred, dominated the trade in livestock at Poissy and Sceaux. These merchants purchased at seasonal fairs and weekly markets and then moved their goods to urban areas. They organized the transport of herds numbering twenty, forty, or even several hundred head of livestock. Such trade could take a month or more to move from regional fairs to an urban provisioning market. Hence a clear geographical distinction existed between the stock raising areas on the one hand and the grazing areas on the other. The animals lost weight during the migration (the drove), and had to be corralled and fed at local country inns or grazed in open pastures and woods. The so-called drove roads, along riverbanks and through mountain passes, connected the two zones. They followed special trails (where possible) through sparsely populated districts so that traffic on the ordinary commercial routes would not be blocked by the slow-moving herds that covered about two to four miles a day and had to rest on every third day. There was no point in forcing the pace, because the cattle would then lose too much meat and fat. A number of people accompanied the animals. In northern Europe, one drover handled about twenty oxen together with a "forager" (often the son of the merchant). Cattle merchants sought accommodation at inns that provided enclosed pasture, access to water, and, in some cases, stockades and hay for the animals. Numbers of lodging houses sprang up along the drove roads to serve the needs of animals and men.[2]

Paris enjoyed a privileged position in the kingdom at the center of a half-dozen rivers and major roads that led to and from the capital. The flat, fertile basin in which Paris sat made for easy transport of farm animals. Early extension of artificial meadows through drainage provided pasturage for livestock in the Ile-de-France region surrounding Paris. The extension of meadows brought more livestock that made more manure, lifting the constraints on agriculture that depended upon this organic fertilizer.[3] Cattle drovers rounded up livestock from cattle lands north and southeast of the city and grazed their animals in pastures within a day's distance to the cattle markets at Sceaux and Poissy where Parisian butchers came to buy. Cattle merchants sought livestock throughout France. The ten fairs in the region of Poitou, the two in Marche, and the one in Haute Limousin drew at least 800 oxen a week to the capital according to the butcher guild's own estimates. The eleven fairs in Berry, nine in Bourbonnais, and twelve in Lower Limousin supplied no less than 1,400 head a week.[4] Other regions that supplied the provisioning markets with sheep, the most common livestock, included Champagne to the northeast of Paris along the Seine, the Perche region to the southwest of the city particularly surrounding Alençon, and to the north shepherds drove flocks from the Beauvais region even as far as Flanders where the fair in the city of Lille saw 50,000 sheep during one season. Merchants frequented other northern cities of Bourbourg, Bergues, Furnes, and Ypres nearly every week.[5]

Within the most immediate supply zone surrounding Paris, market towns offered country butchers and farmers a number of choices of where to sell their livestock. There were cattlemen in the trade called *nourrisseurs* who purchased livestock in these smaller markets, often underweight and at a lower price to fatten over the season. Without the same financial resources of cattle merchants, their traffic remained in the region surrounding Paris. This area had no lack of resources for a cattleman especially in Brie where riverbanks along the Seine and Marne offered excellent pasture for grazing animals. The countryside outside of Meaux and Melun was reputed for its veal. The expansive fields of grain that covered the Beauce and Vexin regions also gave ample grazing for both bovine and ovine species. This area, known as the breadbasket of France, allowed for pasturage in the wheat fields after harvest while fields lay fallow. Livestock also grazed in local forests and along the king's highways to economize on hay and other animal feed. Many of these smaller traders–farmers, shepherds, and cattlemen among them–chose to avoid the large cattle merchants, dealing instead with merchant butchers directly.[6]

Royal administrators and the Paris Parlement would try throughout the eighteenth century to discourage these informal trading practices surrounding the urban center. They passed several police ordinances and royal acts that limited the sale and purchase of livestock first within 7 leagues (about 28 kilometers), then in 1635, extended to the 20-league (80 kilometers) area surrounding the capital (see Figure 3). By the end of the seventeenth century, royal ordinances required all butchers within this zone to make their purchases within the public cattle markets at Poissy and Sceaux.[7] Officials considered any other exchange illegal and subject to stiff fines (500 livres). Such regulation reflected the character of government intervention in provisioning that aimed to ensure the greatest number of market transactions in a single area.

The single most important rule concerning the provisioning trade was the requirement that all transactions occur in the marketplace. Keeping trade visible and systematic, first and foremost, would guarantee a level of honesty and efficiency. Such a move would also centralize the meat trade by concentrating all commerce within one or two locations; this focus would attract more sellers and increase supply at the marketplace. The twenty-league provisioning zone acted as perhaps the best guarantee for the viability of the two provisioning markets during periods of dearth as well as giving greater stability to prices.[8]

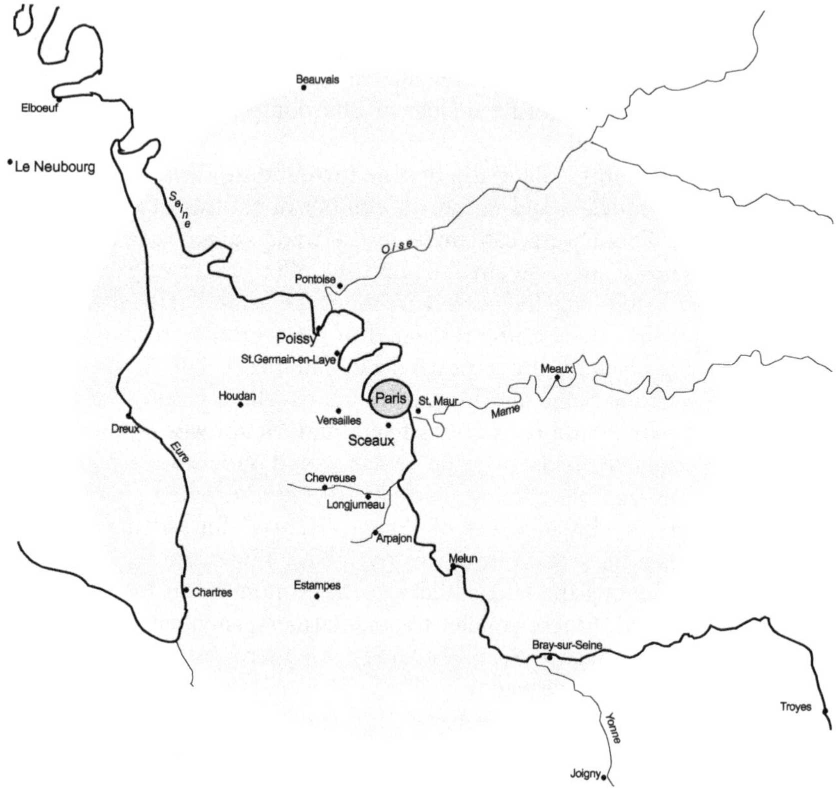

Figure 3: Approximate area of the twenty-league provisioning zone. All livestock raised in this area supplied the Paris meat markets

The regulation of the cattle trade, like the meat trade, operated within moral obligations and financial imperatives. These governing principles engendered a certain degree of opposition from butchers whose countervailing impulse appears, to our twenty-first century eyes, laissez-faire. In their vociferous legal battles carried out by lawyers hired by the guild, butchers called for "liberty" to seek out cattle purchases wherever they wanted and with terms that suited their own interests. But rather than seeing this as a deregulatory demand, we must consider how their cries for freedom in the marketplace also accompanied a long defense of their traditional merchant practices and guild privileges that made them honorable men. Butchers, who were less concerned with the fight between regulatory and laissez-faire doctrines, focused their attention on their reputation as guild merchants whose expertise and honor in the cattle markets eschewed any royal interference.

Urban-Rural Networks of Trade

For Parisian butchers, the traffic between countryside and city was literally the lifeblood of their trade. Urban butcheries could not maintain gross purchases of twenty to fifty head, sometimes more, and thus livestock had to be held in rural farmyards, barns, and meadows in suburban areas. Butchers drew from their supplies to piece and sell in their stalls according to demand. Most merchant butchers relied upon shepherds and farm laborers to tend to their livestock for which they received a meager wage.[9] They leased sheds and barns and purchased hay and other feed. The most prominent merchant butchers maintained a second residence, a kind of ranch house in the countryside where they could stock and fatten their cattle for slaughter. Though not all butchers held property outside the city or even second residences, many relied on family connections in the outlying areas to gain access to their herds and the weekly cattle markets. Outside of kinship ties, butchers employed shepherds and cattlemen to increase the returns on their investments. In addition to the trade links Parisian butchers maintained with the countryside, many had agricultural origins; others held extensive lands outside the city; their sons and daughters married wealthy farmers; in essence, their links to rural agriculture remained a constitutive part of their everyday lives.

Parisian butchers built systems of exchange with farmers, nourrisseurs, and forain merchants. Rarely did they draw up formal contracts with their suppliers.[10] Most butchers relied on what they called their agreements of "good faith" (*la bonne foi*). These business relationships could regularly feed merchant butchers' demand directly, if not through their employed cattlemen and shepherds whose homes extended throughout the Parisian countryside. The revised 1744 guild statutes allowed butchers and their journeymen to buy livestock from farmers and ploughmen and drive them back to their homes without being troubled by anyone.[11] Merchant butchers kept abreast of supplies in regional cattle markets, most likely through their cattle merchants or buyers. Perhaps as much out of their own interest as in the interest of the frequently touted public good, the guild released reports to royal officials about cattle population shortages and expected periods of dearth. With access to information and supply markets throughout the country, Parisian butchers were linked to a network of exchange that allowed them to overcome the domination of the provisioning markets at Sceaux and Poissy.[12]

In an effort to enforce compliance with the five percent tax on hoofed animals (managed by tax farmers at Sceaux and Poissy), royal officers charged those who evaded the levy with fraud.[13] Butchers, who sought out sites of exchange throughout the countryside surrounding Paris, were the first to face such accusations. This hidden activity frustrated one outspoken tax farmer, Nicolas Fauvet, who saw "abuses that are committed each day by the butchers of our good city and the cattle merchants, to the prejudice of the levies (droits) of our farm, of 12 *deniers* [or 1 sol] per livre on the hoofed animals sold at the market of our said city of Paris." He claimed that "butchers and cattle merchants have of their authority erected several markets to which they go to make their sales and purchases of the said livestock, without coming to the very said market of Paris, because at the said places, they pay no tax."[14] The loudest objections to the flagrant circumvention of levies came from these collectors. Like Fauvet, they pushed further regulation through parlement and the king's council. In one case, tax farmer Jean Laurent publicly reproached the Parisian butchers' "immoderate lust" that hastens butchers to bypass the marketplace "to underhandedly extract an illicit profit for themselves."[15]

Royal administrators and tax collectors could not correct such transgressions easily. The localized, informal trade in the Ile-de-France region around Paris would remain an important part of provisioning the city until the nineteenth century. Butchers who circumvented the highly regulated markets in Sceaux and Poissy did so for reasons beyond their own economic interests. Merchant butchers maintained strong ties with their suppliers that often rendered a day at Sceaux or Poissy unnecessary. They operated under a set of conditions in keeping with their own customs and expectations of what constituted good trade.

Changing merchants' habits to draw them exclusively to the two provisioning markets was no easy task. Aware of the myriad commercial routes and the exigencies of provisioning the capital, one would question how every transaction that brought cattle and sheep to Paris could possibly be monitored. The flow of goods followed a kind of logic where supply did not always meet demand, but rather butchers built exchange relationships upon systems of trust that followed and forged social relations. To be sure, most parties understood that exchanges made outside these designated areas could cut costs. Bringing in cattle and slaughtered meat without paying entry duties was also a savings as much as it was illegal. Beyond the directives of self-interest, butchers held to an urban-rural exchange network deeply embedded in traditional merchant culture. Certainly royal administrators were not indifferent to commercial imperatives that drove merchants to settle outside the marketplace as well as the social bonds that kept them there. The difficulty remained in finding an effective policy that would redirect these commercial practices.

Part of this difficulty laid in the inability to chart the urban-rural exchange, the inability to control, in fact, all movements in and out of the capital. As the urban population grew 30 percent or more in the eighteenth century, no one was quite sure where the city began and ended. Urban migration and settlement around the capital upset claims as to where the city limits could be drawn.[16] It was not until the end of the 1780s when the tax farmers physically enclosed Paris with fortifications (the *mur des fermiers-généraux*) to control fiscal matters more effectively. The new perimeter embraced a vast zone, often undeveloped, with fields and vineyards, a temporary no man's land that was difficult to control, encouraging fraud and, in the eyes of the police, crime. As the reliance upon a continual flow of goods between the agricultural producers outside and the mass consumers inside increased with the growth of the city, the effort to monitor and regulate became more essential.

Although it is difficult, if not impossible, to determine what part of their trade bypassed the provisioning markets at Sceaux and Poissy throughout this period, evidence suggests that it was hardly insignificant. In 1729, an anonymous report made to the Paris Parlement named twenty-one merchant butchers (*jurés* and *syndic* among them) who purchased over 15,000 sheep outside of Sceaux and Poissy from July 20 to August 6 of that year. The report reminds us that "the infractions listed above only form a very small part of those glaring practices and monopolies exercised daily that divert from the markets every week more than ten to twelve thousand sheep since the first of July through Carnival."[17] On June 16, 1730, a similar report revealed the dealings of Parisian cattle merchant, Sieur Barnabé. From his stock of 6,800 sheep purchased at a fair in Berry on June 11 only 1,500 head reached the provisioning markets that day. "The rest had been sold at a profit" to eighteen merchant butchers named in the report. These purchases made by the elite butchers of the guild suggest how successful butchers were in maintaining their own direct links to suppliers without the need for cattle market supervision and regulation.[18]

Admittedly, the police could only control what they could see. Limited in their manpower, the authorities focused upon the major thoroughfares and marketplaces throughout the sprawling metropolis. Their surveillance included smaller communities within the twenty-league zone around Paris where suburban butchers, village butcheries, and local markets operated. Although it is difficult to know exactly what percentage of the trade evaded the fiscal reach of the state, the actual contribution that these butcheries brought to the city should not be underestimated. Guild butchers in the 1770s claimed the rural butcher population to be over three hundred.[19] Although many of these butchers frequented the markets at Sceaux and Poissy, many others contended that they were under no obligation to buy there.[20] As contemporaries well understood, any conclusions on the Parisian cattle trade must account for a certain number of transactions outside the two provisioning markets, particularly for those country butchers and farmers whose meat business served as a small part of their livelihood. Still, government officials, police, and tax farmers made efforts to stop the leaks from the provisioning funnel.

How significant was the "black market" for meat? Determining the numbers of agricultural workers whose surplus escaped the purview of police and tax farmers is nearly impossible. Understanding the significance of this backdoor meat trade for those who tried to shut it out, however, seems more plausible. One way to measure its importance is through royal proclamation. Voices grew louder as this activity expanded beyond local consumption and drew upon Parisian commerce. Police and parlementary regulation focused on butchers from smaller communities such as Chartres, Saint Germain, Nanterre, Argenteuil, Versailles, Clamart, and Chatillon who frequented local markets drawing cattle merchants away from Poissy and Sceaux. A 1704 arrêt stated that villages constituting a parish could only allow two butchers to practice their trade. This rule encompassed the villages of Passy, Auteuil, and Villejuif that sat just outside of the city gates. Authorities went after the owners of competing marketplaces. In 1746, seigneurs, who by custom held rights over the sale of farm animals in their domain, had to prove so by presenting their letters of concession and other documentary evidence to lieutenant general of police de Marville. The repeated royal ordinances and police sentences only reinforce the fact that this kind of trade persisted, if not encroached upon the legal limits of provisioning.[21]

Royal Failures and Contradictions of Policing

For the lieutenant general of police, whose courts at the Châtelet upheld civil law as well as criminal law within the capital, the containment of the illegal trade meant maintaining a careful equilibrium between liberty and regulation. This balance involved a sleight of hand that often produced more fumbling than a clear policy. Despite the apparent tightening of the provisioning surveillance, it would be wrong to assert that the Châtelet defended these laws in a mechanically rigid and oppressive fashion. The police abstained from direct coercion not out of indulgence for the merchants but rather to avoid provoking "alarms" and "anxieties" among consumers. Rather than clamp down on those involved in a black market or secondary trade, the presence of inspectors and royal officials who reported to the lieutenant general of police centered on the proper functioning of Sceaux and Poissy to elicit a wider number of merchants. They strove to maximize practices that were visible, equitable, and followed a certain discipline and to minimize activity that was secretive, speculative, collusive, and hazardous. In the police rationale, regulating the marketplace aimed to limit confusion and conflict that "troubles commerce" and limits the "the natural liberty" of trade. In this way, their presence as peacekeepers, traffic cops, and health inspectors offered a public service to Parisian consumers.[22]

For example, the surveillance of cattle droves aimed to stave off the unnecessary herding and driving of cattle. Further transport only tired the animals and made them more susceptible to exhaustion and dehydration. The police saw that livestock was protected from exposure to the elements and not crowded into small stockyards and barns.[23] The police placed strict guidelines on the timing of exchange, giving butchers nine days to determine the health of their purchases before cattle merchants could refuse to refund their money.[24] Cattle that showed signs of infection were quickly identified and isolated from their herds.[25]

Inspectors and local police berated cattle merchants for their minor annoyances (e.g., arriving too early, demanding the same spot in the market square, keeping a select stock in nearby country inns for private sale) especially when it showed a kind of prejudice against other merchants. Here, their policing action was limited. According to Nicolas Delamare's treatise on policing, market regulation meant limiting the number of abuses that would show ill will or malfeasance. He typified such abusers in seven categories:

1. Those who keep their livestock too long at their homes or on the roads to make it appear that there is a dearth in the market and raise the price.
2. Those who sell at the stable on their way to market or elsewhere than in the market and in other times than the hours prescribed by the regulations.
3. Those who buy from other merchants and from secondhand merchants for resale use and to make profit.
4. Those who work together to control all commerce in a province; what one calls a monopoly.
5. Those who have agents or representatives residing where markets take place, so that they are not pressured to sell to return, that they refuse to deliver their goods only when they are offered a reasonable price where they find legitimate and sufficient earnings.
6. Those who take away or return with cattle before having shown it for sale for three consecutive days, and for having wanted to sell it above the just price.
7. Those who show cattle that they know to be harmful or sick, or that they falsely (*par artifice*) make appear to be fatter than they are in fact.[26]

According to this list, police were to be on the lookout for dishonest merchants, particularly for those engaging in graft and collusion born of market libertinage. Such vigilance suggests the extent to which fraudulent sales pervaded the marketplace. Or perhaps that is too naive an assumption. After all, many of these same rules appear in the butcher guild statutes suggesting that they were party to these illegal maneuvers.[27] Merchant butchers who frequented Poissy and Sceaux had to be wary of fraud from suppliers, but such activity could easily be checked by boycotting, even accusing a cattle merchant of less than honorable behavior. The few cases of merchants actually arrested for such activity point to weak surveillance, the lack of criminal activity, or a limited civilian policing system.

The tax farmers and administrators who governed the fiscal system at Poissy and Sceaux, however, held a greater interest in the surveillance of the trade in livestock than the police. They were strict with forain merchants, especially on the roads going and coming from the two market towns. The tax farmer of the Caisse de Poissy along with his crew of *commis* made efforts to account for the number of livestock that passed through the provisioning markets with registering procedures required of all merchants. In addition, tax farmers stopped butchers at the gates surrounding the capital to collect entry duties. And once within the urban zone, butchery inspectors entered the stalls of city butchers to verify cattle purchases and collect their dues. Butchers had to show passports for foreign cattle purchases and other visas for their livestock. Although these policing efforts were less strict for country butchers who purchased in smaller livestock markets such as Chevreuse, Houdan, Longjumeau, and Pontoise and operated on smaller margins, there were some tax farmers who sought out all the surrounding trade to guarantee the greatest accumulation of revenue. These hungry collectors allowed their private interests to overcome merchant traditions, leading to predatory practices that went beyond what many contemporaries saw as the legitimate limits of policing.

One example comes from a farmer in the village of Sarcelles who brought his high-profile case before the Paris Parlement. Bouquet was a well-to-do agriculturist and butcher[28] who maintained a large farm with about a thousand sheep, admittedly not all purchased at Sceaux or Poissy. On September 28, 1758 officers employed under tax farmer Durivault arrived at Bouquet's farm to question him about these purchases. In his absence, Bouquet's son observed that the officers "did not make evident the right that they claimed to have to pry around his house." Once realizing their intentions to reclaim goods he "declared that he was against all that they claimed and wanted to do."[29] Less than a week later, the tax farmer's four inspectors and his deputies arrived with three *archers de robe-courte,* sporting rifles with bayonets, followed by two shepherds and three sheep dogs. They asked Madame Bouquet to tell them where *their* sheep could be found. She, wondering how they had a claim on her sheep, said they were out to pasture. Whereupon the cohort left to reclaim the flock and to herd them back to Poissy. Bouquet's farm hands, witnessing the seizure of their animals from the fields, responded instantly and a scuttle ensued. As the inspectors confiscated the goods, the deputies beat the unarmed shepherds and farm laborers and killed one sheep. Despite the farmer's attempt to gain some proof of seizure, the tax farmer's men managed to rustle the flock without proper cause. As Bouquet told the investigator, "No title, no ordinance, no judgment, no sheep."[30] The same tax farmer, Durivault, used similar aggressive tactics to seize property from country butchers in Hyères, Boissy-Saint-Leger, and Villiers-sur-Marne.[31]

This move to extract a greater share of all transactions led to the perceived loss of trade in other market towns. The Marquis de la Lande, governor of Neuf Brisac and lieutenant general of the king's army, returned from a tour abroad only to find his weekly market at Chartres "empty of cattle merchants." He accused the "avidity of the tax farmer and his officers" who forced cattle merchants to Poissy and Sceaux with the threat of fines and imprisonment to increase their collections. In the words of the seigneur, this was a move "to abolish this market in Chartres," a market that served the royal troops as well as local needs of the city. Moreover, the Marquis de la Lande contended that his marketplace sat just outside of the seven-league circle around Paris and by law was exempt from the provisioning rules. The office of the controller general reminded la Lande that the zone had been extended to twenty-leagues and now included his territory. To avoid future disputes, the royal officers published maps under the direction of cartographer Cassini and the Royal Academy of Sciences and charted the zone surrounding Poissy and Sceaux markets with markers that highlighted the residences of country butchers. The tax farmer presented the map to the parlement in 1759 for approval and posted it in the marketplaces at Poissy and Sceaux.[32]

Markets remained a means of power and domination in a world of limited supply. Farmers from the regions surrounding Paris watched the city drain their own stockyards as the enormous fiscal shadow spread beyond the two provisioning markets. Indeed, much of this shift occurred out of the necessity of state finances to reach farther and dig deeper into the world of taxable, consumable goods. In other ways, the contests over the marketplace reveal the inability of bureaucratic intervention to resolve issues of supply. These issues were dire in an economy built upon credit.

Credit Practices and Merchant Culture

Butchers' commercial practices, particularly those that encompassed *bonne foi* or good faith agreements, although difficult if not impossible to uncover from written sources, must be considered a part of butchers' daily interactions as well as lifelong economic growth. Building a business meant building relationships upon which to found a system of exchange, one that would be flexible enough to allow for the great distances of time and space that separated buyer from seller, not to mention the exigencies of periodic shortfalls and great misfortune.

The extension of credit responded to the ongoing needs of butchers as they conducted their affairs. Butchers took credit as freely as they could in small amounts from trading partners, in large amounts from bankers and wealthy Parisians. Their credit practices varied as their needs for credit changed. Butchers had a wide selection of credit options that varied in function of who the lender was, the amount of the loan, the loan period, and the social and physical distance between the parties involved. Many butchers utilized this opportunity to spread their credit over a great number of people.[33] Although it may have been in creditors' interests to have butchers as their primary clients to ensure repayment, butchers chose to spread out their debts among creditors in order to increase their flexibility. The fragility of credit relations and butchers' heavy dependency on credit cannot be understated.

Often in early banking or prebanking systems, difficulties arise in credit transactions because of the limited information on what lenders know about borrowers. Participants who are only partially informed about each other may limit their credit practices to a few borrowers whom they know well, or specialists may appear with greater access to resources that are better able to handle short-term shocks in the market. In the case of the meat trade, the lack of information about butchers and their financial histories–perhaps even a butcher's lack of accounting–forced creditors to take risks. Added to this was the fact that butchers benefited from several layers of protection against peremptory seizure. Even though the chief collateral was the livestock a butcher bought on credit, law prohibited its repossession.[34]

Given that creditors could not rely on the supply of direct collateral to guarantee a loan, they centered their reciprocal obligations on personal criteria, namely reputation. Reputation served as public information accessible to anyone interested in another person's affairs. A good reputation could provide the personal capital to give an individual access to credit; it could also extend a person's credit. As lenders learned more about their clientele, the creditor-debtor relationship could develop trust in a highly personalized setting.

The marketplace as site of exchange also represents a center of sociability where men and women came to conduct business and fraternize. Thursdays at Poissy often began the night before in taverns and inns and continued through the main meal at midday. The kinds of relationships built upon these regular exchanges overcame doubts that suppliers may have had about their clients. They reinforced bonds of trust and perhaps engendered the will to cooperate even in times of hardship.

Yet these credit relationships could only go so far before the need for cash payment became immediate. The demand for loans became especially fierce in periods of dearth and rising prices on livestock. At these moments, butchers turned to moneylenders. However hated and mistrusted, these men played an important role in the economy of the Old Regime. Their ability to extend credit in a cash-poor society was essential in greasing the wheels of the provisioning machine as cattle merchants were reluctant to leave the city without cashing out their notes from butchers. Cattle traders depended upon a secure currency with which to make their own purchases in distant markets and fairs. Moneylenders who brokered the trade in cattle were most often called bankers, or the more pejorative title butchers gave them: *grimbelins* from the verb to sift, perhaps also to cut a deal or take a share (sift out). Most butchers relied on these merchants to supply them with needed capital for the weekly cattle markets where big outlays for livestock took place.

Conflicts arose as butchers watched their creditors wield enormous power over their transactions, bleeding them for more money. There was little public control over their operations and little competition from others to drive their interest rates down. Many butchers were left with no option but to succumb to their creditors' usurious practice. Bankers engaged in a profit making enterprise in which expenses were paid by the butcher and, more often than not, passed along to the consumer.

The cries of usury and the blame put on moneylenders for inflating meat prices hailed the attention of royal ministers and administrators. The controller general of finance responded by creating a community chest for butchers managed by treasurers called the *Tresoriers de la Bourse,* backed with the ensurance of "an open [and accountable] office" (*un bureau ouvert*). With the implementation of the treasurers, and later the Caisse de Poissy, strict guidelines multiplied in the steps required to obtain credit. These guidelines brought the continued surveillance of commercial transactions at provisioning markets. This institution inculcated a new set of rules and social relations that had a direct influence on butchers and how they practiced their trade.[35]

The fact that the treasurers as members of the caisse operated partly out of their own interests and partly out of the crown's gave them a different status vis-à-vis those merchants caught in the mutually dependent network of the meat trade. These brokers purchased their offices from the king, and with that, they brought the prestige of royal patronage and the privilege of managing the king's affairs. It is important to remember how these offices provided a service to smooth the inconsistencies of the credit market; however, the reciprocal obligations based on trust and human relations for these titled men did not always apply. To ensure consistency, the officers of the caisse pushed for a change in the way commerce behaved, trying to break the chain of credit. By this, I mean that the government's ambition centered on reforming the practice of linking commercial relationships through IOUs or promissory notes, by requiring butchers to pay their suppliers in cash.

When butchers bought their herds outside the marketplace, brought their newly purchased herds to graze on lands outside the city, and smuggled either livestock or fresh meat into the city, officers of the caisse seized these goods by force. Yet this heavy-handed policing could not ensure compliance. As as result, the caisse installed a pass system by introducing the *laissez-passer*, which both documented the movement of cattle and sheep between buyer and seller to the city gates as well as certified that the livestock were purchased at the two provisioning markets. Butchers and cattle drivers obtained the numbered form from clerks at the caisse office upon presentation of receipts for purchase. Clerks took the receipts and filled in the *laissez-passer* form with the same information: the date, the number and type of livestock, the place of purchase, the names of the buyer and seller. Once acquired, butchers could legally leave the marketplace and enter their livestock into the city. This document had to be presented to the tax farmers who ran the entry duties at the edge of Paris. The number of sheep and cattle recorded on the pass had to correspond to the number accompanying the butcher or cattle driver at the city gate. Those who tried to falsify the document faced heavy fines (500 livres).

The tax farmers quickly adapted the pass system as a valuable bureaucratic tool. In a published mémoire supporting the newly reinstated caisse of 1735 and its director, Jean-Baptiste Hayon, the controller general argued that the *laissez-passer* was "absolutely indispensable." It acted as the "touchstone" that uncovered the inside dealings of butchers and created an obstacle for clandestine purchases that butchers are "in the habit of making." The formality of the pass system, Hayon argued, imposed "inconveniences" upon butchers. Echoing the complaints of these merchants, Hayon added that butchers assumed that such formalities were "prejudicial" to their trade. Hayon's sarcastic tone points to the lack of sympathy that he and other royal administrators shared toward merchant butchers who evaded the cattle markets. For him, the pass system brought transparency to what he assumed was primarily a hidden and often fraudulent trade.[36]

Nevertheless, this pass system encountered logistical problems even among those honest merchants who bought and sold at Sceaux and Poissy. For example, difficulties arose when butchers purchased livestock for other butchers and would divide up the herds by lottery the following day, or when butchers bought large quantities to fill their stockyards and sheds outside the city to be later driven into the city as need be. How then would a butcher show proof of his purchase at market once he arrived at the city gate?

In mémoires written and published by the guild, the objections to the laissez-passer most often point to these kinds of practical difficulties. The debate centered on typical situations such as "one butcher who on one market day makes a purchase and takes a laissez-passer for 600 sheep, and who brings them into Paris at different times, ten or twelve at a time, how would one comply to the formality expressed in the laissez-passer?"[37] The answer was relatively straightforward: let livestock purchasers have as many passes as they need. In fact, by the middle of the eighteenth century, the caisse printed these passes like coupon books so that livestock could be divided along with their coupons after the sale and accounted for in part (even individually) as they passed through their final checkpoint.

But the butchers still complained. They objected to the formalities engendered by the laissez-passer and decried that other systems of surveillance hindered, even ruined their trade.[38] For the directors of the caisse, the formality was its genius. Without the precise tracking record of livestock moving from provisioning market to butcher stall, the policing efforts to end fraudulent practices in the cattle trade would be severely handicapped, if not useless.[39]

Butchers, like apprentice Barthélemy Nicolas, learned the importance of these slips of paper the hard way. The twenty-three-year-old native of Metz was sent by his Parisian master LeRoy with two passes to bring in nine sheep purchased at Sceaux from his stockyard in Montrouge. He arrived at the St. Jacques crossing where the offices of the tax farmers stood waiting to collect the passes and entry duties. There, he realized that one of his two passes was missing and all he had was one pass for one sheep. So he innocently took the second pass for "*un mouton*" and changed it for "*onze moutons,*" albeit paying the duty on the nine sheep he herded. Nevertheless, the two-sheep discrepancy made the controllers at the gate immediately suspicious. They examined the pass closely and got a confession out of Nicolas. He was promptly arrested and taken to the police at the Châtelet. Asked why he chose to write "*onze*" instead of "*neuf,*" the number of sheep he actually had, he replied, "It seemed too difficult to make the word *neuf* out of *un,* and I could easily change the word *onze* out of the word *un.*"[40] Admittedly, his only motive was to get the animals to the shop in Paris where his master was waiting. A royal procurator at a higher court prosecuted Nicolas three months following the incident and fined him 3 livres. The parlement's Grande Chambre posted the falsified laissez-passer.[41]

Conclusion

Credit would always remain an integral part of merchant butchers' commercial lives. They operated in highly leveraged businesses, many without the proper bookkeeping skills that would keep them apprised of their finances. The credit system offered by the Caisse de Poissy forcibly changed merchant traditions toward formalized banking procedures. The structural characteristics of the system, the laws, regulations, and practices that governed its behavior conflicted with the customary practices of butchers and cattle merchants. The caisse held political power within a certain jurisdiction whereby everyone had to pass by the caisse. The role of the tax farmer or moneylender would be short-lived, but fairly important in shaping the prejudice for or against the caisse. Its legal status as a royal tax farm bestowed power and legitimacy to its officers while feeding the enmity of merchants and traders.

At the same time, the system of the caisse brought greater accountability and closer regulation to the cattle trade. The presence of officials to monitor trade and facilitate payment, to police conditions of graft and collusion were elements that gave confidence and reliability to markets. Its mandatory supply zone and on-site presence helped to reinforce its primary role in the market. These aspects were far more important determinants of the caisse's eventual adaptation than its success as a lending institution. In sum, given its meager funds, compared to the entire money in circulation (800,000 livres funded fewer than a quarter of all transactions at market), the caisse serves as a weak example of an early bank. It demonstrated minimal monetary power as opposed to forms of exchange embedded in social relationships (i.e., IOUs and good faith agreements). Given the caisse's minor role in the credit market at Poissy and Sceaux on the one hand, and its attempt to impose strict limits on the traffic in livestock on the other hand, one would be hard-pressed to point to the institution as a leading force in fostering economic development in the early meat industry. Yet the fact that the caisse persisted as a lending institution through the middle of the nineteenth century reveals its ability to serve the needs of butchers and cattle traders. It could not accomplish this without reforms, born of contentious debate, successive boycotts, and occasional rebellion that accompanied the long life of the institution.

The livestock trade faced enormous obstacles. Nonetheless suppliers found ways to trade livestock with merchant butchers with greater efficiency than the methods of market regulation laid out. The fact that merchants did not comply with official rules or that police did not regularly enforce these rules did not mean that provisioning failed. In many ways, this illegal traffic was neither evil nor dangerous but rational and beneficial. The full expression of a market economy could not be reached without overcoming the many mental and physical obstacles that the police, merchants, and royal administrators faced. For all three groups, the liberty of commerce would weigh in differently on the scale of commercial imperatives. For merchants, liberty meant the freedom to keep the urban-rural exchange open and fluid, to seek out suppliers wherever they could, and paradoxically, to protect their privileges from other "unlicensed" workers. For those responsible for keeping funds flowing into the royal treasury, liberty meant expanding markets and increasing revenues through directed measures. But they attained this through controlling central markets and gaining control over the greatest number of market transactions possible. For the police of Paris, a necessary degree of liberty was to be held in check with regulation, as both remained embedded in the social and political institutions they subscribed to and defended. Once inside the city walls, these rules changed as the market for fresh meat, "a good necessary for the people's subsistence," raised different policing concerns that centered on the public health and safety of the city's half-a-million residents.

Figure 4: A country butcher in the act of slaughter. Cattle provided important contributions to agricultural labor as beasts of burden and were often slaughtered at the end of their working lives. Used with permission of the Bibliothèque Nationale de France.

Chapter 4

Order and Disorder in the Urban Meat Markets

On July 23, 1729 a group of angry and frightened residents from the Saint-Bernard district banded together to complain to the city police about a neighboring butchery, in particular its scalding house that rendered fat from the animals slaughtered there on a daily basis. The neighbors' previous complaints focused on the nuisance (that forced them to live with their windows shut in the heat of the summer), and for the wealthy nobleman who lived among them, the potential property losses (his tarnished silver and his apartments that rented out at a "vile price"). After several attempts to alert the city about the thick, black smoke that poured out of the scalding house, the animal waste that rotted in the alley, and the pools of coagulated blood that filled the gutters, the police finally took notice of the potential fire hazard and the threat the butchery posed to the public's health and safety. According to the commissaire's report:

> . . . in as much as the noise, there is the bad smell that comes out of it that is capable of corrupting the purity of the air, not to mention the continuous dread that they are to see each other burn . . . it poses an infinite danger.[1]

Clearly, the incendiary threat far outweighed all other forms of pollution that this butchery inflicted on the neighborhood, giving the city grounds to alert the landlords and force them to close the butchery. Yet, for some of the residents, the imposing presence of butchers and their horrendous sights and sounds struck a nerve.

> That the plaintiffs being near this scalding house hear nearly every night the noise made by nearly twenty pork butchers, the majority drunk on wine and spirits, in addition to this are dreadful screams, from the quantity of pigs that one kills and from something frightening especially at night, by the resemblance that the screams have with all that one murders, also along with the barking of several large dogs that the workers have with them, [all] of which happens even on Sundays and holy days. . . .[2]

The close proximity of butcheries and gangs of butchers heightened the fears of many Parisians and contributed to a growing problem of how to manage their imposing, but necessary presence. On the one hand, butchers performed the duties of urban food providers in which they were given control over an important part of the city's subsistence needs. On the other hand, the growing sensibilities of urban individuals reacted unfavorably to butchers' violent and polluting work habits. At best, their work generated a level of waste that had to be constantly managed. At worst, slaughterhouse workers and their workplace became an urban menace.

This chapter explains the problems tied to the practice of the urban meat trade and the attempts to instill order on disorder in a variety of ways. As the population of Paris grew over the eighteenth century to somewhere between 600,000 and 700,000 by 1789, the government grappled with modern problems of traffic flow, access to markets, and the commercial expansion of butcher stalls. City administrators made efforts to maintain social order that included the maintenance of a regular meat supply while limiting risks to public health and safety. These goals were not always compatible with the will of butchers and the needs of their businesses. Nor were they a concern of individual meat sellers seeking to gain a living from the trade. The government tried to ensure that supply met demand, yet it did not want to interfere in the free flow of commerce. Nevertheless, throughout the eighteenth century, the municipal authorities at the Châtelet increasingly took on the regulation of the butcheries, going beyond the internal guidelines of the corporate community to command standards of cleanliness and to control unruly behavior. More often, police reports sided with the complaints of residents, but were ineffective in eliminating their all too visible presence from the city. Instead, commissaires responded by trying to limit the hazards and noisome conditions that inflicted a certain level of anxiety upon Parisians.

One way in which the civil authorities contained the polluting effects of this trade was through the allocation of workspace. As the demand for fresh meat drove market expansion, increasing the number of stalls from 1674 to 1782 by nearly 90 percent,[3] the police made efforts to control the placement of butcheries. They approved the location of new stalls and meat markets and oversaw the yearly registration of commercial leases. Policing the butchers meant directing their pathways and carving out specific locations for animal slaughter and meat sales, thereby guaranteeing the stability and constancy of the sites of provisioning while minimizing Parisians' daily exposure to public slaughter. Such an objective sprang from the Parisians' new vision of their city which extolled refinement and taste, leaving little room for such barbaric acts as infecting the capital's air and water. These enlightened individuals focused on the savagery of butchers' work that irritated their bourgeois sensibilities. For these observers of popular city life, the skills of butchering did not represent the ingenuity of the mechanical arts. Rather, the violent and bloody medium in which butchers worked debased them. They were inured to killing and, as a result, posed a collective threat to the urban community.

The Spectacle of Slaughter and Butcher Violence

The visceral reactions to public slaughter impelled Parisians (like the plaintiffs of Saint-Bernard) to voice their unease with the authorities. As their police report attests, the primal screams emanating from the slaughterhouse were frighteningly similar "to all that one murders." Popular belief maintained that the repeated sight of slaughter could desensitize workers (and passersby) to the act of killing, thereby engendering violent criminal activity. Louis-Sebastian Mercier, in his eighteenth-century chronicles of Paris scenes, described in horrid detail the social contagion inherent in the public slaughter of animals.

> . . . It is neither good nor wise to butcher a lamb within the sight of children, to allow blood to run into the streets. These bloody streams affect the morality of man as much as his body: emitting a double corruption for them both. Who knows if some man has not become a murderer from crossing these streets and bringing home shoes red with blood? He has heard the wailing animals being slaughtered alive; and perhaps by consequence made him less sensible to the smothered cries of someone he has struck.[4]

The unfavorable image of the Parisian butcher sprung from an overriding pathology of the city, namely its crowded conditions that bred violence. Parisians saw an environment filled with blood and pollution that begot a kind of barbarism. For Mercier, this repeated activity dehumanized the worker as his description of butchers shows:

> . . . ferocious and blood-thirsty with their naked arms, a thick neck, bloodshot eye, dirty legs, bloody apron; a knobby and massive baton arms their heavy hands and always ready for a brawl which they enjoy. One punishes them more severely than other professions, to quell their ferocity; experience proves that this is the right thing to do.[5]

Butchers, like other trades associated with blood and violence, such as surgeons and executioners, faced strong prejudice from urban elites. In the close coexistence of butchers and town dwellers, the slippage from a form of culturally sanctioned behavior to a deviant form such as murder or cannibalism filled the social imagination. Popular children's tales such as the *croquemitaine* propel the image of the cannibalistic butcher, in this case, one who cuts up and eats small children.[6] The proximity of "savage" butcher to "civilized" Parisian made for a great deal of discomfort that required close surveillance.

Figure 5: *La Bouchère* (The Female Butcher), as represented here, evoked ambivalent notions of gender in a highly masculine trade. Used with permission of the Bibliothèque Nationale de France.

Women's participation in the more common practices of butchering generated deeper forms of ambivalence. Seemingly, they could be accepted as merchants as long as they remained beyond the threshold of the slaughterhouse, away from carcasses and blood. As the contemporary illustration of *la bouchère* demonstrates (see Figure 5), the matron with her delicate waist and bourgeois dress is a far cry from other illustrations of working butchers

Figure 6: *La Boucherie* (The Butchery) taken from the eighteenth-century *Encyclopedia*. Used with permission of the Bibliothèque Nationale de France.

with bloodied hands and aprons, emptying carcasses of entrails and holding axes over their heads (see Figure 6). Here, the rendition juxtaposes a stylish *bouchère* in ruffled, high collar and delicate shoes with the overgrown, ferocious canine and a table of delicately arranged meats. In this pristine portrait of the feminized butcher both the hands of the butcher and all signs of slaughter are absent. We can only discern her trade from the cuts of meat hanging on the wall and the tools sitting on the butcher block. These details are foregrounded by the proud stance of a bourgeois merchant with her spiky-collared guard dog in an oxymoronic visual play of woman and beast, order and disorder, the civilized and the barbaric.

Parisians' imaginary fears stemmed from the association of knife-wielding meat cutters that promoted their own elements of identification. Butchers distinguished themselves from other artisans by their physique, their dress, their work habits, their working conditions, and even a spoken dialect.[7] Over the course of several centuries, they had become ensconced in several areas of the city near covered meat markets and central food halls. Prominent butcher families constructed a kind of corporate oligopoly built upon family firms and the transmission of property and title. Not surprisingly, butchers earned the reputation as a community made up of tightly knit clans. For reasons of public peace, segregating the community of workers was absolutely necessary. According to Diderot and d'Alembert's *Encyclopédie méthodique:*

> . . . in a large city especially, butcheries and slaughterhouses must be widely separated. One could offer an infinite number of reasons for this: but the most striking is taken from the public peace. Each butcher has four workers [*garçons*]; and many have six. They are all violent undisciplined men whose hands and eyes are accustomed to blood. One sees the danger in putting them in a position where they could draw from this, and if one could gather eleven to twelve hundred in three or four places, it would be very difficult to contain them and to prevent them from beating each other to death. But occasions arise where their natural furor could take them further. One only has to return to the time of Charles VI and the past experience to feel the power of this consideration.[8]

The fear of butcher violence lay in the potential threat that this group of killers wielded–the everyday violence that could become riotous behavior. This fear multiplied as the butcher population become more concentrated alongside a city that could barely manage to contain its general population. Anxiety over the potential threat of butcher violence conflicted with the problems of animal waste. Throughout the early modern period, the butcher shops and stalls appeared throughout the city without a central slaughterhouse (*abbatoir*) to contain the putrid smells and animal waste. One explanation for this dispersed, piecemeal growth was to stave off the collective violence of butchers. The writers of the *Encyclopédie* pointed to the Cabochien Revolt of 1413 as one of the "occasions" when butchers' innate fury led them to a bloody popular revolt. The memory of this urban revolt and the havoc it unleashed on the social order underscored the dangers of butcher gangs as potential warriors. Although in the *longue durée,* the history of butcher involvement in popular revolts may carry some truth,[9] elite claims of a barbarous esprit de corps leading a popular uprising never manifested in the eighteenth century–even during the height of the Revolution of 1789. What the historical record shows are forms of everyday violence and aggression that contributed to a troublesome reputation and the disquiet of Parisians.

Butchers' Work and Workplace

The meat trade required an elect group of trained workers to engage in violent acts to secure one of life's basic necessities. Because the act of animal sacrifice invested the butcher with both savagery and beneficence, the ambivalence between taking life and sustaining life was always a paradoxical aspect of his trade. Most contemporaries lived with this cultural contradiction, pointing out that slaughter in no way violates the sanctity of life because God created animals to sustain human beings. The destruction and depiecing of livestock was for butchers an act of production. Yet for many outside the trade, these tasks (however distinctly human and skillful) disturbed a given order of things, just as pollution and disgust, culturally speaking, are the result of matter out of place.[10] They are visceral reactions to the sights and smells of slaughter that varied according to the custom and reason of eighteenth-century Parisians.

Most outsiders unaccustomed to the work of slaughter and butchering saw it as filthy work. In the stalls and the private slaughterhouses that adjoined them, workers plunged their hands in steaming carcasses to remove entrails. They stood in pools of blood and bile. They filled tubs with toxic animal waste, flushed their stalls with streams of fresh water, and swept away coagulated blood. They collected skins and salted them to preserve the flesh from rot before selling them to tanners. They washed and cooked the lining of the stomach and small intestines to sell to tripe dealers. Butchers' work polluted the city not only with animal waste, but also with the noise of animals that screamed out before their deaths. Butchers' work polluted the air with the stench of rotting flesh, steaming organs, and rendering fat. Most significantly, their work desensitized them to the act of killing, and in the imaginations of some contemporaries, made them unruly brutes.

Butchers who held the highest positions in this highly stratified community of masters, journeymen, and apprentice butchers, also distanced themselves the furthest from the work of slaughter. Most masters who hired journeymen to work in their stalls positioned themselves as guild merchants not meat cutters. Intent on constructing an honorable reputation in their dealings at the cattle markets, the work of merchant butchers (negotiating purchases and provisioning contracts, borrowing and lending small sums, supervising the shop) was decidedly patrician. The merchants' wardrobe, as evidenced in afterdeath inventories, included fine cloth overcoats, white ruffled shirts, and wigs–clothing that was not fit for the butchery, but would be worn in financial dealings in the cattle markets and elite households.[11] Even though it is impossible to know how these men occupied their time, the fact that many had designated a small portion of their living space as offices (*cabinets*) where they kept their chests of gold pieces and promissory notes, suggests that much of it was spent in secretarial and banking duties, not engaged in the manual labor.

Similarly, the division of labor that separated heads of households from wage earners also separated butcher's work along gender lines. A butcher's wife or widow, although an integral member of the working household, maintained her distance from the slaughterhouse floor. The work of butcher's wives, daughters, and widows focused on managing household finances and domestic chores: washing, preparing food, and childcare. Yet as living space and workshop melded together, "women's work," which included cleaning linens, boiling carcasses, and rendering fat, was also productive, and, in the case of child rearing, reproductive. In households with several children and five to six stall workers, wives and daughters with the help of domestic servants kept the crew clothed and fed. Each butcher household, even the most modest, had at least one domestic who as nurse, housekeeper, or cook, allowed for butchers' wives and widows to focus their energy on the family business.[12]

The primary duties of a butcher's wife or widow involved serving clients at the storefront, collecting money from stall sales, and keeping track of revenue and expenses. Bookkeeping among butchers made no distinction between family and business funds. In many butcher account books, scribbled in the odd pages are shopping lists, laundry lists, and the accounts for the washing woman (*blanchisseuse*).[13] As bookkeeper, she was also responsible for keeping records on clients who often paid on credit. She corresponded with clients whose accounts were past due. In the case of butcher Antoine Danet, his wife's rhetorical skills also proved to be a powerful asset. During a period when he fell into deep debt with the officers of the Caisse de Poissy, she wrote emotional pleas to creditors to beg for extensions on loans.[14] In this household, the butcher's wife was as much his business partner as his helpmeet; the needs of efficiency entailed a coordination of efforts that could require women to fulfill a variety of tasks separate from her husband.

In any assessment of women's contribution to the trade, the historian has to consider the cultural assumptions that placed invisible boundaries around the women's workplace, as well as the gender roles that structured and were structured by a sexual division of labor. For example, when minding the stall, would a butcher's wife be expected to trim and distribute cuts of meat according to the customer's wants? Did she enter the area where livestock was slaughtered to assist other workers? Certainly, much of butchers' work that involved lifting, hanging, cutting, and piecing meat required a certain level of upper body strength that women lacked. These jobs were not simply gender-specific, but also demeaning and polluting to status-minded masters, their wives and children, hence reserved for wage laborers. Even mistress widows who undertook their husband's businesses most commonly relied upon journeymen to work behind the stalls.

For many anxious Parisians living in proximity to the butcheries, the focal point was the gang of journeymen who worked as wage earners in the daily tasks of slaughter and butchering. Their position outside the guild made them less likely to subscribe to the ethic of serving the public good. And their status as nonkin, seasonal labor working for a family firm, made them less invested in the family's short- and long-term success. Instead, other forces served to curb their behavior. Masters enforced military-like discipline at work through a system of rank for each task. The bad conduct of a worker reflected directly upon his master who suffered penalties to his reputation. Police surveyed the behavior of journeymen, commonly referred to as "boy butchers" (*garçons bouchers*), especially when these boys were outside of their masters' supervision. At the same time, these authorities allowed youths a certain amount of play and revelry.[15]

The demands of the trade meant journeymen labored with little respite. They lived and worked under the same roof around the clock, even sleeping in the market stalls on wooden planks.[16] Like the butchers in Saint Bernard quarter, one habit that these butchers acquired on the job was the practice of drinking–too much and too often. Journeymen drank to be sociable as much as journeymen worked to drink. Master butchers regularly plied their cellars with enough wine to keep their working household full of alcohol. The accounts of the Hôtel-Dieu allot a certain amount of drink to each garçon who worked at the hospital's meat stalls that operated during Lent. Those who worked in the slaughterhouse received two pints a day, others a pint-and-a-half.[17] No doubt alcohol profoundly influenced their behavior in the shop and in the streets.

The cabaret served as a place to settle disputes. The danger of combining drink with boisterous crowds often led to heated altercations.[18] Garçons who found themselves in trouble with the police for rowdy behavior did not always need drink to incite them. Typically, police records show groups of three or more who, after carousing, were caught in one fray or another. For Leonard Lefebvre, an unsuspecting food seller, the evening's revelry of three garçons bouchers was enough to merit a knock on the head. The three workers entered the city from the north along rue Montmartre and commenced fighting with the man selling skewers of meat. The unprovoked attack left the victim with a lump on his head and "in fear for his well being." All that can be determined from the complaint was that the butchers wanted something of Lefebvre's–perhaps a bit of food? Was this reason enough for a band of butchers to make trouble?[19] As the police archives attest, the struggle to maintain civility and order was not always successful. The flaring of tempers and a show of force occurred, often as journeymen became defiant toward those who challenged their position in the world of work.

Journeymen's dogs became a means for workers to provoke fear and gain respect. Dogs also served more productive uses to herd animals in the stalls and along the crowded streets. They offered a certain amount of security against robbery. But when journeymen intentionally raised them to attack other dogs or people, the police intervened, viewing their actions as "contrary to the security of the public streets." Dog fights often became sites of male competition between rival journeymen. Witnesses of a dog fight on rue Saint Martin one Friday afternoon blamed two garçons bouchers for their avidity to "excite the animals and provoke them," leading to the injury of an innocent bystander.[20] Clients knowingly took risks when entering a butcher stall as journeymen could enlist their bloodthirsty hounds to intimidate them. For Marguerite Forest, who brazenly stepped across the threshold of a shop full of journeymen to settle a dispute, the boundary she crossed would prove nearly fatal. The journeymen present had little to do except give the command and she left with several bites over her hands and one on her stomach. These aggressive acts elevated the power journeymen held over their own territory, one they could guard with temerity.[21]

Although these incidents point to particular cases of butcher unrest, they are not representative of the entire working population. The characterization of butchers as savages reveals more about an elite's fear of these men than their actual reputation evinced. The archival record shows that butchers were never singled out as a dangerous group by the police. Their criminal record did not in any way stand out among those of other manual trades.[22] More often, the cases that filled the commissaires' reports represented the escapades of youthful and undisciplined garçons bouchers who sought the pleasures of drink and group high jinks. On the rare occasion when they harmed innocent pedestrians, journeymen faced harsh consequences not only from their masters, but also from the police at the Châtelet. More typical was the harm that came to Parisians indirectly or unintentionally. These complaints centered on butchers' work itself perceived as a public annoyance that threatened the relative peace and tranquility of the city.

A Public Nuisance

Butchers who transported livestock from provisioning market to stall contributed to the congestion and traffic hazards in the city. Police regulations required that butchers herd animals through the city at times when the streets were free of pedestrians, with at least two men driving the herd–one in front, one behind.[23] Once safely at the slaughterhouse, stall butchers tethered and enclosed the livestock within the courtyard or small sheds behind the butcher's house. By law, slaughterhouse doors remained closed to prevent wounded and frightened animals from fleeing their imminent death. Yet even if butchers followed these prudent measures, animals could escape causing havoc. The frenzy and danger of the streets of Paris is where butchers' work appears as one of the multiple urban hazards with which Parisians had to contend.

On June 26, 1785, a steer freed itself from the hands of two stall workers under Master Butcher Eustache Homme of rue Montmartre. In its fury to escape certain death, the animal charged through the streets of Paris, injuring ten or twelve and killing two or three persons, according to reports sent to the procurator general of the Paris Parlement. The injuries included broken legs and arms, impaled stomachs, and minor cuts and bruises. Apparently, the raging animal could not be stopped before it crossed nearly half the city throwing people from its way.[24] Less than a week later, a steer belonging to butcher Lefebvre escaped from the ropes that held its horns. The two stall workers who led the steer across the street from the cowshed to the slaughterhouse ran after the animal. The running of the horned beast toppled carts and caused minor injuries. The only fatality came to a horse at the Porte de Sèvres.[25]

A high number of such incidents in 1785 (known as *boeufs échappés*) greatly troubled city authorities who tried to protect innocent Parisians from harm. Their investigation finally ended in a parlementary arrêt published on September 2, 1785 over the traffic of livestock in the city of Paris. The police viewed these cases as "a veritable offense" and urged the leader of the city's parlement to press charges.[26] Paris, with its densely populated city center, could not manage the continuous traffic in livestock. By September 1785, a police ordinance prohibited any circulation of livestock in the city after 6:00 A.M. during the summer and 8:00 A.M. during the winter.[27]

Without taking these precautions, butchers risked injuring themselves and others. Such was the case on December 14, 1737 when a garçon butcher working for Master Butcher Barré drove seven steer through a crowded intersection at the rue Verrerie and rue Poterie at about 11:00 A.M. The garçon spurred on his herd through the crowd of pushcarts and other wagons, only to drive them straight into the carriage of Madame Francoise Richard, widow of Jacques Fauveau, a robe noble.[28] The steer's impact broke the door and shattered a window of her carriage, leaving her unharmed but quite agitated. She left the scene of the accident to scold the boy's master and file a complaint with Commissaire Blanchard.[29] In another incident, Nicolas Porteur took his life into his hands when making a delivery of 60 pounds of fresh meat on December 29, 1751. Carrying the merchandise on his back, he left his workplace on rue Saint-Denis and headed toward rue Vivienne at 9:00 A.M. Along the rue Montorgeuil, Porteur was struck by a four-wheeled carriage driven by a team of horses. The accident left him with a broken arm and a bruised left leg as well as a load of meat flung into the mud. For these stall butchers, crossing the city occasioned as much of a battle as overcoming a steer.[30]

Beyond the movement of cattle and sheep, Parisians living next to the butcheries and stalls confronted the emanating stench from meat processing. The worst odors came from the scalding works where workers removed the skins and fat from animal carcasses. The refining process consisted of running fresh hides and offal through large cauldrons of boiling water that had to be drained and replenished at regular intervals. The work provided an important link in the production (or deconstruction) process whereby butchers could reap value from every part of the raw product. Typically, butchers set up the large kettles within their residence, but far enough outside the living quarters and into the courtyard so as not to be a nuisance to neighbors. Needless to say, the thick, black smoke and heavy odor of rotting flesh filled the area, engendering numerous complaints.

Police made attempts to minimize the polluting effects of butchering through a variety of regulations to maintain standards of hygiene. The police required that butchers put grills over their drains to prevent "the escape of any blood or foul matter."[31] The city government appointed a sanitation director who oversaw the meatcutters and tripe cleaners at the Place aux Veaux.[32] The police also required butchers to dump their solid waste in designated pits. Most stalls contained tubs that held liquid waste to be dumped into the river or in dumping grounds. By 1758, with pressure from Lieutenant General of Police Bertin, the municipal authorities moved many of these public dumps outside of the city.[33]

Most butcheries were located within easy reach of a water supply, which allowed them to flush out their stalls regularly. The oldest covered butcheries were located along the river Seine. Others had access to the many fountains and wells located throughout the city.[34] Despite efforts to clean the most unsightly areas that surrounded the butcheries, their location upstream and along the tributaries leading into the Seine meant that a good deal of waste flowed into the city.

Aware to some extent that this pollution was an undesirable and unhealthy presence in drinking water, the police made a crude effort to protect Parisians by designating places along the river from which vendors might draw the water they sold. Ideally, butchers would work where the river ran free, as far away from sewer openings as possible. But most butchers sought locations near market squares and busy thoroughfares, where customers and transportation was most accessible. As the city grew, these areas became more congested with the traffic in cattle and fresh meat, not to mention the waste that fed into open sewers, contributing to the infamous Parisian bog. The location of new stalls and shops became a critical issue for the city authorities whose aim was to benefit the safety and health of Parisians.

Controlling the Growth of Meat Markets

As much as possible, the city authorities monitored the expansion of the butcher trade to ensure the "safety" (*sureté*) and "public health" (*salubrité publique*) of the people of Paris.[35] Increasingly, the police had to weigh the demands of provisioning against the nuisance and disorder caused by butcher trade practices. Even more troublesome was the threat of butcher violence. The history of the Grande Boucherie, one of the oldest covered butcheries dating from the Roman period, reminded city leaders of how high the stakes could be. Concentrating the majority of the city's butchers in a central location (in this case behind the Châtelet) would make it all too easy for them to organize an insurrection. Charles VI realized this only after the Cabochien Revolt of 1413. His response was to raze the prominent edifice as a way to lessen the strategic hold of the butcher rebel. After this show of force, the crown won back the allegiance of the masters by building them another covered butchery on a smaller scale than the original, adding several other meat markets throughout the city.

During the latter half of the eighteenth century, as food markets expanded, the police took active measures to diffuse the butcher population further by granting the construction of new stalls away from the city center. Rather than concentrate all food merchants in one central marketplace such as Les Halles, the city approved the creation of several, smaller food markets in other public squares such as the Place aux Veaux and the Place Maubert. The government granted other locations along central throughways that allowed for the traffic of people, animals, and goods, these included rue Saint Martin that led north from the city center, and rue des Boucheries that led west from the Left Bank near the Luxembourg quarter. Other butcher markets grew within bounded spaces such as inside the walls of abbeys in the Faubourg Saint Germain or the priory of Saint Martin des Champs.[36]

These new meat markets fanned out from the city center where the oldest covered butcheries stood. The Grande Boucherie (also called *l'Apport Paris*) was the largest with twenty-nine stalls. The three other covered butcheries held their fixed location; one, at the Saint-Jean cemetery with eight stalls, at the Saint Denis gate with six stalls, and on the major street leading to Montmartre with six stalls. These butcheries did not relocate nor augment their number of stalls as other meat markets did throughout the eighteenth century. Rather their permanent constructions reinforced the stable position they held within the city. Their enclosed space also set physical boundaries on sites of exchange and concentrated trade in select areas.[37]

Although the locations of meat markets were fairly evenly dispersed, the city confined each of these retail centers, to cemeteries or sites where human waste was dumped. At least in the minds of the city administrators, all butcher stalls were supposed to operate within a restricted space that allowed for better surveillance and control, and ideally, to prevent expansion. According to the Châtelet's registers of the stalls (*étaux),* the majority of butchers worked in covered butcheries and open markets rather than in single shops (a stall attached to a house). This arrangement remained intact for most of the eighteenth century, as it corresponded to urban authorities' demands for central markets that they could regulate and control. It also fulfilled their desire to restrict butchers' workspaces to locations that did not threaten public safety.[38]

Parisians, increasingly more aware of the effect the urban environment had upon their health, grew less tolerant and more fearful of butcher quarters where waste and effluvia collected in the streets and water supply. By the end of the eighteenth century, city planners sought to modify the urban trade beginning with the location of central slaughterhouses outside the city center. But even before the construction of the first abbatoirs, the Châtelet granted the establishment of single butcher shops within residential neighborhoods, as retail boutiques became more commonplace. At the same time, many new stalls in open markets on the outskirts of Paris appeared as a response to the demographic shift that pushed the city outward into the faubourgs. The new butcher stalls on the fringe of the city offered added space for holding livestock, slaughtering animals, and processing meat, hides, and tallow. The butcher shops in residential areas offered another venue for butchers to gain access to different clientele who lived far from food markets. Overall, the number of stalls grew along the city periphery, while the number of stalls near the city center decreased.[39]

Officials, who reviewed the requests for new butcher stalls, based their decisions upon criteria that most often related to issues of traffic flow and occasionally to the convenience of consumers. An example resides in the report of Commissaire Dupré submitted to the royal authorities in March 1658 to build eight new stalls in a covered butchery at the Porte Saint-Jacques. His opinion rests on principles of city management, saying that the establishment of a new butchery would be necessary:

> . . . in order to free the rue Saint-Jacques that is the principle [street] of this city, from the confusion of the market that is held there, [the area] from the gate to the Jesuit college is filled with numbers of benches, tubs, and goods exposed for sale that occupy the street in its principal thoroughfare, that the free movement of coaches, carts, and wagons are considerably

hindered by them, that they often cause many disturbances and quarrels, even hinder the passage. . . .[40]

Many of the petitions presented to the courts at the Châtelet to construct additional stalls and covered butcheries were never approved because of their imposition on the urban space. Butcher François Maindorge made numerous appeals to build four new stalls in 1787 and 1788 and had his letters patent revoked at least twice after exceeding the geographic limits designated in the legal document. The police opinion written on February 22, 1788 clearly specified the boundaries within which Maindorge's proposal had to remain.[41] Another police opinion on a proposal dated December 20, 1776 expressed concern over the crowding that an additional butchery would cause in the Saint-Gervais parish that would only result in "the ruin" of the neighborhood.[42] The proposal was denied.

When the police did grant licenses to construct butcher shops in residential areas, they often awarded these to property seeking notables. In one case, the nobleman, "Monsieur le Comte de Persan," acquired a stall adjacent to a house near the Faubourg du Temple (an area now known as the Marais). According to the written police opinion, the proposal met "the motives of utility and public good."[43] The stall augmented those in the neighboring quarters to satisfy the needs of local residents, giving them easy access to goods. Another successful appeal that year gave the residents of the same quarter another butcher shop. The police opinion states:

> In effect the inhabitants of this quarter, of which the number has grown considerably in the past few years, force us to see a marked advantage in this establishment, as it only makes it easier to procure and to put in better reach one of the most essential goods for their subsistence. Given how important these views are, they cannot be ignored, arousing our zeal to concur and favor this establishment.[44]

In calling for better access to meat markets, the police reiterated the essential conditions of eighteenth-century food policy, namely access to supply. The regulation surrounding market placement followed other primary food issues, as it was "one of the most essential goods" for the people's subsistence.

In addition to new butcher stalls in established markets, owned by property investors, leased and operated by guild butchers, Paris saw the rise of the "privileged stalls" (*étaux privilegiés*). Those interested in such a venture, either by way of a personal bequest or the purchase of the title "privileged butcher," could find an easy entré in the growing meat trade. In 1721, the police registered ten privileged stalls in the Châtelet rolls. By 1781, the number totaled fifty-nine. The greatest change came between 1772 and 1781 when the number of privileged stalls grew from twenty-nine to fifty-nine. Many of these earlier privileged stalls represent a transfer of ownership from stalls previously held as part of royal domain or ecclesiastical property to individual property. The sharp increase in the number of privileged stalls suggests a kind of privatization of the trade. Whereas previously the king or the church owned and managed several central butcheries (usually with the oversight of guild leaders), now individual entrepreneurs were building or acquiring the property. While these stalls had to be run by master butchers, wealthy proprietors could invest in a new stall out of a single residence and benefit from the additional revenue of this commercial property.[45]

Many merchants circumvented this legal procedure and set up their own businesses independently. Butcher Leonard Paramour, who held two legitimate stalls in the butchery at Saint-Eustache, attempted to build a third without the consent of the police by placing a bench at the end of one of his stalls. Remarkably, this unofficial stall appeared on the police rolls of the following year, 1721. This brazen move troubled the church wardens of Saint-Eustache who owned the butchery. They complained to the police and sought an injunction against the butcher. This police intervention did not end the dispute between landlord and tenant as the church wardens returned to the commissaire at the Châtelet to file complaints about the harsh treatment they received from Paramour, his wife, and workers.[46]

Although the new privileged stalls competed with well-established butcheries, it was the nonguild meat sellers who troubled the guild masters most of all, especially as their presence encroached upon the masters' privileged urban space. When these unlicensed merchants (*métiers sans qualité*) came into the city and set up shop along marketplaces and butcheries, the guild responded by driving them out as they threatened the status of guild masters. Here, policing took another turn away from the public good toward defending honor and reputation.

The Threat of "Rogue" Butchers

In theory (and in limited geographical areas) master butchers held a monopoly; but in practice, they by no means controlled the sale of meat to Parisians. Numerous meat-sellers existed outside the guild community and competed with master butchers. The most common were meat sellers with mobile stands (*échoppes*) who congregated across from the butcheries or in the open space of the market squares. Police also reported the illegal presence of peddlers (*colporteurs*) and female meat sellers (*regrattières*) who came to the central food market, Les Halles, to hawk their own butchered meat as well as cooked and recycled meat scraps. The law clearly stated that these itinerant merchants could not sell meat in Paris. A parlement's decision (arrêt) dated April 1, 1704 clearly defined the territory that threatened the guild butchers' markets, which included virtually all the gates and barriers at the city limits.[47] Country butchers whose volume of sales attempted to overtake the trade of guild butchers faced heavy fines and possible arrest. Yet, the prominence of these forain traders suggests that there were plenty of opportunities for butchers in the outlying faubourgs.[48]

Considering the fact that the guild population could never exceed 240 master members and remained under 200,[49] each master operating no more than three stalls in a city of half-a-million people,[50] many outside the guild saw room for more Parisian butchers. Even master butchers depended heavily on hired labor (journeymen) to staff their one or two supplemental stalls throughout the week, some of whom operated more or less independent of any master. No doubt, the common perception of huge Parisian market and the relative ease in which a peasant could gain access to this agricultural commodity lured any fortune-seeking country butcher or farmer into Paris. These rogue butchers added to the Parisian meat supply as they furnished households directly from their farms. Contemporaries estimated the butcher population that resided in the Parisian suburbs and villages of Ile-de-France to number anywhere from 100 to 300 hundred.[51] These meat sellers, who either brought fresh meat from outside the city or produced it illegally within the city, offered an alternative source of meat for consumers, one that did not subscribe to guild standards or the police regulations. Only when their volume of sales attempted to overtake the trade of guild butchers did these interlopers face heavy fines and possible arrest.[52]

Peddlers and forain butchers who sold meat in Paris threatened the concept of the corporate community. Exclusionary rhetoric surrounded the policing of nonguild butchers, many of whom worked clandestinely. Their meat was either without merit or far from any standards of quality. Guild leaders, as standard bearers to their trade, took on the responsibility of policing (and criminalizing) these illegal sellers. Guild officers together with commissaires participated in seizures of "very defective meat" that was "inedible" or arrested those "selling unqualified meats" in public squares and along busy streets. Their discourse against the nonguild trade bespeaks a language of disorder, incompetence, and immorality; it serves to reinforce the corporate distinction that masters made such efforts to maintain.[53] Only guild butchers had the expertise and social standing that guaranteed meat that was healthy, if not well portioned.

The men and women who engaged in this black market trade took risks, often facing penalties of imprisonment. On occasion, the butchers and police pursued them with force, typically employing the police strength of city archers. Their goal was to seize the goods carried illegally into the city and try to extract the name of the butcher supplier from the peddlers or carriers who were caught. Commissaire Blanchard led a series of raids in the winter of 1722–1723. During this time, when supply and demand reached their height, the single trader reached for the opportunity to enter into the black market.

On November 29, 1722 at 7:00 A.M., Jean Baptiste Bertrand butcher guild officer and Commissaire Blanchard, along with the first archer named Prevost as their armed guard, patrolled the neighborhood near the Saint-Antoine gate. Other merchant butchers had notified them of the frequent passages of itinerant butchers who peddled meat to passersby. Within a short time, they spotted two butchers with large baskets full of fresh meat. They approached the young men who immediately fled the scene knowing they were done for. The officials eventually caught them and managed (after a great deal of struggle with Prevost) to get them to confess their crimes. One of the carriers, Jean Moniquet, worked for DuChastel a wholesale butcher in Montreuil. According to his statement, he was to deliver 65 pounds of meat in the baskets to the house of Madame La Marquise Duchastelet, whereupon he would receive roughly 50 livres, a price per pound that was nearly double the standard rate. His partner, a frightened shepherd named Philippe Rossignol, although employed by DuChastel to tend his herds, declared that this was the first time he had ever come to Paris to do such a thing. He begged forgiveness.[54]

Many of the seizures focused on female peddlers known as regrattières who marketed lesser cuts of meat and meat scraps. By definition, these female merchants sold a number of small goods second hand: herbs, fruits, vegetables, dairy products, as well as flowers. The professional category of regrattières, however, precluded the sale of meat. This area of commerce, though not necessarily beyond their physical capabilities, entered into the well-protected territory of the butchers' guild. The illegal trade that occurred on the fringes of the city was not insignificant for the women arrested on December 1, 1722. The dismantling of their butcher business required two wagons to carry off the seized goods; these included sixty-three fore- and hindquarters of mutton, plus other organ meats that together weighed nearly eight hundred pounds.[55]

Separate but not unequal in the minds of the guild officers were the nonguild butchers who practiced the trade in privileged zones such as the faubourg Saint-Antoine. Guild leaders referred to these "illegitimate workers" (*faux ouvriers*) or "unlicensed workers" (*ouvriers sans qualité*), a menace to the guildsman's cultural and economic capital. Their freedom was perceived to thrive in an unlicensed mayhem and lacked any concern for standards of quality. It is not surprising that the guild leaders were the first to pursue the workers, seizing their smuggled goods, and bringing them to the attention of commissaires at the Châtelet who imprisoned them for sham operations.[56]

Officials who seized the goods of unincorporated workers reported the meat "defective" and "unfit for human consumption." Most often, we can infer from the inventory of goods that the meat was simply rotten.[57] Several cases included meat that was "incapable of entering the human body," namely stillborn veal and totally spoiled meat. Regrattières who sold cooked meat could only claim to its freshness or its wholesomeness. Shoppers beware! Even though the police were interested in protecting the public's health, they turned a blind eye to many of these sellers whose survival depended upon their own resourcefulness.

When peddlers dealt in taboo foods such as goat and horsemeat, the police of Paris acted with little compassion. In March 1739, two dayworkers suffered the *grande peine* of a 300 livre fine for trying to smuggle in fresh horsemeat through the Saint-Denis gate.[58] Geneviève Jasmin, wife of a butcher, faced repeated incarcerations at Salpetrière prison in the spring and summer of 1728 for selling horsemeat and stillborn veal in the faubourg Saint-Marcel. Police accused her (a recognized bouchère) of practicing the trade freely, not under guild or police supervision. She had learnt her butchering skills as the wife of a journeyman butcher. After he abandoned her, she continued the trade alone. According to the police reports, her illegal status and Lenten commerce were lesser evils than the sale of ersatz butcher's meat.[59]

The stigma these workers faced goes beyond the prejudice of gender and rank that guild butchers upheld to reveal contemporary judgments about the urban evils born of harsh economic realities. Namely, those desperately seeking a means of livelihood posed the greatest threat to the city, especially when they endangered the safety and security of the food supply. For many Parisians, the survival strategies of the working poor that threatened the health of the innocent, only highlighted the moral disorder and backwardness of popular urban life. Of the faubourg Saint-Marcel, Mercier writes,

> It's the quarter where the Parisian populace lives, the poorest, the most turbulent, and the most undisciplined. There is more money in a single house of the faubourg Saint-Honoré than in all of the faubourg Saint-Marcel, or Saint-Marceau, taken together. It is in these settlements far from the central movement of the city, that hides ruined (impoverished) men, the misanthropes. . . . No one ever seeks out this corner of the city. If one makes a journey to this land, it is out of curiosity, nothing calls you here; there isn't a single monument to see; these people have no connection with Parisians, polite dwellers of the Seine riverbank. . . . The houses have no other clock than the height of the sun; these are men of three centuries back in time.[60]

Such accounts as this one, couched in the misapprehension of the urban poor, tell us more about the social conscience of the ruling elite than the real experience of those who lived in these areas. In many ways, Mercier's description appeals to the cult of misery, the ignorance, the danger, and the isolation that Enlightenment thinkers observed in the absence of effective urban policy. For him, Paris was a cesspool, a "filthy den of every vice and evil, where people are all crammed together in air poisoned by a thousand putrid vapors, amid cemeteries, hospitals, slaughter-houses, drains. . . ."[61] While many contemporaries may have agreed with Mercier, there were those who made efforts to make dramatic changes to the urban landscape. These entrepreneurs aimed far beyond the limited scope of the police, whose meek efforts did little to maintain standards of health and sanitation for butchers. Châtelet may have influenced the placement of butcheries to lessen the polluting presence of slaughter, but it was not able to eliminate them entirely from the city center.[62] The attempt to free Paris from the polluting and dangerous elements of butcheries would require an outside force–one that was willing to reconfigure the meat trade altogether.

The New City

For centuries, attempts to move the work of slaughter outside the city walls failed in the face of a powerful community of butchers.[63] The Paris Parlement passed several arrêts that attempted to legislate this move, decrying the "annoyance" (*incommodité*) that the butchers cause the public, but with little avail. Numerous proposals were forwarded by "entrepreneurs" and "bourgeois" to complete what the state could not. In 1664, Nicolas Rebuy, Bourgeois de Paris, desired "to do something advantageous for the public and to carry out the laws of the king's council and the parlement. . . ."[64] Many of these proposals, though claiming to serve the public, also sought the opportunity to privately invest in the construction of central slaughterhouses. One entrepreneur offered 100,000 livres to the king for the privilege of building and managing the new slaughterhouses.[65]

Despite these citywide initiatives, the butcher guild and its lawyers managed effectively to keep their privately held stalls and shops through powerful arguments that looked to the greater interests of the population. One argument rested upon the public health: that meat had to be processed on location to ensure quality. Fresh meat carried into the city had greater chance of spoilage and adulteration. The second relied upon safety, as it was the difficulty for master butchers to manage two locations where journeymen would work unsupervised while masters traveled to and from their shops in Paris. Finally was the cost, as a move would incur additional fees for transport and workers wages that would in turn raise the price of meat. These reasons centered on the fact that butchers' work (slaughtering and butchering) entailed two processes that were inextricably linked. The progression from animal to edible could not be interrupted nor could its production site be split in two.[66]

Nicolas Delamare considered the location of the slaughterhouses outside the city as an unnecessary move. In his treatise on policing, he agrees that the cost of transporting fresh meat from a remote slaughterhouse to the city butcher stalls was too high, as well as being an inconvenience to the butcher. The master butcher could not be in two places at the same time. Even if the master butcher's wife managed the market stall in the city (a popular proposal) while he worked in the outlying slaughterhouse, who would oversee the work of their group of journeymen and apprentices? The master was needed to organize and supervise their work. The danger of allowing these "violent and undisciplined" workers to travel throughout the city, to and from the slaughterhouse, needed to be seriously considered.[67]

These arguments kept the private slaughterhouses in central Paris for nearly three centuries because they appealed to the greater good. Such a successful defense points to the power of the guild and its ability to appeal to the most common fears of Parisians: the undisciplined gangs of boy butchers. Any effort to oust these workers and their dogs from their debauched enclaves met with little success until a more effective central authority, Emperor Napoleon, took power.[68]

Conclusion

Parisian meat markets and butcheries held vital yet problematic positions within the urban environment. The location of meat production within the city limits was on the one hand absolutely necessary. Meat, because of its easy corruptibility (whether by nature or man), required the strict surveillance of inspectors and police and the close proximity of producers to consumers. On the other hand, the visible presence of slaughterhouses evoked disgust and engendered complaints because of the polluting nature of butchers' work. The public spectacle of animal sacrifice propelled some observers to question the safety and security of those who resided near butcheries and open markets. The location of the butcheries in the center of Paris encumbered the city and threatened the public health. Finding the balance between the demand for fresh meat and the management of the urban space became increasingly important for city administrators as the city grew and the taste for beef spread. In many ways, the issues of urban provisioning hinge upon the symbolic paradoxes of meat that pit a healthful food of necessity against its violent and defiling production.

The market for meat in Paris saw significant changes throughout the eighteenth century. The emergence of these new stalls and boutiques and their subsequent royal approval throughout the century appear as a response to the growing demand for fresh meat. The government regarded the placement of meat markets as crucial to maintaining the public health and safety. Because meat was highly perishable and easily tainted, stalls and the work that went on inside them needed to be visible and within the consumer's reach. By the end of the century, the police increasingly gave shoppers greater access to local boutiques in their residential area. Following subsistence policy, the needs of local consumers won out over complaints of the polluting slaughterhouses and dangers of runaway cattle.

For guild butchers, their corporate organization imposed a kind of order that set them apart from other meat sellers. Their privileged position within Old Regime society gave them leverage over others who impinged upon their exclusive rights over the marketplace. Their corporate identity resided in standards of expertise and a pledge of quality and trustworthiness that bolstered their reputation as public merchants. They looked to the encroachment of "illegal workers" as a constant threat to their elite status in the trade. This expanding workforce below the leading masters and merchants contributed to reform in the corporate organization as we shall see in the following chapter.

The police took a different position to the threat of nonguild butchers, allowing for the distribution of meat to reach locations along the barriers of the capital. They granted a certain level of commerce that competed with the guild and at moments threatened its privileged position within the trade, focusing instead on the circulation of tainted and ersatz meat as a threat to the public health. These officials contended with the urban pressures of commercial expansion of the meat trade, not able to effectively alter the system by which meat was produced and distributed throughout the city's stalls. The introduction of central slaughterhouses would have to wait until the dissolution of the guild and the rise of a new regulatory authority at the close of the Revolution of 1789. This turning point not only saw the reconfiguration of the urban meat trade, but also a new vision of the city free from blood and violence.

Chapter 5

Guild Unity and Discord

During the period of Carnival, usually the Thursday morning before Lent, the butcher guild chose their prize fattened ox, known as the *boeuf gras,* decorated it with garlands of flowers and plumes of feathers, paraded it throughout the city, and finally offered it to the first president of parlement on the steps of the palace. On this ceremonial animal's back rode either a young butcher's daughter, or more often, a young boy, named king for the day, donned with a sash of royal blue, a sword, and a scepter. A dozen or more master butchers and their journeymen joined the parade, carrying their knives on their belts like swords, sporting ceremonial dress fitted with red stays, white trusses, and topped with turbans of the same colors. Two butchers led the procession in which they pulled the prized steer along by its horns. Musicians accompanied the others playing tambourines, violins, and fifes.

The tradition of le boeuf gras was one of many such celebratory events that marked the height of meat-eating season, in anticipation of the Lenten fast. For the butchers, this festivity also fell at the end of their working season–no doubt a reason to celebrate. Carnival called for play and mockery as people disguised themselves in costume and indulged in a litany of transgressions. License, gluttony, and crazed disorder ruled in this liminal phase, freed from the hierarchies of Old Regime society. In a world turned upside down, butchers who represented the commoners' interests could parade through the city and to the steps of the old palais (home of the Parlement of Paris) to "hold court," all the while displaying the pride of their trade. This march of revelry could only succeed with the mindful presence of master butchers. Occasionally, the tightly ordered procession could end in the beast's escape, turning the festive event into a bullfight with the young butchers playing matador. The ritual continued until 1790 when artisans abandoned such "backward" corporate traditions, considered part of the Old Regime.[1]

From the early Middle Ages, public rituals and processions of the numerous guilds and corporate ranks, as well as obligatory gifts, modes of dress and forms of address served to reinforce the hierarchy that characterized French society. In this case, by carrying swords and holding court, guild butchers parodied the most discriminatory social cleavage in French society that separated noble from commoner. A noble, by virtue of birth, encountered honors and privileges that no commoner could attain. The social inversions of Carnival and le boeuf gras relied on mockery and role-play to make visible the entrenched social categories that Parisians lived by year round.[2]

Under the Old Regime, commoners struggled for a worthy place within the limits of a society of orders. This social universe was composed of interlocking corporate entities, bound in an elaborate hierarchy known as "the Great Chain of Being" that led directly to the authority of the throne.[3] Although for most, the noble rank remained an impossibility, the fortunate commoner found avenues to gain positions of privilege either through venality or marriage or both. In these cases, wealth meant a great deal in one's quest for a corporate niche that would distinguish a person from most of his fellow commoners. For the person who aspired to guild membership, a title of mastership not only granted that person a living, but a specific position within the social order. The choice of becoming a master butcher entailed a whole set of social meanings, and conferred a particular rank along with its corresponding social value. Traditionally speaking, the profit gained from businesses was second to the symbolic displays that proclaimed social position as a point of honor. For butchers, membership in one of the oldest and most prestigious guilds brought them social esteem. Yet this membership varied widely as butchers increasingly relied upon multiple forms of capital (social, cultural, and economic) to further themselves in this corporate system.

By the end of the century, new conceptions of liberty and equality would decry and eventually abolish this system of hierarchy and privilege. First, in the failed attempt at liberalization under Turgot's Six Edicts of 1776, and then, more successfully, on the night of August 4, 1789, when the Constituent Assembly denounced privileges along with feudalism, implicitly dissolving the corporate guild system. This chapter explains the rise and fall of the butcher guild from its feudal beginnings through its guild formation to its first dissolution as a way to understand the social nature and function of the guild. In the revolutionary narrative, however, ending the privileges of elite groups to make way for the freedoms of independent workers in an unfettered marketplace oversimplifies what was a complicated battle between the social hierarchy and *communitas,* collective property and natural rights. The history of the guild was characterized by competing groups of butchers struggling to gain a position within the corporate system, as well as a succession of royal edicts that further unified and rationalized the butcher community under the authority of the king. Rather than an association of merchants with equal standing, the butcher community's historically skewed membership bred a great deal of diversity and strife, particularly in regard to recruitment and internal governance. Institutional nepotism, corruption, and fraud bred contention within the highly stratified ranks of guild masters and merchants who pledged to protect their fellow members. Given the social hierarchies and political divisions among butchers, the guild cannot be viewed as singular, but rather as a composite entity whose formation and dissolution was characterized by internal and external conflicts. As much as guild rituals and symbols aimed to inculcate a collective identity for guild masters and tighten the social fabric, hierarchies and modes of distinction characteristic of Old Regime Paris fostered a culture of inclusion and exclusion that spurred the cries for equal access to the world of work through the reform of corporate membership long before revolutionaries abolished the guild in 1791.

Guild Heritage and Corporate Identity

Guild histories from the eighteenth and nineteenth centuries give homage to the butcher guild as a powerful, unified (even clannish) community that was bound by a single corporate identity. Commonly referred to as one of the oldest and most stalwart of Parisian trade corporations–dating back "from time immemorial"–the butchers captured their esprit de corps in pictorial representations on ruins and medallions that celebrated the guild's classical Roman tradition.[4]

The butcher guild held one of the most prominent positions within the corporate chain of being. At the height of its prestige, the guild had the honor of escorting Henry VI of England at his coronation in Paris. During the fifteenth century, master butchers aligned themselves with the elite group called the Six Corps who maintained official leadership for public ceremonies. The six leading guilds varied over the centuries, and the butchers never regained the ranks of this prestigious group after their brief tenure.[5] Yet, even late into the sixteenth century, butchers achieved a level of distinction just below the Six Corps in a list of all guilds ranked in order of *bonté et valeur,* qualities that imply benevolence, gallantry, and largess.[6]

Butchers also built their prestige through family history, in particular the butcher families of the city's original covered market, the Grande Boucherie, for whom that market's ownership conferred special privileges that also evoked noble status. Nobles perpetuated their bloodline through the male line and with it, the racial distinctions of honor, privilege and power–in short, their place at the summit of society. Artisan family firms, even dynasties, were formed out of kinship ties, but not exclusively. Certainly for butcher families of the Grande Boucherie, who held onto their property as long as their male line endured, the names Thibert, Saintyon, and de La Dehors held immense power and prestige. Yet, this is not to say that butchers actively formed some kind of caste, born into a trade that they were destined to practice at birth. But they nonetheless demonstrated a level of professional identity that was replicated from generation to generation.

The eighteenth-century claims of a long-established artisan organization echoed the defensive posturing of a guild dominated by privileged family enterprises that reinforced their own long-held customs. In reality, the history of this powerful community pitted wealthy, property-owning merchant dynasties against small shop workers who sold meat à la cheville (hung meat, literally "by the ankles"). Throughout its history, the guild's leaders aspired to gain greater control over the city's meat markets through the acquisition of property and the institution of family firms. Even though these successful merchants held to their patrimony, the guild itself never became the ultimate guardian of the Parisian meat trade. As we have seen in the last chapter, the infusion of nonguild meat sellers into the Paris markets followed the ever-growing demand for fresh meat, yet the royal government largely ignored the interlopers' presence. The crown's greatest reforms occurred earlier in the fifteenth and sixteenth centuries when it brought order to rival communities of masters and merchants in the meat trade and lessened the exclusive privileges of butcher clans. Their push to unify competing butcheries and meat markets under one corporate structure would be constantly challenged by the pull of individual interests. This century-long battle centered on the formation of the first unified association of butchers who owned and operated the Grande Boucherie.

The Grande Boucherie

The Grande Boucherie is the historic site of the first butcher community. As Paris's primary meat market located just north of the Ile-de-la-Cité, it dominated the city center with anywhere from twenty-three to twenty-nine operating butcher stalls. Historical descriptions of the Grande Boucherie give credence to its architectural splendor; the eighteenth-century *Encyclopédie méthodique* tells of an edifice comparable to the magnificence of Roman baths, circuses, aqueducts, and amphitheaters.[7] Over the covered market was the guild hall where members assembled for their weekly meetings and banquets. Nearby was the parish church of Saint Jacques-de-la-boucherie. Today, the Saint Jacques Tower is the last remaining edifice from this ancient butcher quarter, a section of the church built, in part, with the guild's own funds.

By the thirteenth century, the butchers of the Grande Boucherie wielded their exceptional juridical and administrative status as a privileged domain rooted in this central meat market. Their joint possession of the Grande Boucherie (passed from father to son) was the basis of their union, one that rested in common law, not transferable privilege or title. This market acquisition demonstrated not only their financial prowess, but also their avidity as property-owning, Parisian merchants.[8] Not until 1381, did the butchers outline a complete list of their statutes in forty-two articles, the twenty-third of which stated "No one shall be butcher of the Grande Boucherie of Paris who is not a son of a butcher from the said butchery."[9] Their statutes reveal how the Grande Boucherie operated within a feudal system of justice that mimicked a small kingdom or barony. Aristocratic in nature, the political power of this early guild nonetheless resided in a single head, a *primus inter pares.* This seigneurial leader or chief was a master elected for life. While representing the collective will of the Grande Boucherie butchers, he held the ultimate power in managing not only their affairs, but also the entire meat trade in the city. In principle, his authority allowed him to close any butcher stall in the city for an infraction of the community's unwritten rules (part of their oral testimonies upon entry to the trade). A contingent of clearly ranked officers supported this leader: two deputy masters, a mayor or judge, four officers, and three sergeant *écorcheurs.*[10]

The independent authority of the butcher proprietors of the Grande Boucherie reached its apogee in the early fifteenth century during the Cabochien Revolt of 1413. According to one historian, the urban revolt pointed to "a crisis of the moral order" whereby heavily taxed Parisians aimed to oust the corrupt elite for what the Cabochien Ordinance claimed to be the common good (*le bien commun*). The city's artisans and ecclesiastics joined forces to recreate a hierarchy of functionaries according to their intellectual capacity. The butchers of the Grande Boucherie served in waging war against the royal government. Acting as a kind of private militia, masters and journeymen fought side by side in the several days of slaughter that followed the attack on the city. The butcher proprietors of the Grande Boucherie also lent financial support to the three-year war through loans to the Duke of Burgundy, the crown's enemy. Unfortunately, these merchants suffered the misfortunes of choosing the wrong side. By May of 1416, their ruin was guaranteed: Charles VI demolished the workplace that exemplified their power and wealth, La Grande Boucherie. The king also revoked the legal privileges that secured the community's autonomy.[11]

The city government allowed the butchers of the Grande Boucherie to return to the city to rebuild their famed central marketplace, completed in 1421. Even though many of these butchers contributed to the financing of the new covered butchery, they could not replace its grand splendor. The new edifice was much more modest than its predecessor. This royal retribution considerably diminished the seigneurial claims over the Grande Boucherie. A century later, Henri II dissolved the lifetime master seigneur position and established a royally appointed office in direct contact with the crown. With this final blow, the most prominent butchery in Paris lost a great deal of its economic power and political independence.[12]

For at least five centuries, the butchers of the Grande Boucherie ruled over the Parisian meat trade, if not in terms of their commercial domination, at least in their level of social distinction. Entitled "Master Butchers of the Grande Boucherie," these men represented several families who maintained their hold on this property through rights of primogeniture.[13] Beginning with at least twenty members in the thirteenth century, the dynasties of the central butchery reached their height in 1491 when their numbers grew to thirty-one members of eight families. Whether for lack of male heirs, or by simple attrition, the blood ties of this "butcher aristocracy" shrank to four families in 1637.[14] At this time, Louis XIII granted the surviving four families (D'Auvergne, Thibert, de La Dehors, and Saintyon) *lettres patentes* for a sum of 90,000 livres conserving their ancient privileges of ownership in perpetuity.[15]

The considerable wealth of these butcher dynasties put them at the top of this stratified community of butchers. The Saintyons and Thiberts owned twenty-seven of the thirty-two stalls in the Grande Boucherie, in addition to other shops throughout the city.[16] They also held a strong participatory role in municipal and royal administrations, gaining titled positions as royal procurators and judges, notaries, and city magistrates (*échevins*).[17] Clearly the title, "Merchant Butcher of the Grande Boucherie," bestowed certain influence in the king's court as long as one avoided work, for those who held titles often distanced themselves from the day-to-day dealings in the meat trade.

Until the later half of the sixteenth century, when formal recruitment occurred through apprenticeship and journeymanship, butcher proprietors of the Grande Boucherie relied almost exclusively on wage laborers to operate their businesses. Called *valets détaillants,* these workers assisted master butchers with no expectation of mastership. Many complained of these "unqualified" laborers, some of whom worked like journeymen under masters, others among them rented stalls and practiced their trade more as independent butchers than as servants to the masters of the Grande Boucherie. There was no legal objection to the right of these men to work, rather the objection focused on their lack of supervision and training that resulted from the high rate of master absenteeism. Allowing wage labor was one thing, but allowing untitled butchers into the central meat market meant lowering standards of quality that came with a master's expertise in the trade. Frequent reports of these butcher proprietors claim they "abused" their privileges by leaving the practice of their trade to hired labor and renting out their property at high prices, thereby driving up the price of meat. Critics cited even worse abuses when masters abandoned their profession altogether (although they retained their titles) and made their wealth through property management and investment as true bourgeois.[18]

The legal and commercial position of these masters allowed them to dominate the Parisian meat trade, even as the central marketplace could not fill the demand for fresh meat. This situation forced the hand of the butcher proprietors of the Grande Boucherie to allow other butchers to set up butcheries and meat markets in outlying areas.[19] Yet these competing marketplaces could not seek establishment without the approval of the masters at the Grande Boucherie. Their oligarchic rule forced the lesser, independent butchers into a subordinate position because they did not hold membership in their elite society.

By the mid-sixteenth century, the butchers of the Grande Boucherie had been confronted with repeated parlementary edicts and royal proclamations against the "enormous abuses" that the people of Paris "suffered" under the neglectful meat cutters. The independent authority of the Grande Boucherie had bred butcher absenteeism and unqualified trade practices. As a result, the royal government took action not only with the butchers, but with all trades, placing itself as the sole creator and supreme arbitrator of the corporate system. The making of a single guild first required the submission of the butchers of the Grande Boucherie who held their power over several localized, merchant-run markets throughout Paris.

The Making of a Unified Guild

In 1587, the king broke the oligarchy of the butchers of the Grande Boucherie forcing them to submit to a list of royally sanctioned statutes as lettres patentes. The royal letters patent established a system of guild inspectors and officers in direct communication with city officials. They visited the shops and stalls throughout Paris and enforced the numerous regulations surrounding the meat trade. The statutes of 1587 also dictated that the leaders within the butcher guild relinquish control over the expansion of their trade.

Most importantly, the new statutes acknowledged not only the privileges of the butcher proprietors of the Grande Boucherie, but those artisans who leased property in the Grande Boucherie and who essentially performed the work of butchers without the title. By giving these wage laborers titles to mastership, the crown subjected them to the guild's discipline, and in turn, ensured that these practicing butchers would uphold the moral and professional standards of their trade. Suddenly, the proprietors' elite status gave way to a higher authority to regulate the trade.

The assertion of royal authority was in response to the tight limits on meat production and distribution that the Grande Boucherie put on Parisians. By incorporating all butchers at the Grande Boucherie under open mastership, the king meant to take away the special jurisdiction of the butcher aristocratic families and place the power to grant new butcheries in the hands of the royal authorities. The extension of the numbers of butcheries and the increasing population of master butchers around the city occurred within the king's realm. In more subtle ways, the rules of admission, as dictated by the crown, preserved the patriarchal traditions of this early butcher association, giving favor to the sons of butchers. Those who were not from butcher families paid the required apprenticeship fee (often prohibitively expensive) to enter the profession.

The butcher proprietors of the Grande Boucherie opposed the registration of the letters patent, appealing to the Paris Parlement–the highest court of appeals–to resist the royal will. This legal battle with the parlement continued until Henry IV gave into their demands to entitlement with letters patent in May 1594, adapting a corporate status that–at least on paper–was separate from but equal to the rest of the Parisian butcher population.[20] Nevertheless, the four families of the central butchery guaranteed their titles of distinction and rights over stalls through royal letters patent under Louis XIII in return for the payment of 90,000 livres.[21] Clearly, the crown's financial dependence upon these butchers "for the needs of the affairs of war and the extraordinary expenditure and training of our armies" determined royal policy more than the government admitted.

The now unified butchers of the Grande Boucherie and the remainder of Parisian master butchers coexisted as separate corporate systems until 1650 when they all "submitted" to the same list of rules as those set forth over a half century earlier. Published as a "*Concordat des Bouchers de toutes les boucheries de Paris,*" this formal agreement united all butchers under the Grande Boucherie's privileges. It also affirmed the legal access to mastership by way of apprenticeship for all Parisian butchers. The agreement demonstrated the first step at breaking down rivalries among these various butcher communities and creating a unified legal status that aimed to safeguard the commercial, moral, and political interests of all master members.

How did these men come to such a decision? On the one hand, the coalition of all master butchers made the guild a more powerful collective force when dealing with royal authority. The pooling of their resources under a single corporate body doubled the guild's membership and its operating budget. For the master butchers outside the central marketplace, the alliance with the most notable butchers of Paris brought them greater prestige and raised the value of mastership throughout the city.

On the other hand, by signing this agreement, these butchers submitted their trade to royal control. No longer would they be able to practice as individual merchants or as small competing groups, but rather the agreement forced all butchers into a seemingly equitable association, even those with greater authority and power. Yet, putting all masters under a single set of rules provided a kind of protection from the individual will of powerful butcher families. It also avoided the threat of lawsuits from other butchers. By pooling their resources, the guild could police the trade and defend their members' interests more effectively. In a revitalized and enlarged form, the merger of all Parisian butchers would put the guild in a better position to finance the purchase of royal offices directly related to the meat trade.

The unification remained attractive to the fiscal circle in the royal government because the Grande Boucherie, given its special jurisdiction and its internal disorders, had escaped the series of extortionate measures (creation of offices of controllers, visitors, auditors, etc.) imposed on the other corporations. With all these resources pooled together, the guild would be in a position to contribute more generously to the royal treasury. Mazarin no doubt saw an opportunity, in the name of the public good, to bind the butchers to a single modernized set of rules, codifying the profession for more efficient policing. Multiple and rival corporate systems in the same craft created confusion and made the profession difficult to regulate. Furthermore, the agreement lessened the exceptional power held by the butcher proprietors of the Grande Boucherie, seen as anachronistic and defiant. On this ground alone, the action was a measure of good police.

Thus, butchers began as an aristocratic group of merchant proprietors and, throughout the early modern period, developed into a more socially and economically diverse association of privileged merchants. As in many other trades, the corporate initiative took a broad population of artisans and placed them under one umbrella group with a single set of guidelines. Rather than seeing these institutional decisions as closing off the trade in the name of monopoly, we should regard them as an opening up for development and growth. Later statutes published in 1744 and 1782 went even further to regularize the trade under a single set of statutes that outlined standard procedures for recruitment and commercial practices. For example, masters were not allowed to operate businesses out of more than three stalls, two in the same location. In principle, such uniform guidelines gave each master member of the guild the same opportunity to succeed within the group. In reality, the two-tiered division of labor, similar to the protocorporate system that existed at the Grande Boucherie, persisted throughout the eighteenth century. At one level were merchant butchers who controlled the wholesale to retail trade and hired laborers on a seasonal and weekly basis to run their shops and stalls while they invested their capital in cattle futures and annuities. Below them in wealth and status were master butchers who sold meat à la cheville or simply retail and purchased sides of beef, mutton, or veal directly from other merchant butchers. In effect, all guild members held the same guild privileges and corporate status, even though each master competed for his market share.

The later statutes systematized the work habits as well as the group's administrative functions. Guild members had to collectively determine the specificity of these codes and regulations, otherwise each individual was insecure. In their oath to the king and to each other, master butchers pledged their allegiance to the guild and invested themselves more or less equally in an association to protect their common interests. Yet, in reality, the vision of an artisan brotherhood on equal footing was far from true. Two avenues to mastership separated the insiders with family connections from outsiders who acquired mastership through conventional means. Guild members and leaders were a highly stratified group and to a certain extent divided against themselves. How did this work out on a daily basis?

Guild Leadership

From what we can glean about the size and nature of guild membership, master butchers limited their membership well below the 240 statute-limit throughout most of the eighteenth century, to as little as 187 members.[22] They divided their ranks into several categories based upon seniority and administrative positions within the guild. According to the guild election record from 1747, the largest group, listed as *modernes et jeunes,* consisted of 162 of the 187 butchers, the young (*jeunes*) butchers were the most recent guild members and the moderns had at least ten years membership. Above them stood the senior (*anciens*) butchers consisting of twenty butcher elders, many of whom had been guild officers.

The highest ranking leadership positions within the guild were the jurés led by the "*Sindic* [sic] *de present en charge.*" These elected corporate officials included five regional jurés, each one representing a different section of the city: the faubourg Saint-Germain, the quarters of Saint-Martin, Saint-Paul, and Montmartre, along with the central area known as the Port (or L'Apport) de Paris. Also known as the bureau, these masters managed guild affairs, called assembly meetings, presided over them, counted votes, led deliberations over important guild issues, and oversaw admission to mastership. They also played an important role in policing the meat trade, and in visiting butcher shops, butcheries, and open markets throughout Paris and its surroundings. They met weekly at the guild hall, located at the rue de la Mortellerie, just off the Place des Veaux. Meetings were held every Friday for the jurés, their clerks, and accountants to expedite everyday matters. The office provided a communal space for guild assemblies and housed the guild records and accounts.

The guild assembly, made up of twelve elders, six moderns, and six juniors, constituted the second tier of guild administration. The jurés brought important affairs before the assembly for discussion and ratification. By obtaining the assembly's explicit approval, the jurés sought to avoid personal responsibility for decisions made on the guild's behalf. Those who sat on the assembly included the current and all previously elected jurés. The fact that these men once held office did not preclude them from being reelected for another term. Simon Tripperet and Vincent Lelievre, both anciens, were later elected as syndic, Butcher Tripperet for three terms

(1763–1769) and Butcher Lelievre for five terms (1749–1759). Beyond the two-year period of active administration, the guild position thus conferred lifelong, remunerated participation in its administration. The anciens' influence in guild affairs resulted from their control of this assembly in addition to an informal aura of honor or prestige.

The final (and ultimate) level of authority resided in the king's procurator at the Châtelet who acted as the government's chief interlocutor with the guilds. He, or his representative, received the oaths of new guild members and presided over guild elections, keeping records of both events throughout the eighteenth century.[23] The royal procurator also served as the magistrate for lawsuits involving the guilds. After 1658 he bore the title of "first judge and preserver of the privileges of the corps of merchants, crafts, masterships, and sworn trades (*jurande*) of the city, faubourgs, and suburbs of Paris."[24]

In accordance with the statutes, members elected half the jurés among the butcher masters annually, with each juré serving a two-year term. This rotating system ensured continuity in the guild's administration and the presence of experienced leaders at its head. Elections took place at the annual meeting where the police adjudicated the registration of all butcher stalls, before the beginning of the working season. Not all guild members were eligible for office. The junior members had to wait at least ten years until they were eligible as *modernes*.

Guild government hardly operated under democratic principles, instead it followed a corporate model of representation that was exclusionary.[25] Only a small group of master butchers voted; the elders were by far the most influential voting block. According to the ballots of elections that took place from 1708–1775, the total number of votes for a single office never exceeded 100 and often remained below 50. Among the roll of 187 members present for the March 1747 vote for syndic and 3 jurés, only 50 votes are counted for each office. This would have to include assembly members made up of the 6 present officers, the 20 elder members, and only 24 of the third category of young members, leaving 137 nonvoting members of the guild. Which masters were given the vote and why remains unclear. Perhaps the roll reflects the entire guild membership present at the election to nominate members or to oversee or "approve" the outcome of the election. In any case, the limited participation in elections bespeaks a formal process to perpetuate a small elite of butchers within the guild's leadership rather than as an open and democratic means of selecting new jurés.

A closer look at the election results over the eighteenth century suggests that some kind of term limits applied, although none were expressly stated in the guild statutes. The vast majority of elected officers held their positions for at least two terms (four years), usually consecutively. The syndic never stayed in office for more than three terms with the exception of Vincent

Lelievre who held the title for five consecutive terms (ten years). After having served their first term, most incumbents easily won the reelection with a healthy majority of votes, if not unanimously.[26]

Rarely did guild elections go unopposed and many candidates entering office for the first time won with thin margins. Such evidence indicates an active electoral process that had long evolved from the dynastic origins of the guild. Masters relied upon their reputation and family alliances as they vied for positions of power and influence within the guild. The syndic election on March 20, 1708, is one example where three candidates nearly split the ballot, in which Christophe Frère won with a three-vote margin. The guild syndic pulled one of two names from a hat when a tie did occur, such as in the March 17, 1722 election for the juré of the Saint Martin quarter.

Levels of seniority informed the strict rules that governed the guild administration. Ideally, voting members elected officers of the guild who were "persons known for their experience and probity . . . among the most notable of the masters of the guild." The guild statutes of 1744 spelled out the minimum requirements, saying that no syndic could be elected without having had the experience of being a juré, and that jurés had to have ten years of experience as masters. Guild leadership came to mature men with established careers in the trade. For forty of the jurés elected from 1708 to 1775, their tenure as master butchers before taking office was on the average twenty years, the median was sixteen years.[27] Syndics elected over the century came from some of the largest butcher clans, all of whom gained their mastership through their fathers.[28]

Union and Division in Guild Government

The guild took an active role to maintain its own integrity as a corps and fend off any attempt to dislodge its hold over the meat trade. The guild statutes clearly designate the commercial territory butchers held within the confines of the capital, as well as those competing trades that were obliged to buy from them directly. Those who sold prepared meats in Paris such as pastry cooks, roast meat vendors (*rôtisseurs*), cabaret owners, and country innkeepers were required to buy from master butchers or could face a 30-livre fine.[29]

When guild jurisdictions overlapped, such as with the leather dressers *(megissiers)* and tanners, the butchers lobbied hard to keep the upper hand in commercial dealings by requiring that all purchasing contracts be negotiated at the beginning of the season for at least six months.[30] This way butchers could not only guarantee the price of their animal hides but also the loyalty of their buyers. The guild advanced their interest, winning such commercial privileges through legal battles. The guild hired lawyers and procurators to present their case, published as mémoires that declaimed their opponents in order to gain public support.

The guild jurés also policed the businesses of their own members who, by and large, viewed the stronghold of guild controls as providing the necessary discipline to ensure that work achieved its own proper degree of perfection. They oversaw the reception of masters and approved their masterpiece for admission to the guild. Officers visited the stalls and shops of master butchers on a regular basis, fining delinquent butchers and demanding dues (*droits de visite*) upon each visit. They also collected the tax levied on stalls that formed an important part of the guild's revenue. No doubt these visits and the manner in which they taxed a master's trade caused some strife in the guild.

Masters who freely joined the ranks of the corporate hierarchy had to swallow certain inequities and injustices that guild membership entailed. Their strength rested in their union. Rarely did masters publicly take sides over administrative issues. However, butchers were not timid in taking their leaders to task when, as one faction stated, the "weight of the administration [. . .] was so violent and prejudicial to all the members who make up the corps of the guild"[31] that formal measures of opposition ensued. On this occasion, conflict arose over the excessive taxation on butcher stalls (25 sous weekly) as well as over the mismanagement of guild accounts in which fellow guildsmen accused certain syndics of embezzlement. Here, the corruption of guild jurés had become so blatant as to require some kind of official reprimand.

This case appeared around 1718, shortly after the establishment of the Royal Commission on the Affairs and Debts of the Parisian Guilds. Then, twenty-six master butchers and "their consorts" published a remonstrance against a number of guild elders. The printed source includes the accounts of the guild from 1689 to 1717 and contests the amounts levied on each butcher stall. The collected taxes (which were grossly underestimated by the *syndic*) could never be accounted for. It is difficult to say whether this action denotes corruption or negligence, but subsequent police sentences gave clear instructions to future syndics as to the methods of bookkeeping and banking to ensure a level of honesty.[32]

Perhaps the greatest amount of strife within the guild concerned decisions over the regulations surrounding the commerce in livestock and the tariffs on heads of cattle collected by those who operated the marketplace. The guild had purchased the rights to the cattle markets at Sceaux and Poissy for several years at the beginning of the eighteenth century. During this period, they collected tariffs from butchers to finance their tax farm. By 1719, the guild had paid 49,000 livres, a small fraction of the 450,000 livres they owed on the title to the tax farm. The commission to audit guild accounts could only give credence to the fact that the guild had bitten off more than it could chew. Their inability to manage the marketplace opened up opportunities for other tax farmers who proposed financial solutions to the insolvent guild. As a result, the controller general of finance established the Caisse de Poissy in 1707, not only to regulate commerce at the two provisioning markets, but also to supply butchers with a reliable system of credit by which they could finance their livestock purchases.

The issue of whether to support or suppress the caisse divided the guild butchers throughout the century. At the center of the debate was whether it benefited the commercial enterprise of butchers or locked them into strict rules of debt repayment–something they were not accustomed to. Seen as a blow to the special jurisdiction the guild held over the marketplace, the caisse run by a financier named Dominique Antoine Huel undermined the "good faith" of butchers to pay their debts in due time. But it also provided needed capital to butchers with smaller budgets whose cash flow was not so flexible. When eighty guild butchers (none of them officers, many with small businesses from lesser-known families) came out to publicly support the caisse's renewal in 1737, the guild retaliated with slander, naming each master butcher who had signed the mémoire as a "drunkard," "a lowly man," "a cheat," "bankrupt for twenty years," and so on.[33] The debate over the caisse, perhaps one of the most contentious issues among the butcher trade, split the guild along lines of wealth and power.

Not long after this moment of crisis, the guild took measures to protect its less fortunate members. In a gesture meant to take into consideration the economic diversity of butchers, the guild reevaluated its fiscal policies. As a result, the administration reformed its collection of the inspection fees based upon a graduated tax plan. A 1749 royal arrêt that outlined the regulations governing the guild syndic and jurés, divides the guild members into three classes. The first is made up of masters and widows who kept their own shops and who "are in a situation [*état*] to [be able to] pay the droits de visite." The second class is made up of sons of masters still living with their fathers or other masters as "*garçons de boutique ou compagnons*." The third class consists of those who are reputed as being "without means [*hors d'état*] to pay the dues," or who would only be able to pay in part. The guild stipulated that the juré accountant keep this list and the funds collected up to date on a yearly basis.[34] In this way, the guild administration maintained a more equitable system in which they acknowledged the relative position of every member and applied their fiscal imposition according to the member's means.

Charity and Brotherhood

If the guild administration willingly reformed its illegal or discriminatory practices, it was because the community's essential purpose was to safeguard the commercial, moral, and political interests of all its master members. The guild extended its commitment by furnishing its members with charity in times of need. Production standards were collectively determined and maintained not only to guarantee a level of quality, but to proclaim a moral standard that the guild–in a single voice–pledged to the public.

Guild masters demonstrated their spiritual allegiance to their community, which excluded any member who was not of the Roman Catholic faith, through religious devotion. Their own confraternity of Saint-Sacrement, also known as *la Fête-Dieu* or the Feast of the Nativity, cultivated communal rituals such as banquets and feasts to strengthen the bond of the guild.[35] These gatherings, in which all sat together at one table, all contributing to the expense of the meal, were performed in the spirit of commensality. That is, by breaking bread together and drinking wine, the members of the *confrérie* celebrated their faith in God as men who were united in both the temporal and the spiritual worlds.

In the eighteenth century, all master butchers contributed to the brotherhood's operating budget through dues paid to the guild. This money funded gatherings that not only focused on social drinking and feasting rituals, but served as a spiritual center for butchers living and dead, as well as a source of charitable respite for the less fortunate butchers in the community. The ideology of mutual aid suffused these brotherhoods. The personal contributions made by wealthy butchers such Vincent Lelievre, a leader in the guild for several years, further exemplified this ethos. Lelievre supplied the butchers' confraternity with meat provisions throughout his life. In return, his brothers in the confrérie honored him with the recitation of the *te deum* and other prayers for his soul long after his death.[36]

In principle, the brotherhood was open to all artisans in the same trade, whether they were apprentices or journeymen or masters. Whether this principle held true in practice is highly unlikely. Journeymen sought separate associations called confraternities (*confraternités*) based upon their own patron saints. Although butchers may have participated in these mutual aid societies, no confraternity was created exclusively for journeymen butchers.

Unlike the confraternities, the confréries' system of financial and spiritual support was tied to the guild administration, a fact that potentially corrupted the idea of charity for all based upon voluntary will. As long as the corporate statutes required masters to pay confraternal dues, the separate existence of the confrérie put into doubt its spirit of Christian self-sacrifice and its moral strength of free association. Throughout the modern period, the royal government had become increasingly critical of the conduct and management of many confréries in many of the trades. Some "degenerated" into circles of libertinage and irreligion, others served as a pretext for a kind of political subversion, and finally there were those who drained the guilds of their resources. These accusations may have applied to the butcher guild and their accountants (who were often criticized for failing to keep the accounts of the confrérie), yet what evidence that remains of their finances shows a consistent contribution of at least one-tenth of their total outlays "to help poor butchers" and "the parish poor."[37]

Guild officers who used their positions of power to exploit lesser masters and merchants went against the ideology of *communitas* that extended to worldly practices such as lotteries for cattle purchases. The fraudulent exploits of guild leaders only fomented further divisions in the ranks that weakened the association. The account of an eighteenth-century Parisian master glazier, Jacques Ménétra, offers one perspective of how a master felt toward his jurés that is less than favorable. In his *Journal de ma vie,* Ménétra waxes on in a bitter tone about the intrusiveness of the jurés throughout his diary. In 1773–74, he writes a song about the "fat cats of the jury" that challenges the pettiness of the guild's regulations. His diary reveals the way in which an oligarchy could dominate the market and retain power through elections limited to a closed circle of cronies and through manipulation of the guild finances.[38]

After 1750, in a world of work where the meaning of mastership was increasingly put under question, where the possibility of success in the meat trade did not entirely depend upon guild membership as many entrepreneurs demonstrated, the idea of work as a basic human right, equal to all, put the privileged status of guild members in jeopardy. The idea of abolishing the guild, however shocking to guild masters, demonstrated the extent to which the collective value of corporatism had fallen to the individual right to work.

Guild Dissolution and Renewal

The late eighteenth-century opposition to the economic rights of trade corporations and other privileged groups intensified as the public debate grew. Faiguet de Villeneuve in the *Encyclopédie* wrote that mastership had been instituted originally "to maintain good order among artisans and merchants" and had degenerated into "cabal, drunkenness, and monopoly." Contemporaries had come to regard apprenticeship and journeymanship as long, oppressive, and fruitless forms of institutionalized "brigandage" for the master and "servitude" for the laborer. In effect, sons of masters, who were exempt from the requirements of apprenticeship, could become masters at eighteen years old and paid an honorarium of about 50 livres. Outsiders paid 300 livres for the apprenticeship contract and could not become masters until age twenty-eight.[39] The masterpiece was a contrivance meant to keep out even the most frugal and industrious outsiders. Jealous of their authority and hungry for more wealth and power, the corporate fathers had transformed the mastership from a system of renewal into a system of exclusion by means of which, "the richest and the strongest ordinarily succeeded in keeping out the weakest."[40]

Opposition to economic monopoly was particularly evident among the physiocratic circle surrounding Louis XVI's controller general Turgot. As the failure of most of Turgot's reforms demonstrates, however, the groups most affected by his measures were still powerful enough to defend their traditional rights. Turgot's most prominent attack on these rights, published as the Six Edicts, included an attempt to dissolve the corporations entirely, provoking strong protests from guild officials and heated debate in the royal council prior to the presentation of the edicts for parlementary registration in early February 1776. Remonstrances and complaints ended in outright opposition when the Paris Parlement on February 7 refused to register "a project stemming from an inadmissible system of equality, the first effect of which is to throw all the orders of the State into confusion."[41] Turgot persuaded the king to override the parlementary veto, and the Six Edicts were registered on February 22, 1776, but continuing opposition to the decrees and ministerial intrigue led to Turgot's forced resignation on May 12, 1776 and the revocation of the edicts in August.[42]

For the master and merchant butchers of Paris, the attempted measures by Turgot and other liberal thinkers brought responses couched within the political necessity of meat. The dissolution of the guild could only mean the end of quality control ensured by the guild jurés, by the qualifications of mastership that demanded a level of expertise, by the control over production that regulated "this most necessary of staples." According to the logic of the butcher guild, by opening up the profession to any individual without demanding a level of proficiency, or any protection from fraud or abuse, the public's healthy supply of this basic necessity was put in jeopardy.

Other food guilds, such as the caterers and cooks, utilized the same argument over the public's need for healthy food. Their remonstrance published in 1776 was similar to the butchers' logic whereby the increase in the number of masters (and overproduction) would lead to a loss of quality for consumers in the case where meat would "rot"–for only they knew how to prepare and preserve meat. The skills of these food artisans were equated with apothecaries (one of the guilds exempt from the *Six Edicts*) and had to be preserved under the guild structure for the public good. The guilds claimed "their art is as essential to human life as a pharmacy."[43]

The arguments made against the butchers by those supporting liberal policies focused on the usurious monopolies masters held over the meat trade. This explained what critics saw as the poor quality of meat, its meager supply, its inflated price, and the general lack of cheaper cuts for the populace. These critics saw the domination of merchant butchers who catered to an exclusive clientele, speculating in the livestock trade, selling only the best cuts at the highest prices to cover their operating costs. However far from the truth this might have been, the critics and their liberal reforms fought to eradicate the barriers that prevented the free flow of goods and services. By eliminating the tariffs on the cattle trade and expanding the labor market through the abolition of guild privilege, liberal-minded writers in the *Nouvelles Ephémérides,* a physiocratic publication, saw a widening of the market and, through competition, a natural return to what they claimed to be the just price as dictated by the market. No longer would fresh beef and mutton meat be priced together, but each product would fall to useful (or real) value. The liberalization of the cattle trade was the first step in separating "the tyranny" butchers held over the meat supply that would permit all "citizens to join a branch of commerce in which competition and emulation can be placed in true value."[44]

After the revocation of the Six Edicts in August of 1776, the butcher guild returned along with about half the number of guilds that had previously existed. Most changes were made in the regulations surrounding the meat trade, providing greater checks against fraud and inflated prices. Whether or not this liberal lobby and the short experiment that came out of it had any permanent effect upon the guild can be measured in the subsequent changes of the guild statutes published in 1782.[45] Although the number of articles diminished from sixty to fifty, the rules surrounding the employment of apprentices and journeymen became more specific. The authors of the new statutes lowered the age requirements. Apprenticeship began at age fifteen. Mastership could be attained at age twenty-five for outsiders, twenty for those who were apprentices, and eighteen for sons of masters. Even though these new statutes offered no alternative way of entry into the guild other than through apprenticeship, it did begin to open the trade to outsiders.

Other changes helped to protect the rights of unincorporated butchers under the guild oligarchy. For example, apprentices could continue their period of training with another master without losing any time invested. Those who aspired to mastership could perform their masterpiece in front of two masters and two "notable bourgeois, worthy of faith and not suspect." The election of assembly members, now called *deputés,* took place in the presence of the police. Overall, the new statutes incorporated many more police sentences, subjecting the trade to greater outside surveillance and less to the guild's own internal "police."

The reforms of 1776 challenged the need for a corporate world, a system based upon privilege and hierarchies that tied the guild to the state through an elaborate system of regulation. The end of the guild meant a moral loss in the eradication of standards of perfection, and the potential risks to the public's health. For the master and merchant butchers of Paris, the dissolution of their corporate system eliminated their proprietary control over the meat market and jeopardized the solvency of their businesses. Giving access to what appeared to many observers as a highly profitable trade would spur many dabblers to enter the profession and take away business from experienced masters. As we have seen throughout the Old Regime, barriers to mastership existed. The desire to practice the trade within the city of Paris no doubt outweighed the opportunity. Although it is difficult to acquire an accurate measure of the discrimination individuals faced in gaining their letters of mastership, the following chapter explains the many roadblocks journeymen as well as other unincorporated butchers faced.

Conclusion

From its beginnings, the guild built its strength upon the close ties of several butcher families, a kind of urban aristocracy based upon titles to the marketplace. Because several prominent butcher clans stood at the center of this community directing the administrative duties of the guild, they could provide a unity both oligarchic in character and hierarchic in structure. Yet the guild evolved in its own in ways similar to the paths of many of its sister corporations. Using its political and economic leverage, the guild bargained and compromised with royal authority. It protected its members from the intrusions of outside trades while it conferred a distinct corporate identity simply by nature of its existence within a world of orders.

Rather than a democratic alliance of all the city's artisans, the guild's power was backed by the wealthiest meat merchants, who, as guild patriarchs, maintained control over an expanding number of independent butcheries. With the growth of the butcher trade came the establishment of state institutions of royal authority whose centralizing rule directly influenced the legal and financial status of butchers and their guild organization. In their struggles to form and govern a single guild, butchers defended and renegotiated their corporate status among competing factions within the trade.

However, it would be wrong to characterize the guild in this unidimensional way. As the guild evolved, it accommodated a vigorous political life marked by eruptions of dissent that brought down the corrupt practices of its old cronies and solicited substantial numbers of younger butchers to participate in guild politics. It adapted formal routes to mastership that provided greater opportunities to those outside the butcher clans. It policed its own members, dictating hours of operation and numbers of shops a butcher could manage, as well as many other regulations against collusion and fraud, to provide a certain degree of equity for those in the profession, "necessary for the good order of the guild." Although the guild was rotten in many places, characterizations of the guild as crippling and abusive to the meat trade belie its (more or less) democratic self-governance and its regulatory supervision of production and marketing. The more that we learn about both corporation and trade, and the more detailed explanation that we can give of the economy and the social structure of eighteenth-century Paris, the more nuanced the scenario of a corporate world that is less univocal than discordant. Perhaps the clearest understanding of this merchant culture comes forth in the hierarchy and subordination that operated not only within the guild, but in the paths leading to mastership. As subject to culture and subjects of it, these men and women identified with ideas of honor, status, and patrimony while they negotiated the institutions of the market and politics that shaped the meat trade in Old Regime Paris. As historical actors, they played an active role in producing and reproducing this world of work in ways that sought stability and tradition within the challenges and insecurities of eighteenth-century life.

Chapter 6

In the Service of a Master

Apprentices and Journeymen

Four months into the meat-eating season, Jean Baptiste Nez, a *garçon boucher*, suddenly found himself out on the street in the middle of the night, looking for work. Hired by Master Butcher Antoine Rebourg for a weekly wage, room, and board, Nez felt that he had been treated unfairly and went to the commissaire to file a complaint.[1] According to the young stall worker, the master "ordered him to get up [and begin working] at midnight to do four cattle and twelve to fifteen sheep after having supped [and finished his work] at nine-thirty." Nez had not eaten his final meal of the day and had only gotten to bed at a quarter to eleven. An hour later, his master "threw the blanket and sheet from his bed to his feet and then went back downstairs." The master yelling up to his worker challenged him "to get up and defend himself as much as he can defend [himself]." Whereupon, the butcher's wife gave the young man his wages telling him to go out at a certain hour when Profit (a renter in the butcher's house) would give Nez his blanket back so he could sleep outside. Nez reported that, "without knowing for what reason, he found himself on the street, obliged to look for a shop" (presumably where he could find work). Within five days he found a position with Charles Drieux across the city, yet knowing that without an official reprieve–what he called "a certificate," officially known as a *congé*–he would not be able to change jobs. So the young man returned to his former employer where Rebourg again treated him badly, calling him an "insolent" and expelled him from the house for a second time.[2]

Nez made his case before the police, claiming that "he had served in the shop loyally [for which] he [the master] is forced to give the plaintiff [Nez] a certificate." He brought forth his new master as a personal reference. Drieux spoke for Nez claiming that "he was on time [for work] and in his apron." Nez was not concerned with the threats and insults he suffered, the act of being put on the street in the middle of the night, or the demands of his master to produce above and beyond what seemed a "reasonable" amount of work (the fulfillment of which for one stall worker in an evening would be incredible). Rather, he reiterated his loyalty to his previous master, the one who could guarantee his reemployment. Nez chose to go to the authorities not to disparage his former employer, but to defend his reputation as a diligent worker and convince those with the power to influence his master to provide what he felt he deserved.[3]

Even though the nature of the conflict between Nez and his former master remains somewhat clouded by their testimonies, its resolution relied on formal procedures to restitute the honor and reputation of the apprenticed butcher. For a month after his former master, Rebourg, presented Nez the certificate to guarantee his future career as a butcher, Nez formally retracted his complaint against Rebourg. In the notarized retraction, Rebourg, attested to Nez's good character saying "that during this time he served him and worked at his house loyally as a garçon of honor and of probity and incapable of any misbehavior of which facts the said Sieur Rebourg affirms as truthful and having perfect knowledge."[4] Rather than resort to violence or insolence, Nez turned to the legal authorities to provide the just means to move on to a better situation.

During the eighteenth century, the guild exerted greater control in regulating the labor force through formal measures such as the written congé that attested to a butcher's satisfactory release from the previous season's employment. The laws governing the placement of journeymen not only policed the movement of workers, but also limited it. They held that a wage-earning journeyman who left his position midseason faced strict penalties–a kind of banishment from the quarter in which they had worked.[5] For the workers who abandoned their masters and wanted to return to work, the guild required them to pay damages to the wronged master. Masters who took on journeymen midseason also faced penalties, although less severe (only a 50-livre fine). In this case, neither Nez nor Drieux were penalized for the midseason hire. Clearly, the rules of the guild only attempted to guarantee stability to a transitory labor pool that numbered somewhere between 700 and 1,000.[6] For this reason, the royal authorities at the Châtelet supported the strict enforcement of these laws inasmuch as they saw the need to "maintain this order in a profession as horrible as that of the butchers." According to the royal procurator, the constant labor that slaughtering and butchering demanded day and night, required a large number of workers throughout the season who would serve their masters, and more importantly, who would not "plot among themselves."[7] Journeymen were forbidden to associate professionally. Their secret societies, known as *compagnonnages,* were infamously regarded as subversive sects that undermined the stabilizing force of the guilds. The fear of insubordination and plots against masters ran throughout the minds of the municipal authorities. Without legal constraints, they supposed that journeymen would not work. At best they would walk off the job, at worst they would invoke a group rebellion.

Many historians have focused on these fears and the increasing regulation of the workforce to inscribe the conflicts between journeymen and masters with an immanent teleology. These arguments draw on evidence of collective action and violence that presuppose nineteenth-century aspects of class warfare between the increasingly exploitative, commercial-minded masters and the excluded, subordinate, wage-earning journeymen. The question of whether or not the oppressive nature of this Old Regime system galvanized class conflict or even led to an organized labor movement has been effectively challenged by recent guild studies.[8] In effect, these findings have uncovered a large Parisian labor pool made up of apprenticed journeymen and sons of masters who aspired for mastership and those itinerant workers who remained outside the guild. They were a splintered group of workers with various degrees of investment in the corporate system, one that lacked any social cohesion or consciousness of itself as a uniform class.

Similarly, the meat trade was characterized by a complex division of labor born of variegated products and multiform markets that made for a hierarchical and fragmented working community. In addition, the uniqueness of the Paris market for meat meant that journeymen had little opportunity to find employment beyond the capital. When faced with the encroachment of outside workers, the Parisian journeyman with letters of apprenticeship defended his labor market within this guild territory. Workers, like Nez, sought positions within formal rules and prescriptions that reflected certain principles and maintained certain interests of the corporate world such as rank, expertise and prestige. In the long term, these strategies also depended on systems of credit, kinship, and patronage for the community to sustain and reproduce itself. As such, this "institutional" labor market, embedded in the culture of the Old Regime, ensured a place for those willing to (or fortunate enough) to meet the demands that membership required. It rewarded workers with status in the corporate hierarchy. Unlike the neoclassical market, social and political relations trumped purely economic ones.

Even as the liberalizing pressures of the royal government tried to undermine the corporate system through competition and (briefly) through its dissolution, the guild continued to serve as a powerful integrating and stabilizing force. Its role in the registration of apprentices and journeymen, as well as the reception of masters, regulated the labor market in ways that ensured a certain consistency within the trade and benefited longstanding merchant butchers. As liberal-minded physiocrats criticized the guild system of privilege that went against the natural right of liberty and property, apprentices and journeymen held to the promise of mastership. Concurrently, a vast majority of workers who had learned the trade elsewhere and lacked social ties to the community eked out a fragile existence without the stability and social standing of guild membership.

This chapter investigates the friction and modes of coercion inherent in this system of recruitment that favored guild members and their families while excluding a growing population of skilled labor. The guild demanded discipline and subservience from its workers as it instituted barriers to mastership. Yet rather than reject or revolt against their masters, journeymen engaged in strategies to carve out a place in the working world. Career journeymen, without any opportunity for guild membership, performed an integral part in supporting the growing market for meat; many found their niche subcontracting for masters and merchant butchers. Their subordination and exclusion in this hierarchical system, though always potentially contentious, did not provoke class antagonism. As we shall see, butchers who felt disempowered in this system made claims to their legitimate position either through legal or extralegal forms of resistance. The question why so many journeymen complied and so few resisted resides in the possibilities and limitations of this corporatist labor market.

Access to Mastership

The guild's requirements for mastership changed continually over the early modern period in response to pressures from the state as well as pressures from competing butcher communities. The most significant changes were to raise the minimum age for apprenticed masters from twenty-four to twenty-eight and to extend the length of training as a journeyman from three to eight years. These new rules remained in effect throughout most of the eighteenth century.

Sons of master butchers continued to have more advantages in gaining mastership than outsiders (no required apprenticeship, fewer years as an apprentice, mastership as early as eighteen years of age). Not surprisingly, the guild's recruitment throughout the eighteenth century reflects a high degree of family continuity (nearly half of all master butchers were sons of masters). For outsiders, the butcher guild's entry requirements far exceeded most other guilds apart from the prestigious Six Corps.[9] Butchers paid 1,500 livres for their letters of mastership, a heavy price considering the roast-meat sellers and the pork butchers only paid 1,000 livres for their masterships, and many more trades were less than 500 livres. In addition, the new masters were required to pay a *droit d'ouverture de boutique,* which was, in effect, a license to open a shop.[10] The guild fees associated with the cost of mastership also showed a great discrepancy from those who were sons of butchers (51 livres 13 sols) to those who had been apprentices (for a hefty fee of 488 livres).[11]

Access to mastership, in many ways, operated upon a system of seniority. Even for those who gained the required level of expertise, who were prepared to pass their exam and pay their entry fees or not, their opportunity to enter the guild depended upon the retirement (or death) of elder members. It is difficult to know how long some journeymen waited until they could aspire to mastership. For most, the possibility would never come. For others, avenues could open up with a proposal of marriage. According to the guild statutes, a journeyman who had worked under a master for twelve years, having married a daughter or widow of a master, would become a master himself. This method was not any easier than the formal route through apprenticeship, as married journeymen still had to pay the required fees, complete the masterpiece and gain enough experience and capital to be deemed worthy of a butcher's daughter. Nevertheless, the union of a young butcher with a woman who had ties to the trade provided many advantages to the young, aspiring butcher. He gained access to a workplace with the tools and supplies necessary for starting his business. He was also introduced to a commercial network of other butchers, clients, and suppliers who could ensure an easier entry into the trade.

Marie Françoise Roudharte's first husband was a master butcher in Clichy. Upon his death, she married Étalier Butcher Dominique Deschamps who lived in one of the butcher quarters on the Vieille Place aux Veaux. Her contribution to the marriage, while not indicating any figure, includes her first husband's inheritance of tools, large equipment, and a client and creditor base. We can imagine how the match fared from looking at her second husband's contribution. He entered the marriage as a wealthy journeyman with 5,500 livres of his own savings, more than enough to purchase his mastership at 1,500 livres.[12]

The road to mastership aimed to inculcate a young person with the particular values of the community. There was a legal, moral, and biological responsibility that the master held not only toward his workers, but also toward the guild and the public at large. For young aspirants without family ties to Parisian masters, the period of apprenticeship provided the crucial formation of the individual that went beyond simple acquisition of skills, but indoctrination into the ranks of the community.

Apprenticeship

The guild instituted formal training through a three-year apprenticeship followed by a period of work as a journeyman, as much to fill the ranks of the guild as to ensure standards of perfection and reputability in a growing market for meat. Again, sons of butchers had a clear advantage: a minimum age of eighteen with four years' experience, no formal apprenticeship required. Even compared to the requirements of other guilds, which set the minimum age at twenty, sons of master butchers benefited from an early entry.[13] Newcomers faced more stringent requirements: a minimum age of twenty-eight and eleven consecutive years of experience that included the three-year apprenticeship. This age requirement surpassed what most other guilds required (twenty to twenty-two years of age).[14] The particularly unequal conditions under which young butchers entered this trade and the extraordinary limitations for advancement contributed to a large pool of career journeymen.

The master adopted the adolescent boy into his home for a given period of training that also allowed him to keep the apprentice under his watchful eye at all times. Ideally, this paternalistic model established that the master would educate and protect his younger disciple. And like a surrogate parent, he cared for his daily needs, guaranteeing "to house, heat, light, and launder, and to treat gently and humanely as is proper."[15] These contractual stipulations also ensured a relationship based upon industriousness.

The apprenticeship contract (or brevet) embodied a formalized set of conditions under which an apprentice began his working life.[16] The guild required that the document be drawn up in the presence of a notary and the guild jurés to ensure that the agreement followed the rules of apprenticeship as outlined in its statutes, setting standards for all apprentices to follow.[17] For the young person entering the world of work, drawing up an apprenticeship contract represented an important moment of both liberation and servitude. He or she left the security of his or her home and family, perhaps in a village far from the capital and embarked upon several years of training. The apprentice joined a household of working men and women, each having their own set of responsibilities, where he or she would enter as the lowest ranking member.

In principal, the brevet stood as the legal covenant that embodied the will of the guild. Nevertheless, the contract, negotiated between the two main parties, could be modified in accordance to their needs. For Louis Laurent Poupet, son of a merchant butcher, an "accelerated" apprenticeship program of two years, raised the price from 202 livres to 350 livres.[18] This amount corresponded to fees imposed by the master allegedly to cover maintenance and training costs. In addition, the contracts confirmed the payment of fees *(droits)* to register the brevets with the guild at an additional 42 livres.[19]

Rather than place Louis Laurent Poupet into a typical apprenticeship, his guardian found a willing master butcher to take him "as a boarder to learn the trade of butchery" for two years. As he was only six at his father's death, Louis Laurent's guardian and uncle deemed that an abbreviated period of formal training was sufficient to continue his father's trade. His older brother, Louis Charles, who also entered the trade, worked alongside his father and uncles as young as ten years of age, which provided him with an informal (perhaps unavoidable) apprenticeship without a contract. Louis Laurent's agreement followed the format of other apprenticeship contracts except for the missing guild jurés' signatures and a period of two rather than three years. For the Poupet sons, family linkages with the trade overrode the need for a formal certificate of apprenticeship, registered with the guild.[20]

For Nicolas Brichard, son of a ploughman *(laboreur)* from Brouy, a formal contract drawn up in the presence of guild officers was a necessity. Like many other immigrant workers from outlying towns and burgs, he brought to his apprenticeship his experience in farming and animal husbandry.[21] The young Brichard's name appeared along with his uncle's, a farmer from nearby Antony, who acted as patron to finance and guarantee the agreement. Both signed the contract with Claude Daix, master butcher living on rue Montmartre, Saint-Eustache parish at the guild office. This location provided an ample opportunity for the jurés and syndic to judge the candidate, an outsider whose shaky signature suggested a low level of literacy. The guild could also determine the eligibility of the master to take on an apprentice, and to prevent his signing on more than one trainee at a time. Brichard met all the requirements and continued on his career with success. He received his letters of mastership on March 17, 1764, over twelve years after his entry, one year beyond the required training period for apprenticed masters.[22]

Simon Proffit, a stall worker at age twenty-five, and a resident of the Faubourg Saint-Antoine, signed a contract with Merchant Butcher Henry Boursier at the end of Lent in 1751. Proffit's self-proclaimed title garçon boucher denotes a semiskilled butcher who worked in one of the privileged areas of the city outside of guild jurisdiction. Immediately, one would question why a master would take on such a mature apprentice. In theory, the guild wanted masters to sign on apprentices while they were young and impressionable. Perhaps Boursier may have found it in his economic interest to take someone like Proffit who was physically, emotionally, and intellectually more mature and thus able to work harder and more productively. One could assume that Proffit's choice to enter a three-year, formal training at a mature age indicates a certain aspiration to the higher ranks of the guild. Rather than more instruction, Proffit sought the credentials that the apprenticeship would bring him with Boursier in neighboring Saint Paul parish. Conceivably, Simon Proffit not only gained entry to Boursier's shop, but also to the political and commercial realm of one of the most influential merchant families in Paris. Rather than being taught the skills of butchery, he was more likely being groomed for the world of commerce.

Workers, like Proffit and Brichard, who wanted to guarantee a certain level of stability in their professional lives (and a chance at mastership), followed the fold of the guild. Their training involved several years of constant labor under the master's roof with little room for independent living. Most faced this long period of training in a state of prolonged adolescence. In many ways, an apprentice's low position in the workforce made him his master's (or the journeyman's) lackey. He would be expected to do a certain amount of drudgery such as feeding and tending to livestock for slaughter, mopping the floor with buckets of water to wash away the blood and other waste from stalls and shops, hanging and storing cuts of meat, and watching and stirring the kettle of offal for the rendering of tallow. Aside from the menial, time-consuming jobs, he was sent on errands or relayed messages from one stall to another, drove cattle from pen to stall, and delivered whole carcasses, skins, sides of meat, and special orders to clients. Certainly, apprentices spent a great deal of time observing the work of journeymen and masters especially in the more dangerous aspects of slaughter (clubbing and bleeding the animal) and the butchering of large steer. How many of these tasks they actually were given the opportunity to perform is questionable. (Remember, they still had eight years as a journeyman awaiting them.) Yet, it was in the master's interest to train the apprentice to take over the jobs other paid butchers performed, as he provided cheap labor.

More than a simple form of "gate keeping," apprenticeship entailed a rite of passage that initiated skilled workers into the esteemed world of craftsmanship. Becoming a master not only conferred a set of specialized skills, but also a code of conduct occasionally embodied in a corpus of craft lore. As an initiate, the apprentice had to pass through an ordeal or set of examinations including a masterpiece (*chef d'oeuvre*) to prove his competency and be received as a master. The candidate had to prove himself in all areas of the trade by dressing an ox, a sheep, and a calf. That is, he removed the hide, extracted the entrails, and prepared the meat for cutting up and cooking, all this in the presence of guild jurés and eight senior members. The initiate had two opportunities to pass this test and was required to pay each judge an honorarium or droit of 100 sols (5 livres) on each occasion. As newcomers, their training and increased participation in a master's shop gave them the specialized knowledge and legitimacy needed to eventually replace senior members of the working community.

The Social Classification of Journeymen

Once a butcher completed his stint as an apprentice, he was considered a journeyman. Journeymen were "in the service" of master butchers, but unlike apprentices they could travel from master to master on a seasonal basis. These workers, distinct from masters, held a place in the social order that guaranteed everyone his or her place within a long hierarchy. In keeping with this ideology, a worker owed certain obligations to his employer not so much because he was employed by him, but because he was in a subordinate position to him.

Not all journeymen, however, saw themselves in the same place in the world of work. In the two-tiered system of recruitment, some journeymen were destined for mastership, but others remained wage-earning workers. Sons of masters fell into the former category, most often following the guild's clannish profile. Those journeymen with a brevet who signed on with one master for their eight years of training leading to mastership distinguished themselves from seasonal workers by name, *compagnon attendant maitrise*.[23] Journeymen held other titles (garçon, étalier), some that corresponded to their daily tasks in the slaughterhouse, the scalding house, or in their position in the shops and stalls.

The guild placed a high value on credentials, and no doubt a journeyman's career aspirations acted as a crucial marker in this hierarchical system. Yet the distinction between workers who had acquired formal training through an apprenticeship and those who either learned the trade elsewhere or had little or no experience was not always made clear, as the formal title *apprentis* rarely appears in the historical record. Even in cases where the title "apprentice" appears, one cannot be sure that a journeyman held a brevet, and was not simply an unlicensed worker *(alloué)* living under the auspices of his master. More than simply socioprofessional categories in a division of labor, the various titles of journeymen (garçon, étalier, and alloué) evoke different positions of authority and affluence in the trade.

Garçon Boucher

In its literal sense, garçon means boy, young fellow, bachelor, waiter, or workman. Its seventeenth-century usage also includes domestic worker or employee.[24] The title garçon boucher postdates an earlier nomenclature of fifteenth-century workers in the Grande Boucherie who were known as "valets"–a title that is in keeping with the aristocratic nature of the prestigious butchery and the subservience of stall workers. The development of the usage "garçon" to name workers who performed some of the same tasks as valets, reflected a shift in status, and suggested a loss of prestige. The title denoted a subordinate relationship that was both biological and social to a paternal figure–the master. A master butcher had his "boys" working under him. When confronted by the police commissaire, these individuals chose to identify themselves as "garçon boucher de" followed by the name of their master. In doing so, they not only named the person responsible for their conduct, but also reinforced their position relative to a master.[25]

In examining their everyday lives, one soon discovers how the experience of garçons confirmed their identity within this hierarchy, more specifically, as a particular type of journeymen who lived under the authority of their masters working for a weekly wage. For example, master butchers often kept a room (usually on the third floor near the servants' quarters) that they identified as the *chambre des garçons*. These were Spartan quarters that held small cots called *couchettes* with straw bedding and wool blankets for two or more.[26] The rooms housed several boys who worked for a master. The beds offered garçons respite from the crowded conditions, the smells and the noises, and the continual work shifts at the shop.

The work of garçons was the poorest paid and centered on the most ignoble of tasks. Most commonly, masters hired young men to run the scalding houses as *garçons d'échaudoir.* Within Master Thomas Barré's large-scale operation, the title was broken down into various ranks: Nicolas, the *maître garçon,* was paid 9 livres a week; François, *deuxième d'échaudoir,* made 7 a week; and Louis, *le troisième,* made only 3. Each position was commensurate with their weekly wage, roughly half as much as the wages of an étalier boucher.

Their title implied working youths, who were single, living in their masters' home. Yet upon further research, one realizes that garçons bouchers belonged to no particular age group, nor did they necessarily live under their masters' roofs. Garçon Butcher Frot lived independently, married with children.[27] Nicolas Cochard rented a single room on the upper floors of a building which he shared with Widow Talon, a cook who also became his nurse in the last few weeks of his life.[28] Even with this level of autonomy the title garçon remained, reflecting their professional dependence upon their master employer. Few garçons chose to marry, partly out of their financial constraints, partly out of the long hours their work demanded. Their work patterns interfered with a stable home life. Jean Baptiste Nez, garçon to Master Butcher Danet, left his wife, a tripe seller, at 3:00 A.M. to begin work.[29] Garçon Jacques Boucheron, who could barely support his wife and five children, found himself banished from the city after stealing from a cabaret owner.[30]

Garçons who appear in the probate records are the poorest of the butcher population or with a few possessions to their name.[31] Robert Tillois died nearly penniless. He is identified as a garçon boucher, yet lived with his wife on the third floor of a dwelling on rue Jean Beausire above a busy row of butcher shops. The entirety of his worldly goods included a bundle of wood, a few wicker chairs, some wood planks that served as a table, a pan, a grill, two pots of fat, ten plates, three spoons, two forks, a small cot with a straw mattress, a copper candlestick, and some moth-eaten curtains draped over the single window that faced the street. He also had a small, leather-covered trunk and a small chest that also served as a table, a few linens, two plain linen shirts, and some clothes belonging to his wife. Their total value came to 124 livres. The inventory also includes a list of creditors: the surgeon who bled Robert before he died; the landlord, Sieur Louis, whom Tillois owed two terms of unpaid rent; three washer women who loaned money to the couple; and the wood seller. The debts alone exceeded the value of the property by 40 livres, which left the Widow Tillois, a woman who could neither read nor sign her name, destitute.[32]

Étalier Boucher

The title étalier boucher was derived directly from the occupation, that is, butchers who were responsible for the work that took place within the butcher stalls (étaux) on market streets and in covered butcher markets. Most commonly this included the manual labor associated with meat processing: slaughtering, butchering, and blocking of fresh meat. Like garçons, étaliers worked for a weekly wage. Yet, étaliers held a more secure position than their fellow garçons.

According to records of inventoried butchers, the pay étaliers earned was by no means standard. Some étaliers, like Jacques Hervieux, made as little as 8 livres a week.[33] Others such as Louis Marin Guillaume Duval made as much as 20 livres a week working for Master Butcher Paul Felix Vollée.[34] The pay scale could fluctuate even working for the same master butcher. For example, Vincent Gosse paid his three étaliers 24, 20, and 18 livres a week, respectively.[35] Whether this corresponds to levels of experience or responsibility, the documents do not say. Certainly, given the difference in wages, one could conclude that étaliers held positions of higher authority vis-à-vis their fellow garçons.

Most often, masters hired stall butchers to work alone in one of their three shops not under the supervision of the merchant butcher. This division of labor suggests a greater level of skill and responsibility for the étalier. In many ways, he held a public role in the marketplace as someone employed to serve the neighborhood clientele all year long. Yet these stall butchers performed the work of the master, without the benefits or added responsibility of holding their own enterprise as *marchands publics*. Their position outside the guild would prevent them from assuming the financial roles of merchant butchers who traded in livestock at the cattle markets in Sceaux and Poissy. Thus by nature of their status, étaliers remained limited in their economic opportunities to the eighteenth-century labor market.

From what little we know of the labor market, these workers seem well compensated. In comparison with other trades, an étalier's wages were on average 20 livres a week or just over 1,000 livres a year (depending on whether or not his employment was suspended during Lent). This income was well above what wages we know for journeymen in other professions. The average wage for a journeyman baker was just over 4 livres a week; their highest recorded wages–8 and 9 livres were on the eve of the Revolution.[36] At this time, a mason made about 9 livres a week; a master glazier made 12 livres.[37] Part of this discrepancy may be explained through the level of responsibility given to an employee who is not only selling, but guarding a valuable commodity from theft. In addition, the worker benefited from a diet rich in meat, not only for himself, but most likely for his entire family. An étalier's wage was comparable to that of domestics in large houses, who were provided with food and housing in addition to their wages.

Twice as many étaliers than garçons appear among the probate records. The fortunes they accumulated were much larger: median étalier estates of 1,390 livres as against 331 livres for the four garçons on whom we have records.[38] Unlike their coworkers, they were able to amass a certain amount of capital in the form of liquid, coins kept in chests, gold watches, silver plate, and pearl necklaces. Many of them held IOUs for transactions made with tripe dealers and other individuals to whom they sold meat. These men built their own clientele, perhaps in off hours, and practiced the trade as independent merchants.

At their death, étaliers most commonly occupied one- or two-room apartments, usually on the upper floors of a building near the butcher quarters of the city. Depending on the size of their fortunes, homes could be elaborately furnished with tables, chairs, and decorative objects. Often they rented from master butchers, as in the case of Louis Duval, who rented from his employer Paul Felix Vollée.[39] In one case, Stall Butcher Sapin and his family shared the rent on rue Sainte Margueritte with Master Butcher Jean Blanche Francfort.[40] Unlike the wealthy merchant butchers, none of the stall butchers' inventories refer to domestics. Even with their relatively high wages, domestic help remained a luxury that these men could not afford.

Job Placement

The time requirements placed upon young butchers aspiring to mastership, in effect, acted as an extension of their apprenticeship. The four years spent for sons of masters and the eight years for apprenticed journeymen allowed workers to develop their skills in the craft and build capital and commercial networks that would aid them in their ascent into the ranks of guild merchants. Journeymen could choose to leave Paris on a "Tour de France" to work throughout the provinces. With their letters of apprenticeship in hand, they entered other cities with a reputation to defend. Historians writing on journeymanship have argued for the great demand for labor and its systematized recruitment throughout the provinces. Local bourgeois drew on a pool of mobile journeymen through a network of inns run by semiclandestine journeymen associations called compagnonnages.[41]

Yet for journeymen who looked for work in the butcher trade outside of Paris, many would find closed shops. In many provincial cities, the strength of the butcher trade depended upon tightly run cartels where labor remained a family affair. The number of masters in Lyon was more numerous than their apprentices, journeymen, and other hired labor combined (68 percent of all workers in the meat trade).[42] In Dijon, the number of master butchers declined over the eighteenth century, signaling a fall in the output of the meat trade. For Caen, the master butcher population remained stagnant from 1586 to 1789 while the total urban population grew from 25,000 in 1725 to 40,000 in 1775.[43] The reduction of the numbers of businesses in the provinces did not necessarily mean a loss of output. Fewer, more productive businesses in smaller cities could supply their clientele while keeping the price of meat fairly high compared to the budgets of most consumers. Although it is impossible to know exactly how many butchers left Paris for their tour, the weak demand for labor in the meat trade beyond the city walls most likely deterred them. Moreover, there is no evidence that butchers participated in the compagnonnages–at least on a national level.[44]

In Paris, the demand for butchers remained high. Workers could find employment with masters even without an official congé or any evidence of their training. Claude Barré, a master butcher who hired an unregistered worker named Piastre to man his scalding house, faced additional fines for having repeatedly "flaunted the regulations." The police sent Piastre back to his former employer without any penalty. Here, Barré's behavior rather than Piastre's illegal situation seems to be the object of the police's discipline.[45] In another case, the jurés of the guild sided against Master Butcher Noel Martineau and his journeyman Pierre Guibert, a worker who had been "loaned out" by his master. Again, the master who took on the worker suffered the heaviest fine (80 livres) and Guilbert returned to his master to finish out the season.[46] The guild took a stand in enforcing its own justice against those masters who attempted to run their own system of job placement. Masters who engaged in hiring workers without a brevet defied the authority of the guild leaders and circumvented their administration, along with its collection of dues and taxes.

The Barriers to Mastership

Although the number of masterships granted each year could vary considerably, on average, ten aspirants entered the guild per year. Overall, the trend depicts a general rise in the number of masterships awarded to initiates, particularly apprenticed journeymen, after 1776.

Until this time, structural barriers continued to limit the recruitment of apprentices, limitations that prevented a glut of young butchers competing for mastership. Evidence suggests that in periods of low recruitment, the guild favored sons of masters over apprenticed journeymen, adding to the pool of career journeymen.[47] Finding a master who would take on an apprentice may have slowed many who sought letters of mastership. According to the statutes, no master butcher could take on more than one apprentice at a time. And no master without at least twelve years experience could sign one on.[48] For many young men, the cost alone deterred those of little means from enlisting. Certainly, individuals could choose other trades for less than the 300 livres fee, especially in the food trades: bakers paid 40 livres, pork butchers 30 livres, and wine merchants only 12 livres. Those who traded in hides included tanners, who paid 30 livres, and leather dressers, who paid 20 livres for an apprenticeship contract.[49]

The cost could be forgiven in certain cases. In keeping with their religious ideals, the guild showed acts of charity in giving letters of mastership to individuals who trained outside the guild community in privileged areas. Many young artisans with little means benefited from free training that these charitable communities (*hôptiaux*) provided. Nearly every year one or two butchers entered the guild without an apprenticeship but often with several years of experience at one of the city hospitals (either Trinité or l'Hôpital Général).[50]

Every aspiring butcher did not so easily overcome the obstacles to mastership. There were those whose religion prevented them from becoming an artisan at all, as nearly every guild dictated that the apprentice must be a Roman Catholic and of good reputation and manners (*de bonnes moeurs*). This religious requirement excluded both Protestants and Jews, a population that remained hidden from the official meat trade of eighteenth-century Paris. It is feasible that the latter group developed their own kosher butcher markets for their own clientele. But whether or not they followed a system of apprenticeship of their own is difficult, if not impossible, to ascertain.[51]

An outsider or troublemaker could be put off by the subjective criteria "bonnes moeurs" the equivalent of manners or character. The guild panel made up of a syndic and jurés passed decisions to elect those whose honor befitted a master butcher. How could this be measured fairly or objectively? At least in questions of birthright, the candidate had to conform to the laws of patrimony. According to the statutes, a son of a butcher could not claim his "birthright" if he were not "born in a legitimate marriage from [the moment of] the father's entry into mastership."[52]

Although the highly regulatory and exclusive nature of the guild comes forth in their statutes, it is important to remember that these codes were based upon the common interests of the community that sought to uphold standards of skill as much as the status of mastership. There may have been more interest in limiting the number of apprentices to ensure consistency and standards of quality than in opening the trade to those of questionable backgrounds. A master could, however, circumvent these rules and make agreements without the presence of the jurés. He could ask for any amount of time or money from a young wage worker willing to "lend himself" to the shop without any promise of certification. These workers gained employment while they bypassed the formal apprenticeship contract, forfeiting their opportunity to gain access into the higher ranks of the guild.

Other journeymen, who had more than served their time, had to fight for entry into the privileged community of merchants. Pierre Ancel and Jean

LeGrand faced real roadblocks in their careers, even with the completion of all requirements outlined in the guild's statutes. LeGrand, after four years as an apprentice, took his master, Louis Frere, to court for his brevet that would allow him to gain the title of master. Only after five years did Jean LeGrand succeed in gaining his due from the royal procurator at the Châtelet. Pierre Ancel faced a longer wait. Even after eighteen years of service, three as an apprentice and fifteen as a journeyman, he still could not complete his masterpiece and enter the guild. In both cases, the pleas of these workers focused on their completion of the requirements for mastership as specified in the guild statutes. Their arguments quoted the relevant articles from the statutes, utilizing them like a legal code. These cases before the civil courts provide an example in which guild statutes served as a legal contract that bound all members and provided legal recourse for journeymen seeking redress of grievances.[53]

These exceptional cases demonstrate the willingness of some journeymen who considered mastership their due. There were those journeymen whose exclusion from the guild remained an accepted fact: workers who would never go beyond the level of a wage earner. For these men, the seasonal work of slaughter and butchering shaped their everyday lives until their deaths. What kinds of value and motivation did they hold toward their work without the aspiration of guild membership? What kind of leverage did they employ within the constraints of the hierarchical corporate system?

Career Journeymen

The everyday lives of étaliers and garçons with no opportunity for entry into the corporate ranks were predicated upon terms of survival. Although they were at least three times more numerous than master butchers, evidence of their lives appears scattered and haphazard. Most came from rural communities outside of Paris. Few were the sons and brothers of Parisian artisans with modest fortunes. As the following chapter details, few of their marriages show any great success at social mobility, especially within the community of butchers. One reason may be the unbridgeable social gap between these wage earners and their employers.

To a certain extent, the presence of career journeymen as autonomous workers subverted the guild's social order. Career journeymen managed to sustain some prosperity and independence even while formally excluded from guild politics and the wholesale merchant trade. They had acquired the skills and abilities to exercise their trade independently, yet could not enter the higher ranks of the corporate system or advance in the commercial sector. Pressed against its barriers, this rival group provoked conflict and forms of resistance that drew attention to the incoherence of the social taxonomy.

Journeymen who operated their stalls independently managed their own business in defiance of the institutional market. They set up their own stalls, purchased their supply of livestock directly from suppliers or secondhand, and hired their own workers. How they envisioned their autonomy and a sense of identity as equal to masters remains significant. Voices such as Stall Butcher Lesueur's come forth when he orders "one of his garçons" to weigh the meat in the shop for a customer.[54]

Similarly, journeymen who participated in the weekly market for tallow on the Place des Veaux exercised a small commercial sector of the meat trade for their masters, for which they were given a portion of its profits. Working as skilled laborers in the butcheries' foundries, these journeymen were solely responsible for the production and sale of rendered fat called tallow. The Thursday market drew candle makers, perfume makers, polishers (*cireurs*), and other consumers throughout the city. Butchers, with their monopoly of the bovine and ovine industry, fabricated the highest quality tallow. The participation of their journeymen in this market demonstrated an area in which workers could exercise their own business acumen. It also represented a sector of the economy that these wage earners cornered for themselves within the corporate ranks, one they exercised independently of their masters.

The police kept a close eye over the price of tallow as for many other staple commodities. Their objective was to ensure a well-provisioned market and fair trading practices. When the price went too high, it was the butchers who stood accused of speculating. But only their masters could be held legally responsible for these commercial offenses.[55] On September 7, 1741, the police, in an effort to name the master butchers responsible for the inflationary prices, pressed the journeymen to reveal the names of their masters. They refused. One "insolent" butcher responded that "he didn't know the name of his master." The police retaliated, bringing in the royal archers who sparked a violent outburst. They fought off the first band of archers successfully by breaking their swords and tearing their clothes. The riot ended with a single arrest of the insolent butcher. No other informant came forward to give the names of masters. To a certain extent, the journeymen acted in their masters' interest protecting them from inquiry and possible fines. Beyond this, their actions suggest an equal effort to protect themselves and to maintain their own control over the market. The police felt obliged to respond to their unbridled autonomy, for without the authority of their masters, the maintenance of social order was impossible and rebellion inevitable. Or was this outbreak of violence simply provoked? Journeymen without masters subverted the social order, turning the world upside down in a carnavalesque atmosphere. The police of Paris and the guild jurés were obliged to respond by showing who was on top.[56]

Conclusion

The guild system of recruitment provided a certain number of master butchers who reflected the ideal role of master. Either through hereditary right or a formalized process of acculturation (apprenticeship and journeymanship), the world of butchers reproduced the master in its own image. The guild leaders awarded the privilege to those individuals who demonstrated the skills, possessed the means, and expressed the personal qualities of mastership (de bonnes moeurs). The road to mastership permitted those with good fortune and social position to succeed.

It would be wrong, however, to paint this process of recruitment as a teleological system that replicated itself without feeling the stresses of a growing labor pool against the tightening butcher dynasties. Many of the young initiates who fought hard for their place in the guild came from different backgrounds. Their entry into butcher's work as an apprentice was not always purchased or exempt from birthright, but could be sought through charitable organizations. The option of apprenticeship was not for all and, in many cases, could be negotiated. Young men who came with butchering skills from the countryside could find work in Paris without formal credentials, either as an alloué or as a stall worker in the faubourg Saint-Antoine.

With the brevet in hand, butchers could set their sights on mastership while working at least eight more years as a journeyman. During this "holding period," apprenticed butchers had to choose whether the opportunities for guild membership stood as economically and socially viable. Would there be a place for them in the guild? How would they get there?

Many butchers did not exercise the privilege of mastership. Some failed the test. Some were limited by structural barriers–financial, social, political. Others simply did not choose the exclusive membership of the guild, or they simply did not see the need to enter the guild–no motivation nor value. Perhaps they remained content with their station as journeymen. Perhaps the requirements were too great to be met. Many journeymen saw no desire to marry or have a family, choosing to live as "boys" in a state of prolonged adolescence. For many journeymen, the heavy work demands and their low standard of living precluded family life. Many skilled butchers went outside the guild system to sell their wares in the suburbs of the city. Their clientele was limited, and their choice of meat was not as good as the master butchers. These *forain* butchers knowingly operated in fringe areas for a different clientele. They could never hope to achieve the same success as a guild member who held sway over the central Parisian market.

Journeyman butchers functioned as an important part of the workforce that contributed to the growth of the Parisian meat trade. Workers such as étaliers held important positions in the expanding number of butcher shops and stalls. They operated in the retail sector in and around Paris, maintaining a certain autonomy from their masters. Their lives showed a degree of stability not found among most garçons. Nevertheless, their place outside the guild excluded them from gaining any great wealth and prominence among the butcher community. Although far from the servitude of the apprentice, they would never maintain the level of respect shown to a master. Even as a recognized artisan, their social intercourse remained limited to another band of urban life.

As we shall see in the next chapters, the strategies of becoming a master entailed much more than credentials and experience; they also required capital, property, family alliances, and reputation. For sons of butchers, mastership was not only more accessible than for outsiders, but it allowed families to build businesses with greater economies of scale. For the outsiders who may have succeeded in the butcher trade, their integration into the corporate system would never become a mechanical inevitability. Rather, they would build a life for themselves knowing that the world of work existed for them as well.

Chapter 7

Building the Family Firm

Marriage and Succession

The Vollée family chose a wedding day in early February 1745, just at the end of the working season; Master Butcher Pierre Louis Vollée, the father of the groom, had many reasons to be proud. Not only was it the fourth wedding over which he was to preside, but each of his children's marriages built upon two generations of merchant butcher businesses.[1] As a purveyor to the royal household of Madame la Dauphine and the guild's syndic from 1745 to 1749, Pierre Louis Vollée benefited from his family's prominence in the trade to gain access to the most privileged clientele and the most powerful position within the guild. Through his financial and commercial assets, he saw to it that each of his children establish their own households and positions within the guild community.[2] Today was François Alexandre's day to secure his future with Marie Geneviève Crespy, a young girl who had lost her mother as a child. Her father, a prominent roast meat seller, had strong ties with Vollée through their affiliation as the princess' provisioners. The list of attendees (as they appear in the marriage contract[3]) reflects an extensive social network: both the bride and the bridegroom's large extended families included guild merchants and skilled artisans from related trades (grocers, cooks-caterers, roast meat sellers) and petty officials and members of the educated professions (a notary, an architect). The dowry from Crespy amounted to 6,000 livres, capital that would place a young merchant butcher well above his guild peers. More valuable was the stall he received from his father on the rue Saint-Antoine. With this marriage, François Alexandre would establish himself, not only as a head of household, but as an affiliated member of the Vollée family firm.

Marriages like Vollée's may have held great promise, but not all fulfilled the hopes of success. In March 1721, Elizabeth Thérèse Gouet (her maiden name), represented by her procurator, Master Louis LeMasson, presented her case to the lieutenant civil at the Châtelet to dissolve the financial bond between her and her husband of one year, Master Butcher Denis François Bignon. On March 10, the Commissaire Blanchard recorded the depositions of three witnesses, each taken individually, unaware of each other's testimony, none of them servants or relations to the accused Bignon.[4] All three described Bignon's gambling and drinking that had intensified since his marriage to Gouet. One witness, François Brunel *(bourgeois de Paris)* claimed seeing Bignon several times in the cabarets of the Saint-Martin quarter playing cards. He stated that for one month "he knew his affairs were in terrible disorder," and that "he owed money to several individuals." The third witness, Mathurin Feburier, also noted Bignon's financial ruin, saying that "his wife runs the risk of losing her dowry and has been forced to seek a financial separation." After only one year of marriage, Gouet saw the ruin of her property and economic well being, and so took the unusual step of seeking a legal separation of goods (*séparation des biens*). This act split communal property in half, breaking the marital community without going so far as to sever the marriage bond. Although the law provided a woman with some protection against her husband's gambling debts, it also placed the burden on the wife to seek legal representation and furnish testimonies. Such actions, which were rare before divorce was made legal in France,[5] in effect divested women from the communal property established at marriage. The act also dissolved the conjugal partnership (if not the mutual trust) that was so essential to butcher marriages.

These two marriages, taken as a study in contrast, represent two visions of family as an overriding economic, social, and cultural force in the organization and perpetuation of the butcher trade. The first demonstrates the ways in which the ideology and function of the family was enacted through marriage when the butcher household was established. The second shows the struggles and contestations of a woman bound to this social structure that privileged men. This chapter addresses the problem of household structures and family strategies in building butcher businesses as family firms. It examines the form and function of the family firm from the critical moments when households were established and dissolved, as well as from the perspective of individual women and men whose choices shaped and were shaped by these visions of family. How did butchers value family and lineage as the basis of identification and reputation? How did women see their role in the family firm?

Family and Kinship

The idea of the family, especially seen in terms of its patriarchal head of household, has been a governing principal in many early modern studies. Until recently, family historians have exemplified the patriarchal power under the "family-state" compact, which contended that the household, like the state, could only have one head.[6] The husband, who held marital authority over his wife, and the father, who negotiated proper marriage alliances of his children, ruled the family. By viewing the social and legal differences solely within this patriarchal system, however, it is easy to overlook the complex forces at work that show women's agency and independence within the family firm. Moreover, too much emphasis on male authority in the nuclear family obscures the ways in which extended families relied on group strategies to forward the family firm within and across bloodlines through marriage, succession, and collective commercial practices.

Although the Vollée example epitomizes the social profile of an elite group of butchers for whom kinship played an integral part in economic production and expansion, as well as social intercourse and reproduction, the absolute rule of male butchers is far from the case. Even in the most successful families whose extensive resources allowed for a complex division of labor and the relative comforts for some men and women, the trade depended on the pooling of resources and the cooperation of the entire household, not only from day to day, but also from generation to generation.

Such generational cooperation was quite common. For example, Pierre Barré (also the son of a butcher) at the time of his death was survived by seven children (five sons who were master butchers, two daughters who married into related trades) and at least eight grandchildren, two of whom were master butchers.[7] Charles Denis Tripperet and Marie Anne Aubert saw eight of their children prosper as adults, many in the butcher trade. Butcher families not only demonstrated a high degree of fertility, but also a great degree of trade loyalty as parents invested in their children and their children continued to expand their business holdings. Fostering a future generation was desirable to create partners in capital and insurance transactions and not just as suppliers of labor. The child who received support was implicitly bound to compensate his parents by supplying labor and support through their old age. These transactions derive from the complementary life cycle of succeeding generations where children are born when they can be provided for and later they assist their parents.[8] Yet, large families, although providing important benefits to parents, also came at a cost, making demands upon a limited amount of resources for school, training, and dowries, as well as partible inheritance.[9]

The most prominent butchers who built their businesses as family firms dominated the meat trade throughout the eighteenth century despite many significant changes in the labor market. The Barré, Vollée, and other butcher clans held important positions in the guild as jurés and syndics and held a significant market share through their large-scale, well-established enterprises. While the family firm aimed to grow and expand butcher businesses, it operated within a conservative, collective notion that preserved and consolidated fortunes despite many financial obstacles. In a period of economic instability, in a market that faced increasing competition from nonguild meat sellers, and in a trade that required heavy capital investment at great financial risk, the pooled resources of butcher families and their kinship ties provided them with some insurance in difficult times.

It is important to stress how these clans were not the only ones who practiced the trade in Paris. The new guild statutes enacted after 1776 resulted in greater numbers of apprenticed masters. As a result, the city took the lead in changing the labor pool by incorporating outsiders into its fold: allowing entrepreneurs greater access to commercial property and turning a blind eye to the black market for meat. Journeyman launched their own enterprises in the Faubourg Saint-Antoine where the guild jurisdiction did not reign. Other incorporated butchers moved to the countryside or other outlying areas and became forain butchers. A daring upstart could even operate a stall illegally with a false title and a borrowed name and the complicity of a butcher master or widow. This expansion of the trade, however, did not halt the family mode of production nor the social reproduction of butchers, proving that the family firm was the most stable institution to keep butcher businesses solvent through precarious economic times and to grow family enterprises from generation to generation.

For those who entered the trade without extensive kin networks, their success depended upon the acquisition of capital and skilled labor. Butchers' assets included their tools, commercial property, and real estate (discussed in the next chapter). Labor came from children and wives whose relative value to the family business could be measured through their knowledge, efficiency, and low cost. A master's letters of mastership may have ensured his entry into the world of work as a single producer, yet more than any other single choice, marriage brought together significant forms of capital, social networks, and a future labor force that could determine the fate of the business. Although the guild did not require masters to marry, most did so at the moment they entered the guild, showing how important it was to men in establishing the working household.

Given the powerful nature of this ideology, which favored the rule of men, it would appear that the viability of the family firm had little direct benefit for women as they became the object of exchange and reproduction in building family enterprises. But nothing could be further from the case; women had an important role in the not only the establishment and growth of the household, which was also the site of production, but also in the finances and labor relations of butcher businesses.

Women in the Butcher Trade

For women, the moment of marriage, especially to a master, gave her a respected position in a number or ways. First, marriage placed her as a partner in a newly established household. In nearly every one of these cases, the women of butcher families (unlike the men) left their homes at an early age to start new families. On the one hand, this practice reinforced the patrilocal characteristics of butcher households; on the other, it offered women a chance to gain new status as a butcher's wife playing a critical part in the private functioning of the household and the public work of the commerce and trade.

Second, a wife's financial contribution to the household, made at the moment of marriage, provided necessary capital to establish a business or propel it into a higher level of production. By extension, the marriage of a master's daughter to a master in a related trade could provide an added resource of labor or capital. The dowry that may have included a trousseau of linens and clothing, as well as tools (from her father's trade) or other liquid assets, no doubt made women conscious of their own investment in the business.

Third, a woman's role in child rearing and meal preparation, not to mention her semiofficial role as bookkeeper and sales clerk, provided a crucial part in the growth and maintenance and reproduction of the family firm. Her responsibilities to the shop and home, however invisible to guild statutes, made her a de facto partner in the business.

Historians may regard the subordination of working wives, considered a husband's helpmeet, as part of the patriarchal structure of early modern society that devalued women's contributions to the household economy without seeing a woman's level of commitment to and satisfaction from her supportive role in the trade. Anecdotal evidence suggests that her emotional investment was profound. The wife of Butcher Vincent Bignon who kept the accounts of clients and suppliers, inscribed her account book with a loving pledge to her husband, "*mon cher amant.*"[10] She wrote the verse, taken from a popular song, inside the thin leather binding. Such evidence demonstrates the extent to which the marriage bond fused conjugal love and cooperative work, emotional expression and practical chores. The butcher's wife stood alongside her husband as a loyal partner in life.

Another example of conjugal loyalty can be read in the May 13, 1727, report of Commissaire LeConte. In a letter to the Lieutenant General Hérault, he describes his exasperation with trying to police the butchers who did not agree to the price ceiling of 7 sous a pound. One butcher in particular, Pierre Remy, gives LeConte an earful. To the official's surprise, Remy's wife intervenes by turning her back to LeConte, ignoring his solicitation, and telling her husband "Go, go! Leave everything there. We will explain it when we have to." The commissaire, shocked by the woman's brazenness, commented to the lieutenant general, "I confess, Monsieur that if this butcher seems reprehensible to you the impudence of his wife is no less so."[11] In this case, the butcher's wife intervenes to shelter her husband from a heated and inopportune conflict. Yet she deflects the intense situation by showing disrespect to the public official and blatantly disregarding his authority. Here, her allegiance resided with her husband's honor and reputation.

Could a woman be a practicing butcher in her own right? Clearly, the guild thought so. Widows of master butchers, in particular, were a group who were commonly accepted as merchants. According to the guild statutes, they inherited the title of mastership with limited privileges for as long as they remained widowed. Widow mistresses were required to abide by guild statutes that regulated trade practices, but widows could not vote in elections of guild officers. They could sign contracts in their own name, but often included the signatures of their sons and brothers who were masters. Practically speaking, a mistress widow could not assume the managerial and productive tasks of their late husbands without family support. Without denying the gender biases that pervaded the patriarchal structures of the family, it is important to stress the role women played as the head of a family firm. Mistress butchers may not have had the same public recognition as men who held titles as masters of their craft, but maintaining the rights and privileges to practice the trade from late husband to surviving wife acted in the interests of the entire household. The guild, instituted to maintain social order within a clearly defined set of rules, allowed for members to pass on the title as part of their patrimony. To be sure, it was up to the widow whether or not she wished to continue managing the business independently, but the guild statutes made clear that she was not allowed to lend her title to anyone (either directly or indirectly) to any unlicensed butcher without forfeiting her place in the guild.[12]

Widows who retained their husband's title of master and actively engaged in the family business accounted for 3 to 12 percent of all stalls registered throughout the eighteenth century.[13] (A percentage that was comparable to other cities at this time.)[14] From this evidence, we cannot conclude whether they left their marital status to fate or actively forged their own careers in the trade. If they did manage to run the business for any period of time, they were dependent upon strong family ties, especially for legal matters. Marie Françoise Lasnier kept her late husband Louis Thibert's shop running for seven years with the help of her three butcher sons and two sons-in-law, also master butchers.[15] Marie Francoise Ruelle, widow of Pierre Carraque, ran her husband's large butcher business with help from one domestic, Étalier Edme Francfort, and her two daughters, Marie Anne and Rozeline, who lived with her. She also had the support of Claude Simon Aubert, master butcher, who acted as guardian to Marie Anne and Rozeline.[16] Such examples demonstrate the willingness of widows to take the role of public merchant, as well as the merchant community's acceptance of that role.

To be sure, gender distinctions did exist in the butcher trade and influenced women's participation in the world of work. The few, all-female guilds, such as the seamstressess and linendrapers,[17] serve as a profound example of how these differences could be used to carve out a place for women in the corporate system. These communities founded their distinct corporate identity upon their female membership and their female and child clientele. As Clare Crowston effectively argues, the seamstresses made gender a useful category of social and economic organization as the guild defended the legal and economic autonomy it bestowed on women.[18] The title of guild mistress, gained through apprenticeship, gave them legal privileges and a sense of honor as independent artisans. The butcher's wife held no title distinct from her husband's rank, and–even as a widow mistress–her professional identity was defined through her husband, not through any formal training. Yet in practical terms, the mistress widow, given freedom of action and the opportunity to broker agreements, took on a different public role than she was allowed in other domains. However much she may have relied upon sons and other masters, as a senior member of the family firm her business decisions were her own.

Another area of autonomy for women in the meat trade resided in the unregulated marketplaces such as *les Halles*. These women worked outside of licensed butcher stalls and shops as *fausse ouvrières*, or unlicensed workers. In some cases, they set up makeshift stalls in market squares in defiance of guild statutes. They appeared in police records, arrested for illegal sales as was the case with Geneviève Jasmin, a wife of a journeyman butcher. Her crime concerned the transgression of the guild butcher's privileged commerce. Jasmin was not arrested for being a female butcher per se, but for selling illegal meats (e.g., horsemeat) sold outside of the prescribed season (e.g., Lent).[19] The dubious status of female butchers, like many other unincorporated butchers, including peddlers and regrattières who sold recycled meats, placed them in an entirely different level of trade: guild butchers regarded their goods as "unworthy for human consumption." They, along with many other urban women who were part of the working poor, sought any means of earning a living. Most often they chose to trade in cheap, prepared foods and illicit drink, commodities with a wide demand that did not encroach upon corporate professions. Some female entrepreneurs, nonetheless, established themselves as public merchants, selling wine and running taverns, trades which (according to the tax rolls) brought them a relative level of success.[20]

Even though women could, and did, operate businesses independently, most regarded the moment of marriage as an opportunity to establish independent households that functioned as a firm with collective goals. Throughout their lives and their children's lives, husbands and wives based their decisions on the preservation and integrity of the family businesses. These decisions began at the level of daily tasks and a clear division of labor and extended to the couple's decisions over the number of children, their marriage alliances and inheritance. Marriage, therefore, was the critical juncture that configured these social and economic relations. Choosing a spouse involved a number of strategies whose consequences would be played out for many years.

Marriage Strategies

For most butchers (masters and journeymen alike), marriage represented the moment when two families contracted the legal union of husband and wife. This partnership was by far the most important opportunity for a man to establish himself as a butcher and for a woman to invest in a working household, as it set up family linkages and personal assets that were also commercial ones. As the notarial records of marriage contracts attest, butchers demonstrated a high rate of professional endogamy. Men and women married into families whose related trades (cattle trading, tanning, agriculture, candle making, prepared meat selling) made forward and backward linkages to meat production. By doing so, butcher households could exploit their middle position in the chain of production, building a nexus of relationships with suppliers and merchant clients. Moreover, butchers aimed to extend this nexus through their offspring and the marriages they made. These complex family and trade associations, characterized by vertical and horizontal integration, and material interests embedded in property relations, created a strong basis for reciprocity and obligation–an element that could provide security and continuity in the face of uncertainty.

Although it is nearly impossible to know if all master butchers married, nearly every marriage of a Parisian butcher aspiring to mastership occurred after they had gained the title of master. And nearly half the unions represent established butchers who married butchers' daughters. For those few cases where journeymen married a widow in the butcher trade, the guild required the grooms to complete their mastership and pay their fees. Sons of masters who were exempt from mastership fees and a long stint as a journeyman, still waited until they were masters before setting up their own households. Given the importance of the family mode of production, finding a spouse who was familiar with the butcher trade was an added asset. Marriage among butchers became a linkage not only of husband and wife, but of senior generations. Master butchers who married daughters of butchers were most likely sons of masters or merchants themselves and were sons of master butchers themselves eight times out of nine. Taking all marriage records into consideration, nearly a third of them show master butchers marring daughters of master butchers.[21]

Women who married master butchers came from merchant families in half of the cases. Many of their fathers who were not butchers were involved in businesses that demanded great capital investment and extensive credit operations, such as wine merchants, who appeared in several cases. Several of the brides' fathers reported a trade closely related to or in conjunction with the meat trade. Some of these fathers identified themselves as roast meat sellers, caterers, or *cabaretiers,* trades directly involved in selling prepared meats; two were agriculturists, who came from the region surrounding Paris (a rich agricultural area ideal for grazing and stocking farm animals). A ploughman who lived outside Paris handed down extensive properties to his daughter. Brides who married master butchers also came from other backgrounds: one was the daughter of a banker, another was the daughter of a wealthy farmer, the third a mason's daughter. Three women had fathers who held royal offices, and two others a father in the legal profession.

Marriage patterns stress not only the professional identities of kin, but also the residential distinctions of butcher family firms. Parisian masters practiced a local trade and their status as guild members made them loyal to their urban roots. Butchers of the same family tended live in the same neighborhoods. (The Barré and Aubert brothers lived on rue Saint-Martin, the Gallier brothers on rue des Boucheries, the Lelievre clan on rue et Montagne Sainte-Geneviève. The surviving butcher aristocracy of the grande Boucherie, the Thiberts, continued to live and work in the neighborhood of the Vieille Place aux Veaux.)

The work of Parisian butchers linked urban and rural areas. Yet their ties to the countryside did not extend to family alliances. Few master butchers married their daughters into farming families. The one example comes from a family in the village of Groslay. Butcher Lecouvret and his wife witnessed the marriage of one daughter to a butcher in nearby Epinay and their second daughter, Marie Jeanne, to a village officer (*garde*), Martin Hamlin. His title (worth 2,000 livres) brought in 75 livres a year. In addition, his parents bestowed an inheritance that included small landholdings (nearly 100 square *perches* or 0.84 acres) and a house in Epinay. This generous bequest made at the time of marriage brought the country butcher's daughter into a union with a *coq du village*. Clearly her 3,000 livres dowry helped her win this promising young man of the rural community.[22]

For butchers who were not guild members or who had immigrated to Paris, marriage was a time to widen social bonds or to establish those that were of greatest local importance. This fact is attested by the array of guests listed in marriage contracts who witnessed the civil act before the notary. Many nuptials had the signatures of one witness, along with their parents or guardians when necessary. For those young couples who came from the provinces, the person would be listed as a friend who often was a fellow worker.[23] In other cases, the witness was a benefactor: A noble woman's lady in waiting who was daughter of a provincial butcher asked the governor and governess at the Tuilleries Château to be present at her marriage to a Swiss guard.[24] A recent resident of Trinité hospital asked the officers who ran the house for the poor to be present at her wedding.[25] In several of these cases, the witness seems to substitute for a deceased father, even though the couple as legal adults (*majeur*) did not need a guardian to authorize the marriage.

Age mattered in choosing a spouse. The more established the bride's family within the trade, the more likely she would marry a master butcher at a young age: in this case, under twenty-five, the average marriage age for most urban workers. Guild butchers sought young wives in their late teens and early twenties with means as they could bring them large families and ensure important financial backing early on in their careers. Seen conversely, older, well-established merchant butchers made a good match for a young, relatively affluent woman from a merchant family. Not surprisingly, many of the most prominent butcher households were also characterized by large families, ranging from five to seven adult children who contributed to the family production until they were ready to establish their own households.[26]

Clearly these strategies show the advantages for both men and women in gaining social and commercial ties to extended kin networks in new localities as well as a wealth of professional experience that contributed to the workings of the business. Marriage was also a contractual relationship; each party outlined the finances that he or she brought to the marriage. Women and their kin sought to protect their own property in a variety of ways, often delineating procedures for dowry and inheritance in the marriage contract itself. The contract also established the shared holdings of husband and wife, the marriage capital so necessary to the family firm.

Communal Property

At the moment of marriage, the families of both parties sat down with a notary to draw up a marriage contract. This agreement put forth the terms upon which the patrimony would rest during the marriage and when the marriage ended at death. This was done to protect the family of the two parties as much as for the future couple and their potential offspring. Parisian women benefited from customary laws that divided the dowry into two distinct categories upon marriage. One, called the marital *communauté,* specified the assets that both husband and wife brought to the marriage, intended to support the common cost of the household. The other, called the *biens propres,* referred to lineage properties that returned to her on widowhood or passed on to her nearest blood relations. The husband had full authority over the community properties; he could invest them or dispose of them as he pleased. He could not, however, alienate his wife's lineage properties without her consent. Even with her consent he was normally required to reinvest the proceeds of the alienated property in assets that would henceforth acquire the status of lineage properties belonging to her and her heirs.[27]

Communal property represented the shared wealth from both bride and groom. Future husbands pledged a *douaire* at the time of marriage, a sum which was half the inheritable fortune that the bridegroom possessed at the time of his marriage. Upon the husband's death half of this amount would go directly to his wife in addition to her part of the communal property. Even men who did not specify the level of their personal fortune at the time of the contract always included a sum that was to be part of the marital property.[28]

The senior members of butcher families also took an active role in establishing the couple's future. Their contributions included commercial property from their butcher business, given as an advance to their children's inheritance. Widow Hubie, a bouchère, passed along her shop's commercial assets to her son at his marriage. In the contract, she specified the 4,245 livres of clients' accounts payable, the tools of the trade, and the promise of a stall. Another example is the daughter of late Master Butcher Grandjasse, who married Louis Antoine Mabire, a master butcher; she gave him 6,579 livres worth of unpaid accounts, along with 7,792 livres of additional accounts payable that were "doubtful" (*douteuses*). The total of the commercial assets, excluding real estate, amounts to 4,203 livres. This formed nearly half of the average amount for all master butchers (9,269 livres), and 49 percent of the total contributions made by those grooms in the sampling. In other cases, contracts specified large assets such as real estate and annuities that sons and daughters would inherit. Contracts often grouped personal and commercial assets together as they were inextricably linked in the establishment of a family business.[29]

Overall, the range of wealth that master butchers and brides from butcher families brought to their weddings varied widely: a bride's contribution ranged from 250 to 10,000 livres, and a groom's from 200 livres (for a stall butcher) to 20,000 livres (for a prominent master butcher). The amount of communal property in many ways reinforced the economic divide between those who were masters or daughters of masters and those who were not. Another significant correlation points to the importance of brides whose fathers were masters or merchants and who brought greater wealth into marriages to butcher masters than nonbutcher families, many of them farming families. Such evidence reinforces the preference for investing and expanding the kin networks of the family firm.

Even though these brides may have brought greater amounts of capital to the marriage, rarely did they cede property outright to their husbands. The closest example comes from Master Butcher David who gained access to a stall in the Saint-Jean cemetery upon marriage to Louise Marguerritte Barré. Yet, in exchange for the use of the stall, the couple obliged her parents with two-and-a-half years of meals and lodging at the young couple's expense.[30] Butcher property, whether it was stalls, houses, or tools of the trade, by and large remained tightly held within consanguine groups. The one exception is Marie Françoise Roudharte, whose first husband was a master butcher in Clichy. Unlike most widows who chose to remarry within the social strata that separates masters from journeyman, she remarried stall butcher Dominique Deschamps living in one of the butcher quarters on Vieille Place aux Veaux. Her contribution to the marriage, while not indicating any figure, included her first husband's inheritance of tools, large equipment, and a client and creditor base. We can see how the match fared from looking at her second husband's contribution. He entered the marriage as a wealthy étalier with 5,500 livres of his own savings, more than enough to purchase his mastership at 1,500 livres.[31]

Choosing a Second Spouse

For women and men who lost their spouses, the choice of remarriage depended upon a number of pressing circumstances. Could a widow or widower continue the business alone? Did she or he have sufficient help from grown sons and daughters or did the burden of child care force hasty decisions? Did the bereaved live alone or could they depend upon the mutual aid of the guild members or of brothers and sisters? Could these butchers and butchers' wives find partners to support them? In many ways, the decision had far-reaching consequences and had to be made under duress. Marriage at this moment in life turned rapidly on questions of survival, not only for the individual but for the family firm.

Among the master butchers who suffered the loss of a spouse, we find more of those who remarried than those who remained widowed. To be sure, titles obscure many widowers while they pull widows into the foreground. Nevertheless, afterdeath inventories and marriage contracts do offer the historian a certain amount of information concerning the family histories of both men and women. For example, Thomas Barré married three times. We know this because in his probate records children from all three marriages lay claim to a portion of the family inheritance. Barré's first wife died after giving birth to a son, Thomas Nicolas Barré, on August 7, 1719. His second wife passed away on March 13, 1730. Not knowing when they were married we can only surmise that it followed within five years of the death of his first wife, as the second marriage begot two children: Antoine and Marie Thérèse. Two years later on February 19, 1732, he married his third wife, Anne Jacquin, and together they had five children before Thomas died in 1751.[32] Henry Boursier did not wait as long to find a new wife. He lost wife Marie Anne Garnier on Easter of 1711, within the first year of their marriage. Fifteen months later, he remarried Geneviève Proffit.[33]

Widows of butchers often chose to remarry within the same profession. Of twelve widows found within the marriage records, seven were first married to butchers. Of the seven, five married men in the same trade. Widows such as Marie Catherine Fleury, Denise Duval, and Marie Madeleine Gallier, whose husbands had been prominent master butchers with large businesses must have appeared as attractive mates to other unmarried masters. Even though much of the wealth from the first marriage was distributed among the heirs when widows remarried, their ties to clients and suppliers made them valuable partners in the business. For Marie Catherine Fleury, widow of Pierre Barré, four years passed before remarrying Master Butcher Georges Mergery.[34] For Denis Duval, widow of Philippe Boursier with two young children, the need for a new husband was more urgent. She married François Alexandre Vollée within a year of her husband's death.[35]

Not surprisingly the amount of wealth widows contributed to their second marriages exceeded those of brides entering their first marriage. Taking this group of women out of the whole sample above reveals striking contrasts. On average, these women brought 12,855 livres into their second marriages. For some, the jump from the first to the second was dramatic: Marie Catherine Fleury increased her dowry from 10,000 to 50,000 livres.[36] The financial contributions of both husband and wife brought wealth not only gained through savings, but through the inheritance of commercial goods and property from a late husband.

Widows did not necessarily rush to find a new mate. Many kept the mastership title often with their sons' interests in mind. By maintaining the family firm and not passing on the title of master to a new husband and outsider to the group, sons who were masters could form a partnership with their mothers and pool resources. For example, the Widow Carraques registered with Châtelet in March 1761, and named herself and her son, Pierre, as operators of a stall in the butchery at Saint-Germain. By doing so the Carraques family could effectively operate twice the number of stalls within the city than the guild allowed. Thomas Barré's widow did the same thing, a strategy that allowed her to register three stalls in Paris, ten years after her husband's death. Her stepson's name appears in that year's registry under the stall owned by his father on rue Saint Denis at the Ponceau fountain.[37] As the first son of the deceased, Thomas was able to gain access to more stalls by way of his stepmother. One can only surmise that this family holding linked the rented stalls from father to son by way of the widow. The widow held the patrimony in place until the next generation of young masters took over or, in this case, while sons of masters operated their own businesses. These informal arrangements exemplify how male and female butchers maintained claims on their businesses, commercial property being the all-important possession of a Parisian guild merchant. In other cases, these property settlements appear in the marriage contract itself. Thus, widows must be considered within this male-centered system of property holdings. Their independence as marchandes publiques must be taken as part of family strategies that ensured the continuation and expansion of the family firm.

Conflict and Discord

As much as the family firm promoted a value system based upon mutual cooperation and benefit with the establishment of a communal household, individual struggles were inherent in each negotiation of property. The transmission of property that occurred after the death of a head of household or a second marriage threatened family solidarity. In many situations, alliances became more complex and as individuals competed for limited resources. In moments of crisis, the family firm often found itself undermined by conflict and betrayal within the home.

For example, Master Butcher Jean-François Wagner risked losing his place as head of the household from the doings of his wife and brother-in-law. Wagner filed a complaint with Commissaire LeGuay de Premontval that his wife, Jeanne Françoise (from the prominent Thibert clan) was stealing from him. In the brief report, Wagner stated that his wife "withdraws money that comes from his commerce."[38] Having confronted her with the petty theft, Wagner ruptured the trust between merchant and wife. She immediately turned on him, defending her honor as a Thibert, and sought the support of her brother Pierre Thibert (also a master butcher) to strike back at her husband. When Wagner appeared before the commissaire, his situation was desperate. He showed signs of having been beaten. He professed to days of verbal torture from his wife. Even more critical was his financial situation that he feared "not to be able to pay the loans that he owed to maintain his business, such that it forced [him] to abandon them, and causing his total ruin."[39]

Wagner's case raises questions about the accusation of theft. Husbands and wives shared the responsibility of managing the family firm. Although the male head of household maintained the ultimate power over family finances, there is no reason to think that women (who often kept the accounts) did not handle a certain amount of the daily transactions. Confronting his wife with his suspicions brought the two into opposition and severed any bonds of trust they might have had. Did a wife have a legitimate claim to her portion of the income? Did a husband have grounds to charge his wife with larceny when taking money from the business? In this situation, Wagner's lack of support from others and his wife's extended network and well-regarded family name put him in a weak position of authority. No doubt the public shame of having lost face to his wife and her brother as a beaten man meant that he could no longer ensure his reputation in the community. His ruin may have been his own, as much as his in-law's doing.

Master Butcher Michel Sagot, a recent widower, faced a domestic crisis upon the death of his wife. His two sons, Philippe and Michel (also butchers), suspected him of stealing their inheritance and attempted to oust him from his home. On a Saturday evening in July, Sagot senior visited Commissaire Regnard's office at the Châtelet to file a complaint about his domestic troubles. He reported that since January 23 of that year when his wife passed away, his sons "had taken it into their heads to vex their father with their ill will and designs"–to the point that they wanted to chase him out of his home. It would appear that Sagot, the father, conceded his eldest son's right over the property. The father agreed to turn over his three-year lease on the house to Michel, the eldest son, for two years. For Michel, waiting a year to gain control over the site of his business was unacceptable. His brother, Philippe, was equally vexed for not being given any portion of his father's wealth. On Saturday evening as tempers flew over money and property, Philippe became violent and attempted to break into the locked cabinets with a wooden club. According to the father's testimony, Philippe was looking for goods to steal. Michel Sagot senior admitted to the commissaire that he no longer had any authority over his sons, "no longer wanting to react to the violent outbursts and fits of passion against them in a way that he would be able to do by way of paternal discipline having the right to do so. . . ."[40] He had come to the police to seek protection from his sons and to reclaim what authority he had left.

Sagot left the Châtelet that evening and returned to his house in the parish of Saint-Nicolas des champs only to find that his sons had locked him out. Despite several entreaties, his eldest son refused to let him back in, saying that "he refused to feed a thief any longer." As the father went to find a night watchman to help him get back into his house, Michel yelled to his brother to go fetch Commissaire Du Plessis to take their father to the Châtelet prison where he could spend the night. Sagot, once back in his house, saw that his sons had broken the windows to his office and gone through the family documents, that they had taken 39,950 livres in bank notes (*billets de banque*), and that they had broken into and rifled through two other armoires containing dishes, linens, and other things.

The officers of the Châtelet investigated the incident interviewing the night watchman and the armed men who accompanied him. They also summoned the two stall butchers who worked for the Sagot family. All five testimonies confirmed the events, giving few details as to the subject of either the argument or the accusations made to each other. No doubt the police took an interest in the case as it involved a significant amount of money; the war between father and sons threatened the safety and security of person and property.[41]

Without any testimony from the sons themselves, it is difficult to determine the issues at stake in the dispute. Yet we can surmise that it was the death of the wife and the succession of her property that brought forth the domestic crisis. At this moment of rupture, the shift in filial relations became a stressful situation. The transfer of title in the lease, the history of conflict since the wife's death, the accusations of robbery, the destruction of property, and missing money points to a broken family alliance and a battle over the control of property. Having lost any influence he might have had over his sons, Sagot sought the protection of the city authorities.

Succession and Property

In keeping with the ideology of kinship as a mutually beneficial system of support, inheritance served to perpetuate the family and its patrimony. Sagot's example shows how it could also be the center of family disputes. Withholding a young butcher's inheritance posed problems as it limited his ability to further his own commerce and build his own assets. It also limited his prospects for marriage as the tally sheets were drawn up under legal guarantees to assure both sides of the union that the marriage would be beneficial. Conversely, demands for advances on inheritance put parents in a precarious position as they did not always have the liquidity to turn over to their sons and daughters. Claude Hubie lived with his new wife rent-free and operated a stall without paying any costs as part of his financial arrangements with his widowed mother. Their accounts became so entangled with one another that they drew up another contract four years later to delineate his loans to her in exchange for services in kind, and the remaining inheritance owed to Claude that the Widow Hubie eventually paid off.[42]

The acquisitions of Eustache Aubert's family business, however, forms part of a complicated inheritance that reveals a great deal about knotty relationships within the family firm. Aubert's case presents the many contingencies of these successions. According to the marriage contract dated April 23, 1752, the 8,000 livres given to Eustache represents his portion of his mother Marie Anne Thibert's estate. Upon further research, we see that the young Eustache Aubert had held his title of mastership for at least seven years prior to his marriage.[43] Until that time his address remained the same as his father's: rue Saint-Martin, in the parish of Saint-Laurent.

Eustache Aubert's early adulthood was spent like many young journeymen awaiting mastership. Although he had the titles of mastership, he in effect worked alongside his father until he could gain the advancement of his inheritance from his father, nearly fifteen years after his mother's death. An inventory of her wealth is dated April 1737, but notaries were still sorting out the communal property in 1754. No doubt the five children of Marie Anne Thibert and Jean-Baptiste Aubert wanted to be sure that the correct amount of their mother's property (and their inheritance) would be coming to them. Perhaps they anticipated their father's remarriage nine months after his first wife's death to Margueritte Bertembois. By the time of Jean-Baptiste's death in 1770, Eustache Aubert had graduated to the title of butcher elder like his father and settled in the nearby suburb of Vaugirard.[44]

Although butchers' sons were kept waiting for marriage and inheritance, the daughters of butchers married at a young age. Along with their "blessing," fathers gave their daughters dowries as an advance on their inheritance with the understanding that these women renounce their claims upon their parents' estates. This signaled a decisive break from the support of the brides' families. Though the evidence is not conclusive, the sampling of marriage contracts shows many more women than men married with these stipulations, furthering the ties of men to their patrimonies. At its most extreme, fathers held onto their fortunes for their sons and maintained authority as the head of the household with rights over all property until death. Establishing oneself in an independent business meant negotiating the politics of household authority.

Legal Separation

To be sure, patriarchy, as a dominant ideology and instituted practice, limited the choices of minors and wives who lived under the rule of fathers. Women, who had few legal rights over property other than their *biens propres*, entrusted their husbands to manage the household wealth and not squander it. As the case of Elizabeth Thérèse Gouet demonstrates, the law offered them some protection against financial ruin through the legal separation of goods. In another case, Marie Louise Remy told the commissaire that her husband, Nicolas Mergery, had abandoned his butcher business seven years before the inquiry began. Three witnesses testified to Mergery's turn away from the responsibilities of the trade and toward his own pleasure. Louis Claude Beaucreaux, master carriage driver and domestic servant, testified to how frequently Mergery visited the cabarets along rue de Mortellerie where he gambled and lost money, "that his corrupt lifestyle had strongly troubled his business."[45] Joseph Philippe Davoult, bourgeois of Paris attested to Mergery's interest in cabaret life including the prostitutes there. He stated that "around two weeks ago he saw him [Mergery] in a café on rue Gallande with three young harlots [*filles de joie*] with whom he stayed until two in the morning."[46] The same witness concurred to Mergery's neglect of his trade that had disrupted his business. The third witness repeated many of the same stories adding that he spent a day in a cabaret at the Place aux Veaux during the market hours. Mergery spent a gold piece (*un louis d'or*) for his pleasure, "which he said was a mere nothing, and that it was only the price of a calf."[47]

The few women who bravely sought financial separation did so to protect their dowries and avoid financial ruin. But what recourse did women have in the case of physical abuse? In rare cases, the division of the couple's property could be extended to the physical separation of the couple as a *séparation de corps*. The latter, seen as a kind of divorce, occurred in moments of extreme abuse, often when the woman's life was in danger. A financial separation was granted more freely than a physical one, but, in both types, sufficient evidence had to be compiled with statements from at least three witnesses brought before the civil courts at Châtelet.

One example is Marie Marzé, who in 1724 sought protection from her husband, Master Butcher Germain Hebert, after seven years of marriage. According to her statement made in front of Commissaire Blanchard, her first five years of marriage were peaceful. In recent years, beatings had become regular occurrences. The *commissaire* took down her story of physical and emotional abuse. He noted the bruises on her face and neck, read back the statement to her, and began his investigation. It would appear that she did not pursue the charges as no other record of their separation exists.[48] Jeanne Suzanne Leroy's efforts to gain independence failed with her husband's disappearance. According to Blanchard, her case presented to the Lieutenant General of Police was sufficient to grant "a separation of goods and habitation" (*séparation des biens et d'habitation*). Yet when her husband abandoned her, she lost the opportunity to follow through with the action that moved to the court of the lieutenant civil.[49]

In other cases, both husbands and wives used the legal separation of property to protect their assets and the family firm even if there was no visible abuse or neglect. Butchers could seek separations to maintain their solvency by sheltering their wealth under their wives' names. In doing so, master butchers attained a certain advantage when negotiating with their creditors. Legal proclamations point to the fraudulent use of separations. In them they state the grounds necessary to obtain financial separations in order to prevent merchant butchers from exploiting this legal loophole. The police were intent to make the financial shelter of separations public knowledge, especially to cattle merchants at the main provisioning markets. A parlementary decision passed in 1699 required butchers and their wives who separated their wealth to write their names on a bulletin board at the cattle market in Sceaux for all to see.[50] Although there are no records of arrests, the frequency of financial separations by butchers concerned royal authorities only insofar as it disrupted commercial dealings. The abuse of financial separations suggests the ends to which butchers sought protection from creditors and the precariousness of their finances. It also underscores the extent to which butchers' wives were ready to shelter funds that were as much their own as their husbands.'[51]

The next chapter addresses the financial constraints under which butcher businesses operated, and the ways in which they employed strategies to guard their reputation and build credit. For many contemporaries, the meat trade was rife with personal mismanagement and flagrant dissipation of wealth–a problem that perpetuated the exploitation of credit and the burdens of debt. After viewing the grounds for financial separation, one has to question the extent to which its use damaged a butcher's reputation among the merchant community. Declaring business failure (which many butchers did) could easily affect the social standing and commercial viability of the family firm. How could dissolving the marriage contract and the vital partnership between master butcher and butcher's wife be anything but damaging for a butcher business?

Conclusion

The success of the family firm relied upon a stable and lasting form of clientage based on ties of kinship, a clear division of labor in household, and the interdependence of the merchant community. At each critical juncture in the working lives of butchers (marriage, mastership, and death), the family firm carefully negotiated the acquisition of capital (both material and cultural) and the management of patrimony to secure their position in the corporate world of merchants. Yet at such critical moments when butchers forged social linkages through marriage and transmitted property from one generation to the next, families were put under enormous strain as members questioned the authority and legitimacy of such decisions. The solidarity of the family firm faced as many internal threats of competition and discord as external ones, underlining problems in the relationship between the collective constitution of values and the interplay of social relations.

The family firm worked to unite and to protect its individual members. Based upon what we know of their everyday lives and their marriage patterns, the social practices of masters in the guild demonstrated strong bonds across and within generations. Butcher families with kin ties shared resources and held property in common, providing a wider base in which to develop their commerce. It was not uncommon for three generations of butchers to share the same household. Sons tended to continue the same trade as their fathers, inheriting rights on stalls and houses and gaining easier access to mastership. Butchers' daughters and sons had a strong tendency to marry within the trade or with related trades; widows remarried butchers more often than not. Butchers consciously reproduced their communal bonds at moments of marriage and death. Strengthening and widening their social networks through early marriage, the birth of several children, sons who followed their fathers' trade, family alliances with other Parisian master butchers, and inheritance practices that fostered capital accumulation, master butchers built strong allegiances within the trade.

Property exchange between young men and women and their parents secured the perdurability of butcher households within the commercial world. At the moment of marriage, the couple contracted their past, present, and future wealth to each other and future offspring in a legal declaration of rights and obligations. With this formalized agreement between families, butchers could plan strategies to perpetuate the family firm across generations. Masters entering the world of work simultaneously made a lifelong commitment through which monetary and cultural capital could be gained. For fathers and mothers, as well as widows and widowers with children, the contract ensured the continuation of their patrimony as well as some security in their old age. The rights of succession (often outlined in the marriage contract) structured the wealth and property of households. Its rules and practices guarded the patrimony against the will of individuals. It was a collective agreement that gave butcher merchant families their strength and longevity in the face of increasing competition and atomization, economic risk and failure in the marketplace.

Chapter 8

Butcher Fortune and the Workings of Credit

Upon the death of Thomas Barré in January 1751, the public notary came to Barré's home to inventory his entire fortune from his paper assets and butchery tools to every piece of linen stored in his hope chest. Alongside the hundreds of towels that the shop utilized in meat processing, his armoire was full of dozens of leather jackets (*vestes de basane*) that came from the finer pieces of sheepskin his shop produced. Barré stood as a man who not only made his wealth, but also displayed it personally. In his wardrobe, the notary inventoried three blue silk jackets woven with gold thread, wigs, and a walking stick with a golden handle valued at 60 livres. Barré's personal attire marked him as a distinguished gentlemen, whose finery set him apart from the working artisans of his rank and brought him closer to the privileged elite. Likewise, his wife's yellow satin gown, blue and white satin dresses, and black taffeta skirts with gold brocade and lace trim stood out as decidedly uncommon. Her wardrobe alone was estimated at 1,024 livres and her jewelry at over 2,000 livres, well beyond the simple ornaments of most Parisian artisans.[1] Unlike most working butchers–men who dressed in black wool jackets and women who wore black broadcloth and linen–the Barré family held a higher position in the social hierarchy creating an image of a butcher aristocracy among the working population.

Not surprisingly, Barré's privileged place in the world of Parisian butchers came largely through the prominence of his elders. His father held the title of *ancien maître boucher.* His extended family dominated the trade; the 1747 guild roll listed a dozen active master butchers from the Barré clan. Pierre Barré, probably the most successful of the family, managed a big operation that sold more than 6,700 pounds of meat a week. Thomas's business approached that of Pierre, with yearly expenses that included 1,550 livres in rent on two stalls, a house, and a stockyard; and 1,341 livres for his staff of six stall workers, a domestic, and a shepherd. Thomas's father, Antoine, had established the business in the four-story house with adjoining butcher stall on the rue Saint-Denis (a main thoroughfare in the capital), which Thomas inherited along with a several acres of land in the suburb of

Clignancourt. The Saint Denis residence included a kitchen, a "salon" (*salle de compagnie*), office, basement, and seven bedrooms for Thomas, his wife and five young children, at least one domestic servant, and the half-dozen workers he employed at a time. In addition to the butcher stall, Thomas Barré maintained a scalding house and a large courtyard complete with barn and cow shed (*bouverie)* where he stocked twenty or more cattle and sheep and over forty carcasses. During his lifetime, Thomas built a second residence in Clignancourt that consisted of a single-story farmhouse with an attic and three bedrooms, surrounded by several barns, cowsheds, and extensive property for grazing his flocks and herds. In this house lived the gardener Jacques Richard, who was employed by Barré along with shepherd Jean Aleur, and worker Jean Loiseau. Thomas also acquired a butcher stall on the rue Grande Fauxbourg Saint-Martin where he employed Étalier Séjourné. For his weekly trips to market, Barré kept a small house in Poissy with a single bed and some simple furnishings.

Thomas Barré's fortune was extensive. At the time of his death, his total wealth including outstanding accounts amounted to over 82,000 livres, nearly three times the average of other master butchers. At the other extreme were master butchers like Jean Bontemps who died on May 12, 1781, in a room he rented over a shop on the rue Saint Martin, leaving his widow and four children with a meager fortune of 51 livres and nothing but his silver buckles.[2] The trade's division between prominent merchants like Barré and those who operated solely in the retail sale of meat accounts for a wide disparity of fortunes among butchers: the total of assets and liabilities ranged from a surplus of 165,254 livres to a deficit of 14,927 livres.[3] The social profile of Parisian butchers demonstrates wide-ranging levels of wealth that, as a whole, show far greater prosperity than other trades. Forty percent of butchers had a net worth over 20,000 livres where the average fortune of top tier wage earners–journeymen and unskilled laborers among them–stood at 5,385 livres from 1695 to 1715 and 8,182 livres from 1775 to 1790. Even the average baker's fortune (8,932 livres before 1745 and 18,208 livres after 1745) fell far from the butcher average (29,530 livres).[4]

Barré's net worth stands as one measure of his success, a fortune that grew with the enormous scale of his operation. Even though Barré's business model demonstrated no industrial innovation–no mechanized production or large, unskilled labor force–it did manage to overcome transaction costs through the vertical integration of meat processing. A handful of merchant butchers dominated the trade by purchasing large numbers of cattle from wholesale markets to later fatten, slaughter, butcher, and sell at retail meat markets, while profiting from the sale of tallow, hides, and tripe. What distinguishes Barré's success from the standpoint of other guild butchers was his acquisition of capital that allowed him to build a business with a greater economy of scale. Barré's large operation could control costs, weather shortfalls, and gain access to credit with far greater ease than other butchers with smaller businesses who skirted business failure.

More significant to the market culture of eighteenth-century Paris is how Barré had, in fact, established himself less as a successful tradesman than as “a man of credit” (*un homme de crédit*), measured by his appearances as well as by his balance sheets. A merchant butcher in this position hired stall workers and avoided the polluting aspects of slaughter and butchering. He dressed in wigs and silk jackets and adorned his wife with expensive jewelry, knowing full well how the public measured personal worth in monetary means as well as in symbolic forms. Thomas Barré filled his homes with elegant furnishings, family portraits, silver services, silk tapestries, and shelves lined with devotional and travel literature. His country “estate” in Clignancourt included a dovecote and gardens, amenities that reinforced a noblelike stature and allowed for a kind of self-sufficiency as the lord of the manor. Men of credit sought cultural capital (symbolic forms that carried social value) as integral to their economic capital. More important than the acquisition of material goods were the ways in which they were utilized and leveraged in the commercial world. By contrast, butchers with less negotiating power and market share struggled to stay afloat from the flood of demand in the height of the winter season through the meatless days during Lent and the slow summer months. In this way, a successful merchant was one who held sway over his creditors and clientele through his social standing as a reputable merchant. The exchange of goods for credit demonstrated an individual’s worth in as much as the ability to obtain credit was a personal matter tied to one’s reputation among the community. This chapter examines how butchers utilized credit as a means of exchange and a measure of self-worth. Butchers manipulated various systems of credit not only to keep their businesses running but, in the most successful cases, to better their station in life. Credit bought you a reputation as much as reputation gave you access to credit.

Operating on Credit

In the corporate world of work, the individual sought the prestige and security of mastership in order to establish his or her business. Yet even mastership required start-up and working capital. For butchers, these start-up and operating costs were among the highest among the mechanical trades. The fee for letters of mastership (1,500 livres)–well beyond the price of other masterships–stood as the greatest initial investment.[5] In addition, those who purchased (rather than inherited) a business from another master (called the *fonds de commerce*), paid an additional cost of at least 300 livres.[6] Butcher tools made up a small portion of the totality of butcher fortune (1 to 3 percent).

His knives, weights, hooks, splints *(tempes),* wooden benches, and troughs were relatively inexpensive, ranging from 31 to 100 livres.[7] The most expensive equipment included numerous copper kettles and sieves to render and extract fat for tallow. Many of these kettles cost over 80 livres each.[8] Added to this, were the outlays to house and feed household members, to pay the weekly wages of workers and domestics, and to stock, transport, and store meat products. The average value of a butcher's business inventory with evidence of meat processing was 2,586 livres, the median 6,753 livres, showing a wide range of investment in the business. To be sure, a certain minimal amount of equipment was necessary to engage in the trade. And the bigger the business, the more scales, hangers, hooks, knives, tables, cow sheds, stockyards, and feed a butcher needed, not to mention the room (and income) to expand the workforce. A successful business operated on the law of increasing returns in which costs could be surpassed by increasing output and sales. Thomas Barré and those like him who succeeded in large-scale production added variable costs for major purchases of cattle and sheep, transactions that required extensive capital resources and a network of livestock suppliers.

As we have seen in the previous chapters, butchers depended upon kin networks to establish and maintain their businesses. Sons of butchers were given clear advantages in gaining access to the guild. Successful butcher families practiced collective purchasing, held land for grazing in common, and shared the costs of transport. They pooled their resources to overcome high overhead costs. They united their children to keep the wealth within the family and, therefore, the business.

Even though these financial resources were important for operating the business, a master's social standing was perhaps his greatest asset. Cultural capital, in the form of reputation, established and enlarged the circle of clients and creditors who fed the business and provided a vital cushion for merchants who operated on credit. Unlike other merchants who held the majority of their assets in inventory, butchers' paper assets exceeded the value of their tools and livestock more than ten times. The majority of butcher businesses bought and sold on credit that extended throughout the meat-eating season. Constrained by the limits of a fledgling market economy and the weakness of credit institutions, a successful merchant depended upon his perceived status within the corporate world and his ability to secure not only capital, but credit. This may have begun with kin and merchant relations, but the success of a retail merchant's day-to-day operations depended upon the continual flow of goods between suppliers and clientele.

All butchers had to navigate the demands from suppliers and customers, the former who expected immediate payment at the cattle markets, the latter who extended their payments over a year, sometimes two or three. Merchant butchers engaged in commercial transactions that, like much of the early modern economy, were built upon a chain of credit: IOUs and letters of credit kept goods circulating in and out of the cattle pens and butcher stalls; this continual flow fed the economic vitality of the meat trade. Credit was an absolute necessity for the purchase of livestock and a common practice for the provisioning of elite households. Access to credit in the livestock trade allowed butchers to purchase larger herds early in the season and fatten them for the winter feasts. Extending credit to wealthy clientele built important customer relations and added to the reputation of the business.

Liability and Business Failure

Butchers extended credit as much as necessary, they relied on debt to finance their businesses. The daily practice of giving credit and taking on debt remained a necessary risk in a cash-poor society like that of Old Regime Paris, and it was particularly so for butchers whose businesses involved heavy capital investment. For many, their fragile position at the midpoint of these commercial and social linkages was often stretched to the breaking point. According to the cases presented to the Parisian Consular Court from 1700–1789, the number of butchers who declared business failure clearly outnumbered other merchants in related trades.[9] This fact points to the tenuous financial position of butcher businesses and the frequent overextension of butcher credit.

According to the afterdeath inventories, the average total of liabilities for all butchers was 9,621 livres, ranging from zero to as much as 72,070 livres. The vast majority of the reported liabilities (84 percent) fell under the category of commercial accounts payable. These included money owed to cattle merchants and other creditors who financed the butcher with paper assets.[10] Overall, the number of creditors that appeared in butchers' accounts payable averaged twenty-four. According to these same records taken from butchers' registers, merchant butchers kept accounts with at least five cattle merchants, and five to seven sheep merchants on average. On occasion, butchers would have outstanding payments to veal merchants and proprietors of country inns (*aubergistes*). Creditors included bankers and financiers who supplied butchers with *lettres de change*, a kind of redeemable currency. The most prominent moneylender in records of merchant butchers was the Caisse de Poissy that financed cattle purchases. The average amount that these men owed to the caisse came to 6,477 livres or more than half (67.3 percent) of their total liabilities. Compared with the accounts of butchers who claimed business failures, the reliance upon the caisse was not as great, comprising on average only 23 percent of their total accounts payable. No doubt the financial instability of these butchers led the caisse to deny them loans. For certain butchers, such as Gabriel François Sagot, the denial of a loan could prove to be one of the contributing circumstances to business failure and his eventual imprisonment for debts. In his records, submitted to the Consular Court, Sagot includes losses due to the high interest costs he was "obliged" to engage in without access to loans from the caisse.[11] His case suggests the risky environment of the credit market and demonstrates how butchers often submitted to usurious conditions.

Butchers who remained indebted to the caisse at the time of their death were not the wealthiest–their average net worth of 19,177 livres was just below the average net worth of all butchers inventoried (29,530 livres) and far from business failure. Nor did they control a great amount of market share as the prominent merchant butchers who did not depend upon the caisse to finance their cattle purchases.[12] Rather, they represent owners of midrange businesses, merchants who sought short-term loans that the caisse offered. Unlike the more successful merchants who had access to other forms of credit through their annuities and property holdings, who could leverage their reputation as men of credit in more informal ways, these merchants depended on the more institutionalized loan procedure to finance their trade. For these merchants, the caisse provided a valuable banking service.

To be sure, there were those masters to whom the caisse extended credit at great risk. Robert Lauverjat whose assets equaled 3,807 livres carried a debt of 3,202 livres with the caisse. Added to his debts were an additional 1,451 livres wages for his cook, other business expenses, and rent on a house and two butcher stalls that amounted to 1,550 livres a year. Lauverjat's net worth at the time of death amounted to a negative balance of 916 livres.[13] For butcher businesses big and small, the amounts owed for livestock purchases formed the major debt that working butchers carried throughout their careers.

Evidence from afterdeath inventories gives us glimpses of the costs incurred in staffing a butcher business. Most inventories (80 percent) refer to journeymen, domestic workers, and rural laborers who were on the masters' payroll. Overall, the records show few debts to workers, usually in cases where the master died before the end of the working season.[14] Long illnesses brought many butchers into debt, not only because of the costs of medical treatment, which ranged from 60 to 1,500 livres, but the lost earnings due to extended absences. Many butchers facing business failure often explained their dire financial circumstances because of unusually long illnesses that put them out of work for months at a time. They sought protection from creditors until they could return to their normal productive lives.[15]

Butcher Financing

Given the fact that most butchers relied upon large credit purchases to run their businesses, it is surprising that they drew up so few credit agreements.

In a survey of all notarial documents concerning butchers for 1751 and 1761, I uncovered a mere thirty-eight, split evenly between the two years. The sampling includes documents that are receipts of payments (*quittances*) from earlier loan agreements, notarized accounts of the liquidation of goods to pay for accumulated debt, contracts that confer a debt from one party to another (*transport*), and promissory notes (*obligations*).

Promissory notes fell into two categories. One was composed of small loans (between 100 and 1,000 livres) made between family members or other merchants, even butchers. These were simple agreements without any reference to the repayment or other terms of the loan. Together, they account for fourteen of the thirty-eight contracts. The second type of loan was for large amounts (from 2,000 to 17,000 livres). In both of these contracts, a credit relationship had already been well established between two parties. The contract was to ensure repayment. For example, on April 7, 1761, Butcher Jean Jacques Aubert and his wife Marie Florence Trianon, signed a notarized agreement with Jean Etienne Maillet de Grandmaison, collector and loan officer for the Caisse de Poissy. It concerned a debt for 9,500 livres for "meat products" bought by Sr. Aubert in the Sceaux and Poissy markets during the previous year "for which Aubert is content." In the contract, the two parties declared a payment procedure of 400 livres monthly to begin the coming season, and for Aubert to declare himself as the principle debtor to Maillet de Grandmaison until he had been cleared of the debt. Master Rôtisseur Jacques Eustache Trianon (possibly Aubert's father-in-law) appears on the contract as witness and cosigner. The two pledged their residential property as collateral, ensuring the continued repayment of the loan. A short paragraph follows the signatures of both parties and the notary Bellanger, dated February 12, 1763, attesting that the loan had been paid off.

While Aubert was under obligation to repay his debt accumulated over the past year's purchases at market, the contract was set up with this line of credit as a given, stating that the amount lent "for their butcher business for which [Mr. and Mrs. Aubert] recognize and are entirely satisfied."[16] Aubert and his wife established this agreement on their own terms, with a repayment plan that fit into their business cycle. This kind of contract differed greatly from other repayment plans like that of Nicolas LeCornu negotiated under duress. Mr. and Mrs. LeCornu's obligation for 4,693 livres includes a paragraph that describes the consequences of any default on the loan including one missed payment, whereby butcher and his wife consented to the penalty of further imprisonment.

What is striking about these financing contracts is how they neither concern nor make reference to prenegotiated credit agreements between butchers and their moneylenders. Instead, it would seem that these agreements reflected the actions of creditors who had already covered butcher expenses long before drawing up a contract. In only a few examples did merchant butchers draw up notarized agreements with a moneylender in advance of any purchase or at the beginning of his buying season.[17] Merchant butchers saw financing differently than meat provisioning contracts. In the latter case, butchers negotiated terms with noble and religious houses, as well as with hides sold to tanners, the price of which was agreed upon at the beginning of the season.

Rather than use the notary to find creditors, butchers sought their own financial contacts. Notaries, who acted as integral links in the credit market for a vast number of Parisians,[18] appear not to have played as important a role for merchant butchers looking for a reliable creditor, as evidenced by the random selection of notaries in their legal contracts. Instead, moneylenders–aware of the precarious finances of many merchant butchers who spread their debts among a number of creditors–would pursue the legal format of a promissory note to secure their loans. Signing a document in the presence of a notary provided added security in credit dealings, as a kind of analogue to contract law. When the occasion arose (as it often did) and butchers exceeded the limits of the creditor, the notarized copy of the contract was useful to establish collection procedures. In cases like that of Nicolas LeCornu, the butcher found himself pursued not only by his creditor, but the police, and would renegotiate his credit terms (and his freedom) with a notary from behind prison walls.[19]

The Caisse de Poissy appears most frequently in notarized credit agreements with merchant butchers. Of the thirty-eight contracts gathered in this study, roughly one-quarter (nine in all) come from the officers of the caisse and carry nearly two-thirds of the total debt. Clearly, the caisse dominates much of butchers' credit practices–at least in those that appear in the notarial archives. One explanation may be the officers' knowledge and access to legal procedures. Being experienced bankers and investors, they understood the legal apparatus that worked to protect their investments. For most butchers, formal credit agreements written in the elegant hand of the notary were a rarity compared with the good faith agreements and the IOUs scribbled on small slips of paper.

Butchers frequently used IOUs, and on occasion, the more formal bills of credit (lettres de change), drawn up by bankers and *négociants*. The latter carried greater weight in the financial community and were more secure than the former. These two instruments of credit did not include the official signature of a notary, were guaranteed after five years, and circulated widely from market to village to city until they were cashed in. Records of IOUs filled the account books of the merchant butcher community and appeared in the notarial and police records when this exchange system broke down. For butcher Guillaume Rousseau, this happened when his billet for 500 livres, written to the order of Abbé Tiber in April 1760, was then endorsed to the wine merchant Louis Buffault. When Buffault tried to cash this billet payable on February 14, 1761, he found Rousseau without funds and so filed a complaint with the police commissaire the next day. Within three days, Rousseau came up with the funds and cleared himself of the debt. His expeditiousness reflects the seriousness of an unfulfilled obligation that potentially could damage his reputation and in turn severely limit his commerce.[20]

Butchers relied upon these instruments of credit (less often with the intervention and added expense of the notary) to carry out commercial transactions with cattle merchants, bankers, and farmers, as well as tanners, candle makers, and customers. These notes, however, only provide a glimpse of what constituted credit practices on a personal level, such as the number of verbal, "good faith" agreements that permeated most of the local business done between well-known and trusted individuals.

As we have seen in Chapter 3, butchers resisted formal credit agreements, especially when it meant additional transaction costs in cattle purchasing. In their legal briefs and police testimonies, butchers claimed to practice much of their commerce in good faith, meaning that credit was not obtained through formally contracted agreements either in the presence of a notary or evidenced by written IOUs. Here, a merchant butcher's credit-worthiness was founded on trust and long-term relationships with livestock traders and creditors that belied formal guarantees and rules of repayment. For most merchant butchers, credit relations were intricately tied to social relations.

Building a business meant building relationships upon which to found a system of exchange, one that would be supple enough to allow for the exigencies of periodic shortfalls and even great misfortune that beset the cattle trade. In the daily exchanges at the butcher stall, shoppers came to negotiate their food purchases with butchers. In the meat markets, the ground rules differed as this primary good operated within the moral guidelines of healthfulness and fair price. The criteria that determined butchers' credibility in the cattle markets did not apply to the market-goers of Paris.

Credit Abuses in the Meat Market

Louis-Sébastien Mercier, among his many criticisms of Parisian society, harangued against the exploitation of credit, for which there were punishments "without any level of severity." Mercier observed hordes of intrepid buyers who, seeing the weakness of the law, knowingly breeched their own economic limits.[21] According to Mercier, this flagrant irresponsibility of consumers threatened the value of property and the workings of commerce. Pointing to the immoral act of debtors, Mercier rebukes:

> Is it shameful not to not pay your tailor, your cook, your rug dealer, and your butcher? One gladly pays gambling debts, why? Because one

> would no longer be included in society. It would be easy with stricter, more explicit laws, to force debtors to pay back their notes. It is more often unwillingness than inability that undermines the most solemn promises.[22]

Mercier singles out a portion of society that deserves to be scolded, which he names as the prodigious, the libertines, the dissipaters, and the fools. In effect, these are the least valued characteristics of the lesser nobles and the *nouveau riche.* According to Mercier, living an extravagant lifestyle where one is well dressed, well housed, and well fed are the necessary trappings of elites trying to (over)extend themselves into the circles of the wealthy and powerful. Money becomes a means to an end, a tool with which one can gamble to win the favor of others. While on the one hand the extension of credit was the privilege of nobility, Mercier's critique points to another regard of late-eighteenth century society: the highly individualistic point of view characterized the beginning of a modern notion of consumerism, what Daniel Roche has called "the culture of appearances."[23]

> The richer the debtor the less he pays: he defends with a portion of his gold the other portion of his opulence. He envelops his creditor in all the complications of procedure. He throws him in the detours of the quirks of the law. And with the strength of holding back the period of payment, he tires and fatigues his adversary who abandons him in the end with half or three-quarters of his loan.[24]

As Mercier explains, wealth was not only made up of monetary value, but also of the elaborate display of riches. Elites exercised a certain power over their merchant suppliers that allowed them to exploit the system of credit to the detriment of Parisian businesses. Throughout the eighteenth century, the law demonstrated its inability to ensure the sanctity of property and the health of commerce through the enormous liability that merchant lenders faced.

For many merchant butchers, promissory notes, written IOUs, and other records of amounts due for "delivered meat" (*viande fournie*) comprised nearly half of their wealth at the time of their death. It was the largest category of all assets (38 percent) for which the notaries accounted. Known as *dettes actives,* these outstanding debts owed to the butcher drew from his most recent account books; they could also be taken from slips of written promises to pay from a wide variety of clients including tanners and tripe dealers, not to mention other family members. All but four of the inventories include accounts receivable for butcher businesses. On average, their total comes to 18,684 livres. The mean of all accounts receivable inventoried rises to 21,141 livres. Again, the extremes of this sampling are striking, ranging from as little as 200 livres in paper assets to over 112,000 livres.

The particular aspects of this chain of credit left butchers in vulnerable positions. This sampling shows how butchers leveraged their businesses carefully. Among the thirty-four cases, only one butcher's inventory shows a near business failure. At the time of butcher Pierre Feuchez's death, his accounts receivable fell short of his payables by 14,437 livres.[25] One can only wonder whether he was aware that his business was operating at a deficit. His death came early in his life, only eight years after his marriage and at the midpoint of the butcher season. These details suggest that his life ended suddenly, before he could accumulate a healthy amount of nonbusiness assets, a strategy in which the most successful butchers demonstrated great aptitude.

Most butchers established important client relationships in good faith agreements outside of legally binding contracts. While they extended credit to their customers over months, even years, they kept close track of the balance due. In their account books, butchers kept a running total of meat sold to each regular client. The credit butchers extended to these households in many cases halted somewhere midway through their season, marked by the holiday Saint-Remy (October 1) or Saint-Denis (October 9). In all cases, butchers initiated collection at the end of the meat-eating season. Occasionally, butchers stopped accounts suddenly midseason, marking "arreté [sic]" in their books. Whether butchers did this at their clients choosing or the butchers' is not clear. According to accounts of butchers whose failed businesses appear in the city archives, customer activity typically withered away or suddenly disappeared. Whether due to outside financial pressures or internal losses and illness, these butchers lost 10 to 20 percent of their customers within the season.[26]

Probate records offer another perspective on the history of butchers' client relations. The many notes or billets that filled butcher inventories of accounts receivable reveal the commercial transactions of a butcher business season by season. Most often, these receipts come from the butchers' most important clients. Notaries distinguished these IOUs as commercial assets with the phrase "for meat supplies." The date the client signed over the billet to clear his debt with the butcher gives us some idea about the elasticity of client relations and the extension of credit. Of the more than 500 billets listed in the sampling of merchant butcher inventories, the vast majority were signed over to the butcher during Lent when merchants closed their shops and balanced their books. A second smaller grouping appears midseason. There seems to be no fixed ceiling on client credit as billets from clients varied widely from household to household. Rather, it is the seasonal rhythm of payment that appears to be the most consistent factor throughout these records.

The billets that appear in afterdeath inventories provide a limited perspective on commercial transactions in the shop. Rarely do we know the amount of meat (in weight) or the type of meat (veal, beef, or mutton) delivered to these households. It is also impossible to verify if the amount of the note corresponded to part or all of the client's account with the butcher. These financial records also limit the historian in a third way, as they exclude all cash transactions that occurred between butchers and their customers. In sum, these sources must be considered as only a partial view of the totality of exchanges that took place in the shops and stalls of Paris.

The notes which remained in the merchant's possession either at the time of death or when declaring business failure had lost most of their redeemable value. Often these were the IOUs that a butcher held for five years or more with either partial repayment or none at all. Known as *dettes douteuses* these uncollectable debts neared nearly half of the butcher's total commercial paper assets. Jean François Barré's afterdeath inventory totaled 5,193 livres worth of "good" billets and 5,842 livres of long-overdue accounts that the notary termed "doubtful."[27] Jean Baptiste Aubert's complex business affairs, once sorted out by the notary and appraiser, came to 52,879 livres worth of reliable paper assets and 42,953 livres of dubious ones.[28] Even for Aubert, a relatively affluent butcher, nearly half of his business dealings were written off as losses.

Officials who drew up the balance sheets for butchers in arrears clearly distinguished those accounts receivable that butchers had little chance of collecting. By doing so they established a more favorable assessment of a butcher's financial distress and his inability to repay. Even with this strategy in mind, the cases that appear in the consular court do not seem excessive compared with the assessments of deceased butchers. For example, the business failure of Master Butcher André Gout showed outstanding accounts that totaled 41 percent of all his paper assets and 19 percent of his total net worth.[29] For Nicolas LeCornu, the percentage was not as high, uncollectible debts represented 31 percent of all paper assets and 7 percent of his total net worth.[30]

Butcher inventories show how slow clients were to repay. Even if customers signed over a billet at the end or midseason for their meat supplies, they did not necessarily cash out the note with any great expediency. Charles Denis Tripperet, who passed away at the height of a productive season,[31] held over fifty notes from various clients he served, some dating back 10 years. One of his biggest clients named Veret signed over a promissory note on March 14, 1742, for "meat supplies up until that day" that Tripperet had furnished. The amount Veret owed came to 960 livres 12 sous. By May 20 of that year, he had reimbursed Tripperet only 204 livres of the debt. He made his next payment on the account on October 20, 1743. Tripperet died the following month with an outstanding account of 606 livres. Another client of Tripperet named Vendeuil, signed over a billet on March 28, 1740 for 2,446 livres. According to the back of the note, he had made three payments: one for 102 livres on May 13, 1741, a second for the same amount on

July 21 of that year, and a third for 300 livres on March 23, 1742, leaving a balance due of 1,942 livres.[32] In these cases and many others, the repayment schedule is arbitrary and the amount collected was a small portion of the amount owed. Butchers, such as Tripperet, supplied meat throughout the season, putting themselves into debt with their biggest customers.

Guillaume Bazille's accounts offer one point of comparison where two clients' levels of consumption corresponded to their ability (or willingness) to repay. Sieur Marcou purchased 8,145½ pounds of meat between June 24, 1758, and February 27, 1759, at 7 sous a pound. Bazille, at the time of his death in February 1761, had only collected 680 livres of the 2,850 livres due. Another client, Sieur Fouton, purchased 1,039¾ pounds of meat at the same price between April 14 and October 6, 1759. His more modest appetite left him with a bill for 363 livres of which he paid 200 livres.[33] Without knowing more about these two clients, the size of their households, the nature of their relationships with other merchants, and the history of their finances, it is difficult to assess their behavior as in any way typical. Yet it would appear that Mercier's claim–that the more privileged the buyer, the less likely he or she was to repay–at least in this instance, carried some truth.

Collecting Debts

Unlike Mercier's claim, however, butchers did have recourse with their delinquent customers. They pursued only a select few of those clients whose accounts were past due. Butchers turned to the civil courts at the Châtelet to demand repayment first with a police writ (*assignation*) followed by official rulings (known as *sentences* and *condamnations).* The probate records of butchers show several references to such legal procedures but not for all accounts past due. In most cases, butchers hired procurators at the Châtelet to pursue these clients in the city courts.[34] Widow Boursier pursued inn keeper LaFosse who had written three billets amounting to nearly 550 livres. In her effort to collect, she drew on the help of her brother Butcher Duval and paid 131 livres to a city official (*huissier à verge*) who managed to squeeze 114 livres out of the client.[35]

The decision to enter into legal proceedings for debt collection had to be weighed against the potential damage that it caused not only to the client's reputation but also the merchant's. Any demand for payment had to be viewed in the relations of power that existed between merchant and client, as it was the butcher who served his privileged clientele. A butcher's strongest customer base consisted of elites who bought in great quantities on a regular basis. Among these were the robe nobles of parlement and the upper nobility of the king's court whose residences in Paris demanded levels of gastronomic largesse. These were the clients who also conferred the greatest prestige to butchers. Not all could afford to live in the noble lifestyle with elaborate banquets rich in meat. Yet, for a butcher to demand payment in full would mean to transgress rules of social hierarchy and break the trust that cemented credit relations between these two parties. Certain customers were better kept indebted as it strengthened the bonds of clientage.

Given these social boundaries, butchers nonetheless took their noble clients to court in an effort to settle their accounts, albeit with little success. Gabriel Sagot, merchant butcher, pursued Monsieur Deblivierre, a *conseiller* in parlement, for 5,385 livres. Having obtained the sentencing from the Châtelet in December 1768, he continued to await full compensation, collecting the interest on the amount.[36] In another case, Sagot sought payment for sixteen years of provisions totaling 48,373 livres to M. Charles-Henri Roûsselet count d'Estaing, later lieutenant general of the royal navy and his wife Dame Marie Sophie Roûsselet de Château-Regnault. His case was tied up in the courts as the count battled back, contesting the court's first decision.[37] Guillaume Bazille depended upon the efforts of Blondel, a low-ranking officer *(huissier)* of municipal courts, to collect his accounts past due for the Marquis du Châtelet, for which he paid Blondel a fee proportional to the amount collected.[38] Jean François Barré fought alone to recover a relatively insignificant amount (250 livres) owed to him by Sieur Gardier, one of the officers of the household of the duc de Penthièvre. Barré had billed Gardier in April 1778 and the royal servant agreed to pay the bill in the next year. By the end of July 1780, Barré had received nothing and pressed for repayment with an official writ. By September 5 of that year, Barré had obtained a police sentence from the Châtelet. In his afterdeath inventory of March 1786, the notary inventoried these documents as collated, signed, and sealed, yet without any sign that Gardier had paid his debt.[39]

In this last case, Barré dealt directly with the domestic servants responsible for feeding the household. Although his client may have been a duke, his business dealings were with a commoner responsible for the household provisions. Barré's relatively small business and modest situation did not stop him from pursuing what was rightly owed him. As with Sagot and Bazille, he sought legal means to recover what he could to remain solvent and avoid the dishonor of insolvency.

Butchers, as regular purveyors to households, could draw up formal contracts with the backing of a notary, but like loan agreements, these appear as exceptional cases. Pierre Louis Vollée's formal provisioning contract with a royal client (Madame la Dauphine) in the presence of a notary was one example.[40] Clearly, this contractual relationship solidified the formal agreement between a Parisian merchant and a royal household, a highly prized client that Vollée wanted to secure. His choice to enter into a written contract would seem logical to bind the agreement with clients and provide legitimate proof for their accounts receivable. The food habits of most meat eaters in Paris did not correspond to those of the house of Madame la Dauphine whose noble obligation of hospitality included prodigious meat-centered feasts on a regular basis.

With a limited number of royal clientele and a growing number of nonguild butchers competing for customers, merchants with capital sought other, more secure forms of investment to gain affluence. Rather than reinvest their profits into expanding their businesses, many turned to forms of wealth-building that pushed them further away from the market dealings of meat, hides, and tallow toward pure capitalist activities.

Butcher Capitalists

The masters whose fortunes exceeded most guild members diversified their assets in a number of ways. Most sought annuities and other assets that brought greater economic security, purchasing butcher stalls, houses in Paris, and land in the nearby countryside, as well as becoming petty office holders. Others with their accumulated wealth–much of it in stores of ready cash–focused on financial trading in the cattle markets as well as the credit markets that had little association with the butcher trade. Even though they retained the title merchant butcher, many of them had earned the added distinction of being a butcher elder, a title that not only signaled their seniority, but also their economic influence.

Not surprisingly, butcher elders represented the wealthiest guild members. Nicolas Séjourné and Vincent Lelievre, both butcher elders, demonstrated their success as merchants by being able to leave the work of the stall and hire laborers. Their income, however, came less from the sale of meat and meat by-products than from investments and money lending. At the time of his death, Nicolas Séjourné, had as much as 28,858 livres–much of it cash–stored in his home. The inventory of Nicolas Lelievre notes 11,134 livres of hard currency.[41] Other merchant butchers turned to these prominent guildsmen to finance their businesses, if not to supply them with cattle purchased at the livestock markets.

Although the presence of large stores of cash contributed to an elite merchant profile, Butcher capitalists also profited from the real estate investments they had made or had inherited early in their careers as butchers, only later to collect rent from other butchers. Jean-Baptiste Aubert, also a butcher elder, owned a stall valued at 17,000 livres on rue Saint-Martin that he rented to another guild butcher.[42] Butcher Elder Nicolas Berjonneau owned two houses in the butcher quarter of the Vieille Place aux Veaux and three other stalls from which he made 2,850 livres a year. In addition, this wealthy guildsman held annuities (one to the guild itself) that supplied an additional 2,700 livres a year.[43]

In these cases, butchers acquired real estate through a complex process of inheritance that began at marriage. Rarely did a butcher sell his property investments; most often, they were part of the patrimony that butchers passed to their children.[44] Several merchant butchers acquired land outside of Paris that added to their equity. Jean François Claude Proffit, who operated a relatively robust business, inherited a country house and vineyards just outside of Paris from his father, valued at over 2,100 livres.

Many of these prominent merchants added other titles to their name through the purchase of an office. Unlike the letters of mastership, which simply gave butchers a place in the corporate hierarchy, the purchase of royal offices guaranteed a return on their investment. In the case of Louis Mabire, the royal office he purchased related directly to the butcher trade. Mabire, five years after a successful marriage to the daughter of Butcher Louis Grandjasse, acquired the title Inspector for cattle and pigs at a hefty price of 12,000 livres.[45] Another similar example is François Joseph Thenard who purchased the office of poultry inspector (*Jurez controlleur de la volaille*) for 15,875 livres, a title that brought more prestige than income (250 livres annually).[46] For Master Butcher Nicolas Jacques, the offices he held (*porteur de charbon* and *controlleur du décharge des batteau*) had no real relation to the butcher business. Madeleine Barré, widow of Nicolas Jacques, kept the receipts from these titles that brought an annual income of 4,200 livres to the household.[47]

In the sampling of merchant butchers' inventories, just under half can be classified as butcher capitalists who held property either in the form of real estate or royal offices.[48] These holdings that were in excess of the value of personal goods and business inventory comprised over a fifth of butchers' total wealth, averaging 21,659 livres and ranged from as little as 2,150 livres to as much as 83,360 livres. Although many of these assets included property and offices with close ties to their trade, other nonbusiness assets such as annuities and billets, show the extent to which butchers' capital extended beyond their corporate community.

Annuities (called rentes) were largely composed of financial agreements between individuals where the investor made 5 percent on his "loan." Drawn up with a notary, who many times acted as the interlocutor for the investment, rentes filled the portfolios of several wealthy butcher elders, increasing their nonbusiness assets by nearly 40 percent.[49] Jean-Baptiste Aubert held assets of 83,000 livres made up primarily of annuities he held from various individuals, a few with guild titles. The fact that his activity in the credit market extended far beyond the butcher community points to the relative anonymity of these credit relations. Although many wealthy butchers lent money to other guild masters on an informal basis, those who sought out annuities could be assured of a secure investment. The accumulation of annuities also brought butcher capitalists into another social category, far from the laboring classes. Charles Denis Tripperet, a merchant butcher whose annuities and other nonbusiness investments allowed him nearly to divest from the trade, also permitted him to adopted the *rentier* title, "Bourgeois of Paris."[50]

For Nicolas Berjonneau, a butcher elder, success was measured in a variety of ways, most pointedly with his learned lifestyle: 257 books filled his house, including several volumes of European and Classical history, along with devotional literature printed in *octavo* volumes relatively affordable and abundant at the time. His library also included large editions such as Trevoux's dictionary in eight volumes and Savary's *Dictionnaire de Commerce* in three volumes. In addition, Berjonneau collected the published sermons of Saint Augustine and the Jansenist Arnault.[51] Charles Denis Tripperet, son of a master butcher, had a library of 188 volumes including the bible, several dictionaries, Delamare's *Traité de la Police,* atlases, travel literature, military histories, and a Spanish grammar book. His collection points to an enlightened reader who lived in a world of commerce and sought knowledge of foreign lands and language, distant civilizations and history, theological questions and applications. If nothing else, these texts reveal the material culture of prominent butchers who acquired books for their social value, and potentially, for their own education and use. A personal library–whether consulted or not–was the expression of a learned person, it signified a man of letters with time for thought and reading.

These profiles of butcher elders and wealthy merchants demonstrate how after nearly a quarter century of marriage and at the point of retirement, the most prominent guild butchers chose to quit their trade and make money from money. They accumulated pots of gold and shelves of books. They loaned money to other guild members and invested in the expansive credit market. Most importantly, they had arrived as *hommes de crédit* as they were not simply laborers, but men of means able to live off their wealth.

Conclusion

In the chain of credit, butchers took as much as they gave. Yet within this system of mutual indebtedness, these merchants were caught in a double bind. Cattle merchants expected merchant butchers to pay promptly for purchases at the livestock markets, which forced merchants into various loan agreements (some quite usurious). At the other end, butchers faced price limits on their sale of fresh meat and slow payments from their biggest clients who exploited the credit that butchers eagerly extended to them. Merchants who succeeded within these tight margins often had a leg up on the business through capital either accumulated or inherited from butcher kin. These butchers had built their businesses to ensure that they could control the variable costs. They increased their profit margins by vertically integrating their operations, buying cattle cheap and fattening them in the suburbs of Paris before bringing them into the city to slaughter. They profited from the sale of meat by-products such as tripe and hides, much of which they could process and supply in bulk to other merchants. Prominent wholesale butchers benefitted from larger economies of scale with more reliable debts to retail butchers and other merchants, the latter who operated small businesses often with greater credit risks.

The most successful butchers built their reputations as men of credit. They embraced the social status of success and kept the appearance of credit worthiness in mind. Reputation mattered for butchers as it reinforced ongoing exchange relationships and gave entry into other mutually beneficial relationships that supplied credit to butchers. This culturally embedded system of credit shows the cleavages in eighteenth-century commercial life that pitted monetary relations against traditional notions of status and reputation.

Conclusion

The Rise of Meat

The classical interpretation of the French Revolution marks August 4, 1789 as the propitious moment of liberalism. That night, the members of the National Assembly abolished serfdom outright and ended the feudal regime that included seigneurial oppression, inequitable and burdensome taxation, and the absence of adequate representation. This event has been seen traditionally as the starting point of a series of dramatic reforms that broke with the absolutist, corporate structure of eighteenth-century France by eliminating the discriminatory privileges of titled persons and disaggregating the collective body of the corporation. Guild masters and mistresses, as members of this social structure that held the vital links of corporate groups in the "great chain" leading directly to the "authority of the throne,"[1] remained in existence, but not for long. By March 1791, the National Assembly issued the d'Allard law, abolishing guilds across France. In June, the Le Chapelier laws forbade workers associations altogether. The revolutionary ideology that ended the guild focused on its long, oppressive, and fruitless form of institutionalized "brigandage" for the master and "servitude" for the laborer. Jealous of their authority and hungry for more wealth and power, the corporate fathers had transformed mastership from a system of renewal into a system of exclusion by means of which, "the richest and the strongest ordinarily succeeded in keeping out the weakest."[2] The Revolution dissolved this hierarchically ordered society into a collection of free and equal individual citizens, having no links with one another except as fellow citizens of the French nation.

To be sure, the promises of August 4 offered the people of Paris an unbridled opportunity to enter a skilled profession–an offer that unlicensed butchers took to in droves. Almost overnight, meat sellers appeared throughout Paris, outside of the marketplace, in areas leading to public gardens and walkways, and along major thoroughfares. They displayed their goods for sale without bothering to register their stall with the city police. In the Saint Eustache district, near what is now Les Halles, complaints arose as early as September 1789 over the number of meat sellers in push carts selling rotten and unhealthy meat and simple boutiques that polluted the quarter with the stench and effluvia from the private slaughter of animals.

Unofficial reports estimated the number of shops and stalls at nearly 700 in 1790, double the number of licensed sites in 1782. Worse than the flood of meat sellers in moments of plenty was that they suddenly disappeared in periods of want when the price of meat rose as quickly.

These dramatic shifts posed problems for the municipality even with the continued presence of the guild and their newly reconfirmed statutes. Bailly, the mayor of Paris at the time, was a realist, closing his eyes to the abuses that were quickly becoming the norm. He conceded that "resistance [to the guild statutes] was general and universal, the police force was not big enough, one was hard pressed to employ it, and license and infractions were winning ground everyday."[3] Long before the dissolution of the guilds in 1791, many workers, who had previously been excluded from the privileges of operating meat stalls in Paris, decided to sell meat where and when they liked. The radical principles of this new age began with political equality and quickly moved to economic equality. It would appear that under the Old Regime, a large population of meat sellers were excluded from the butcher trade. Once these restrictions were lifted (in principle at least), these entrepreneurs took the initiative to set up shop wherever they could.

Yet this fact ignores the long-held presence of well established, unincorporated workers who practiced this trade covertly in Paris and overtly in the faubourgs Saint Antoine–a fact that also suggests that the practice of corporate privilege was already breaking down throughout the eighteenth century.[4] The August decrees unleashed a frenzied marketplace that brought a new level of disorder to commerce without the power and authority of the guilds to police these "illegal" workers. At the same time, there remained among the working communities a great degree of resistance to the freedom to work and a call for the return of Old Regime regulation that for the meat trade was absolutely necessary for the health and safety of the Parisian population.

As much of this book demonstrates, the butcher trade in eighteenth-century Paris was highly regulated. Royal declarations, police sentences, corporate statutes, and fiscal institutions directed the production, distribution, and sale of fresh meat. The apparatus that employed guild officers, police commissaries, and inspectors, as well as the politics that guided royal ministers and magistrates in the Paris Parlement, aimed at strategic intervention that worked toward meeting the basic needs and safety of Parisians. Although regulation served the public good in word, its reach remained incomplete in deed. The meager resources of the state and the guild to police a city of half-a-million residents could never put a stop to the participation of clandestine nonguild butchers, many of them entrepreneurs, country butchers, and career journeymen who sought free enterprise among the city's licensed shops and stalls. Indeed, government regulatory action to a certain extent reflected an economy that it could not control.

The contrast between the Old Regime corporate system and the new free market system can too easily deceive historians as it brings into relief the repressive nature of regulation–an extension of absolutism that acted as some type of straight jacket on the development of the meat trade. It is a notion that follows the teleological thinking of revolutionary history that presupposes repressive regimes with market restrictions that engender economic entropy, regimes that are suddenly freed by liberal regimes to prosper and develop without the hindrances of regulation. It also confronts historians with the problem of viewing the logic of regulation against the standard of efficiency.

Throughout this book, we have seen how the meat trade experienced significant shifts toward liberalization well before the French Revolution. Paris saw the rise of markets and the influx of entrepreneurs who competed with guild masters. Nevertheless, it would be wrong to overstate the robust nature of this early industry in terms of some kind of Whiggish notion of progress as it would be to see regulation as an impediment to economic growth. The economy of Old Regime France functioned in a realm of incertitude. Royal government intervened in moments of crisis, particularly when the entire cattle population was threatened with virulent infectious diseases (such as the rinderpest epidemic of mid-century), or when peasants faced the loss of their herds due to the failure of forage crops. Government policy responded to as much as it shaped what was a more fundamental shift in livestock production and consumer behavior. Agricultural shortages and losses, market accessibility and prices, as well as tastes and beliefs determined the relative importance of this food. The contingent elements of the cattle trade such as agricultural production, markets, and costs to a great extent defined the place of meat in the Parisian diet and the extent of its economy. In many ways, the constraints under which the meat trade operated originate in particular aspects of French agriculture; where stock rearing was little more than an aid and supplement to the primary sector of agriculture: the cultivation of grains.[5] The commercial growth and development of the cattle trade, dependent upon a surplus of cultivated fodder to feed farm animals, would not take place until well into the nineteenth century.[6] Nevertheless, new agricultural systems appeared after 1750, employing convertible husbandry, clovers, turnips, and other roots that gave new impetus to agricultural productivity.[7] These advancements in agriculture involved a learning process forwarded by agronomists who imported their knowledge from England. During this period, the cattle trade saw greater productivity, especially in the region of Normandy that supplied the cattle markets at Neubourg and Poissy that provisioned Paris.

Contrary to what most historians see as a period of low meat consumption, the archival record confirms that overall a relatively prodigious meat trade grew along with the expansion of the city. Evidence of the rise in the number of butcher stalls registered with the police of Paris attests to the expansion of the urban meat trade across the century. Meat markets penetrated the covered butcheries and by the end of the century had moved into residential areas where butchers set up boutiques in their homes. Guild butchers, themselves, claimed that overall demand had grown significantly. In a legal brief published in 1768, a lawyer speaking for the guild affirmed "a rise in their sales of a fifth for the past several years."[8] The Parisian market for meat filled quarters of the city and its outlying areas offering a wide range of cuts aimed at elite and popular households.

Parisians sought out supplies from more competitive markets outside the guild jurisdiction, namely the growing population of nonguild meat sellers who operated clandestinely within the city and openly in privileged zones such as the Faubourg Saint-Antoine. Contemporary estimates of this population ranged from one hundred to three hundred, as many as twice the number of the guild community. Throughout the eighteenth century, the guild attempted to maintain its hold over the Parisian market as the pressures from nonguild butchers and meat sellers encroached upon their monopoly. Many of these itinerant meat sellers were women who sold the least expensive meat products such as cooked tripe, recycled foods, and meat scraps. In addition, country inns and taverns just outside the city's fiscal barriers offered Parisians places where they could eat cheaply and well. Local eateries (*guinguettes*) in the suburbs of Vaugirard, les Porcherons, and La Courtille were a popular attraction for city folk who spent their Sunday outings feasting on meat stews and roasts. Neighboring residents sought out these establishments for their household meat provisions. Thus, the market for meat fueled by a nonguild labor force that spread into the faubourgs and outside the city walls, following the growth of the urban population.

Another myth that this book undermines is that the expansion of the meat trade resulted in the democratization of meat eating. Throughout most of the early modern period, the distribution of this luxury good corresponded to the social order. More specifically, butchers under certain pressure from the police stratified consumption by classifying meat into the haute and the basse boucherie. Throughout this period, police regulation imposed certain price limits with the intention of reserving a certain share of the meat supply for the poor. In the end, this policy only underlined the social distinctions within eighteenth-century consumer society. Butchers, as mediators of the meat exchange, reserved the best cuts for their most privileged clientele while selling off the lesser cuts to the commoners who visited their stalls. As we saw in Chapter 2, the servant of Monsieur Non exemplified the terms under which she and Master Butcher Drieux battled for a piece of meat to suit her employer. By and large, the market for meat operated in a social taxonomy of prestige, where butchers as intermediaries distributed meat according to their understanding of Old Regime hierarchies.

As a commodity subject to the vagaries of taste and exemplary of rich lifestyles, butcher's meat and its distribution underscore the changes in consumer behavior that influenced meat's social value especially during the late eighteenth century. Culinary fashions for certain cuts of meat that propelled consumers to buy them and producers to market them also contributed to the cultural construction of meat as the food of choice. The demand for refinement in cuisine encouraged diversity in meat preparation along with a more efficient mode of meat distribution for a wide population of meat eaters. The changing position of meat in the social hierarchy evolved with the growing demand. As we have seen, large joints of beef came to be considered "bourgeois meat," a staple of urban elites and therefore a necessity. The development of meat (particularly beef) as a food of necessity, I argue, rose out of its greater market accessibility, wider selection, and the rising expectations of consumers. Although the final claim remains impossible to substantiate for all Parisians, no doubt the complaints of contemporaries such as Mercier as to the quality of meat "for the people of Paris" point to the cleavages and contradictions in the movement toward modernity.

In this book, we have seen the changing regard toward meat among Parisians that also found expression in a growing concern with animal slaughter that took place within the city walls. As the city became more densely populated, residents of the butcher quarters became all too aware of the polluting aspects of the meat trade. Butcheries occupied the popular quarters alongside other workshops on narrow, airless streets. Not only was the natural animal odor of the slaughterhouse dangerous, but the vapors that emanated from rotting corpses in neglected cemeteries and dumps also proved to be lethal. The regulation of the meat trade included many failed attempts to oust the butchers from the city center. But it was precisely because meat was highly perishable and easily tainted that stalls and the work that went on inside them needed to be visible and within the consumer's reach. The placement of stalls had to satisfy the needs of local consumers throughout the urban environment. Hence, the demand for local meat distribution superseded complaints over foul air and blood-filled cesspools. The expansion of meat markets and butcher shops was crucial for the welfare of meat-eating Parisians.

The everyday dealings of butchers and their clients, bound by in social relations, characterized eighteenth-century Parisian market culture. Credit cemented their bonds of exchange while it reinforced distinctions of rank and privilege. By contrast, modern market relations altered how individuals determined their material needs as choices about what goods to buy, and the access to these goods could be regulated solely by the possession of cash. Moreover, the idea that surrounded this conception of free exchange meant that people's lifestyles could be determined solely by their monetary wealth rather than by religious prohibitions on luxury and excess, by juridical prohibitions of certain goods to certain status groups, by traditional and communal surveillance, by the static worldview of the "great chain of being." As Daniel Roche contends, "A rather grim, hierarchic society gave way to a more colorful, shimmering universe."[9] The movement from a corporate society to a liberal society occurred not only in the market, but within a whole world of political, economic, and private associations in which people could be free, convivial, contentedly opportunistic, and self-interested. It also indicated a situation of status instability and ultimately status revolution.

The market culture of merchant and master butchers and their family businesses comes forth through specific acts of solidarity and discord. As we have seen, the moment of marriage, of family succession, of weekly sales of wholesale and retail goods all articulate the points at which the production of social life requires the cooperation of individuals and groups. At the same time, these moments point out fissures in the community, moments of rupture as individual interests clashed with notions of the greater good (of the family firm or the fiscal needs of the state), or the dictates of the public good (the just price, a healthy food supply). Social institutions such as the butchers' guild, the family firm, and the marketplace brought forth the master, the apprentice, the journeyman, the butcher's wife, son and daughter, the merchant, the client, and the creditor who were both the products of these institutions and agents for the creation of social bonds that perpetuated them. Master butchers relied heavily upon social bonds to build family businesses to better succeed in an uncertain economic environment.

Through this examination of the institutions and practices that directed the commerce of meat (and were in turn shaped by it), this study brings into focus the social value and cultural significance of meat in the context of Old Regime Paris. The production, distribution, and consumption of butcher's meat structured the Parisian social life in distinct ways. Its circulation and exchange in the marketplace show the social interactions and the legal and moral boundaries that regulated market exchanges. Simultaneously, this path defined the changing meanings and fluctuating values of meat; its social necessity rang true on several registers: as a perishable food that demanded close regulation, as an item of luxury that demonstrated power and prestige, and as a healthful restorative that evoked subsistence claims. The matters of meat, in all their specificity, offer a way into larger issues of social life, more particularly how Old Regime society reproduced its hierarchical social order through the hierarchy of meat, and later challenged that social order with the rise of consumer society.

Appendix

Table 1 Parisian Butcheries and Growth of Registered Stalls

Parisian Quarter	No. of Stalls–1721	No. of Stalls–1751	No. of Stalls–1781
Cité	13	13	13
Saint-Jacques-de-la-Boucherie	29	29	29
Sainte-Opportune	33	33	32
Louvre	0	0	3
Palais Royale	14	14	18
Montmartre	0	0	4
Saint-Eustache	17	16	15
Les Halles	7	7	6
Saint-Denis	19	21	21
Saint-Martin	30	30	46
La Grève	18	18	15
Saint-Paul	5	5	5
Sainte-Avoie	4	4	7
Temple/Le Marais	10	10	14
Saint-Antoine	10	10	11
Place Maubert	30	31	30
Saint-Benoit	20	24	19
Saint-André-des-Arts	5	6	6
Luxembourg	31	35	32
Saint-Germain-des-près	11	11	16
Paris Subtotal	**312**	**317**	**342**

(continued)

Table 1 Parisian Butcheries and Growth of Registered Stalls–continued

Parisian Quarter	No. of Stalls–1721	No. of Stalls–1751	No. of Stalls–1781
Faubourg Saint-Antoine	10?	10?	10?
Faubourg Saint-Denis	0	1	1
Faubourg Saint-Germain	0	0	1
Faubourg Saint-Honoré	0	7	11
Faubourg Saint-Jacques	0	0	5
Faubourg Saint-Marcel	6	7	7
Faubourg Saint-Martin	0	3	3
Faubourg Subtotal	10	28	38
TOTAL	**322**	**345**	**380**

Source: AN Y 9502, 9503, 9503B.

Table 2 Parisian Butcheries and Dates Established

Name of Butchery or Open Market	Date Established	No. Stalls in 1721	No. Stalls in 1781	City Location
L'Apport Paris or La Grande Boucherie	February 3, 1379	29	29	Quartier Saint-Jacques-de-la-Boucherie
Boucherie de Beauvais	August 1416	28	28	Quartier Saint-Opportune
Boucherie Fb Saint-Germain, la rue des Boucheries	April 1370	22	22	Quartier du Luxembourg
Boucherie Gilles-le-Niais or Villeneuve	n/a	5	6	Quartier Saint-Denis
Boucherie Montmartre, rue Montmartre	n/a	6	6	Quartier Saint-Eustache

(continued)

Name of Butchery or Open Market	Date Established	No. Stalls in 1721	No. Stalls in 1781	City Location
Boucherie Rouge, rue Mouffetard, Fb Saint-Marcel	March 1644	6	6	Quartier Place Maubert
Boucherie Saint-Denis	n/a	6	6	Quartier Saint-Denis
Boucherie Saint-Honoré, près Quinze-Vingts	November 23, 1633	10	10	Quartier Palais Royal
Boucherie Saint-Martin vis-à-vis Saint-Mery	n/a	6	6	Quartier Saint-Martin
Comtesse d'Artois, la rue	June 28, 1651	2	4	Quartier des Halles
Faubourg Saint-Antoine	March 2, 1643	10	10	Quartier Saint-Antoine
Marché d'Aguesseau, Faubourg Saint-Honoré	February 6, 1723	0	8	Faubourg Saint-Honoré
Marché du Boullanvilliers	1780	0	4	Quartier du Luxembourg
Marché du Cimetière Saint-Jean	March 9, 1388	12	9	Quartier de la Grève
Marché la Croix-Rouge, Fb Saint-Germain	July 23, 1652	5	5	Quartier du Luxembourg

(continued)

Table 2 Parisian Butcheries and Dates Established–continued

Name of Butchery or Open Market	Date Established	No. Stalls in 1721	No. Stalls in 1781	City Location
Marché Fb Saint-Germain, petit	1635	9	9	Quartier du Luxembourg
Marché de l'Ile Notre-Dame	ca. 1258	2	2	Quartier de la Cité
Marché du Marais du Temple	September 22, 1615	8	12	Quartier du Temple
Marché Neuf	July 11, 1558	11	9	Quartier de la Cité
Marché Saint-Martin, nouveau	ca. 1771	0	16	Quartier Saint-Martin
Montagne Sainte-Geneviève	1360	14	14	Quartier Place Maubert
Petit Pont de Gloriette	August 1416	10	10	Quartier Saint-Benoit
Place Maubert Maubert	May 4, 1540	6	5	Quartier Place
Pont aux Trippes, Faubourg Saint-Marcel	March 1644	4	6	Quartier Place Maubert
Porte de Bussi	n/a	5	6	Quartier du Luxembourg
Saint-Antoine, la rue	1637, 1639, 1645, 1656	10	10	Quartier Saint-Antoine
Saint-Eustache, rue Montmartre	August 1631	6	8	Quartier Saint-Eustache
Saint-Jacques, la porte	1650–1658	5	4	Quartier Saint-Benoît

(continued)

Name of Butchery or Open Market	Date Established	No. Stalls in 1721	No. Stalls in 1781	City Location
Saint-Jacques, la rue	1650–1658	4	4	Quartier Saint-Benoît
Saint-Martin, la rue, vers Saint-Nicolas-des-Champs	May 4, 1540	21	22	Quartier Saint-Martin
Saint-Michel, la porte	February 1623	2	3	Quartier du Luxembourg
Saint-Paul, la rue	1354	4	5	Quartier Saint-Paul
Porte Saint-Victor	n/a	3	3	Quartier Place Maubert

Source: Delamare, *Traité de la police,* II: 1214–16.

Table 3 Guild Officer Elections 1708–1775, Chambre de Procureur du Roi, Parc Civil, the Châtelet

Date	Syndic	Fb St-Germain	St-Martin	Marais/ St-Paul	Montagne Ste-Geneviève	Port de Paris
March 20, 1708	Christophe Frère	Jean François Marlot		Pierre Thibert	Jean Blou	Pierre Boivin
March 8, 1712	Pierre Thibert	Adam Thibert	Pierre Bignot	n/a	François Drieux	Adam Thibert
March 24, 1716	Jean Magnan	Simon Aubert	François Frère	n/a	Jacques Lejuge	Paul Perceval
March 13, 1719	Jean Magnan	Jacques Geoffroy	Charles Tripperet	Nicolas Cleret	Jean Baptiste Bignot	Pierre Gilbert
1720	Jean Margnan	Jacques Geoffroy	Charles Tripperet	Nicolas Cleret	Jean Baptistet Bignot	Pierre Gilbert
March 26, 1721	Eustache Cleret	Jacques Geoffroy	Charles Denis Tripperet	Nicolas Cleret	Jean Baptiste Bignot	Nicolas Certelet
March 17, 1722	Eustache Cleret	Thomas Bernard	Eustache Depuis	Jean Bertrand		
March 28, 1724		Louis Cottard	Jean Eustache Denis Dupuy	Jean Baptiste Bertrand		
April 1726		Louis Cottard	Andre Danet	Antoine Leroy		
March 9, 1728		Jacques Gallier	Andre Danet	Antoine Leroy		
1734		Pierre Remy	Simon Tripperet	Pierre Aubert		
1735		Pierre Remy	Simon Tripperet	Pierre Aubert		
March 13, 1736		Eloy Bernard	Simon Tripperet	Pierre Aubert		

April 2, 1737	Nicolas Berjonneau	Eloy Bernard	Simon Tripperet	Pierre Aubert	Vincent Lelievre	Louis Thibert
March 18, 1738	Nicolas Berjouneau	Eloy Bernard	Eustache Nicolas Cleret	Jean Baptiste Maurice	Vincent Lelievre	Louis Thibert
March 10, 1739	Nicolas Berjouneau	Eloy Bernard	Eustache Nicolas Cleret	Jean Baptiste Maurice	Jean Charles Garnier	Louis Thibert
March 29, 1740	Nicolas Berjouneau	Nicolas Francfort	Eustache Nicolas Cleret	Jean Baptiste Maurice	Jean Charles Garnier	Louis Thibert
March 14, 1741	Nicolas Berjouneau	Nicolas Francfort	Eustache Nicolas Cleret	Jean Baptiste Maurice	Vincent Gosse	Louis Thibert
March 6, 1742	Nicolas Berjouneau	Nicolas Francfort	François Nicolas Frère	Marc Blou (50/50)	Vincent Gosse	Louis Thibert
March 26, 1743	Louis Thibert	Jacques Adam	François Nicolas Frère (unopposed)	Marc Blou	Vincent Gosse	Clement Bernard
March 17, 1744	Louis Thibert	Jacques Adam	Claude Berthelot	Marc Blou	Vincent Gosse	Clerment Bernard
30 March 1745	Pierre Vollée	Jacques Adam	Claude Berthelot	Jacques Roquet (Quartier St. Paul)	Andre Boivin	Clement Bernard
March 24, 1746	Pierre Vollée	Jean Gallier	Claude Berthelot	Pierre Troquet	André Boivin	Clemence Bernard
March 14, 1747	Pierre Vollée	Jean Gallier	Claude Berthelot	Pierre Troquet	André Boivin	Clemence Bernard

(continued)

Table 3 Guild Officer Elections 1708–1775, Chambre de Procureur du Roi, Parc Civil, the Chatêlet–continued

Date	Syndic	Fb St. Germain	St. Martin	Marais/ St Paul	Montagne Ste-Geneviève	Port de Paris
March 26, 1748	Pierre Vollée	Jean Gallier	Claude Berthelot	Jacques Pierre Troquet	André Boivin	Clemence Bernard
March 18, 1749	Vincent Lelievre	Jean Gallier	Claude Berthelot	Etienne Hureau	André Boivin	Jean Rebour
March 10, 1750	Vincent Lelievre	Jean Gallier	Eloy Housse	Etienne Hureau	André Boisin	Jean Rebours
March 23, 1751	Vincent Lelievre	Jean Gallier	Eloy Housse	Etienne Hureau (78 voice)	Jean Couart	Jean Rebours
March 1752	Vincent Lelievre	Pierre Carraque	Eloy Housse	Etienne Hurault	Jean Couart	Jean Rebours
April 1753 Thibert	Vincent Lelievre	Pierre Carraque	Eloy Housse	Etienne Hureau	Jean Couart	L. Alexandre
March 26, 1754	Vincent Lelievre	Pierre Carraque	Pierre Thion	Etienne Hureau	Jean Couart	L. Alexandre| Thibert
March 11, 1755	Vincent Lelievre	Pierre Carraque	Pierre Thion	Christophe Vollée	Jean Couart	L. Alexandre Thibert
March 30, 1756	Vincent Lelievre	Nicolas Michel Remy	Pierre Thion	Christophe Vollée	Jean Couart	L. Alexandre Thibert
March 22, 1757	Vincent Lelievre	Nicolas Michel Remy	Pierre Thion	Christophe Vollée	Jean Couart	Antoine Danet
March 7, 1758	Vincent Lelievre	Nicolas Michel Remy	Pierre Thion	Christophe Vollée	Jean Couart	Antoine Danet

March 27, 1759	André Boivin	Nicolas Michel Remy	Pierre Thion	Alexandre Vollée	Pierre J.-B. Marquis	André Danet
March 18, 1760	André Boivin	Charles Gallier	Jean-Baptiste Guillain	Alexandre Vollée	Pierre J.-B. Marquis	André Danet
March 31, 1761	André Boivin	Charles Gallier	Jean-Baptiste Guillain	Alexandre Vollée	Pierre J.-B. Marquis	Antoine Danet
March 23, 1762	André Boivin	Charles Gallier	Jean-Baptiste Guillain	Alexandre Vollée	Pierre J.-B. Marquis	Antoine Danet
March 15, 1763	Simon Tripperet	Charles Gallier	Jean-Baptiste Guillain	Pierre Blondel	Pierre J.-B. Marquis	Barthélémy Nicolas Debroy
April 3, 1764	Simon Tripperet	Clement Bernard	Etienne Sejournée	Pierre Blondel	Pierre J-B. Marquis	Barthélémy Nicolas Debroy
March 19, 1765	Simon Tripperet	Clement Bernard	Etienne Sejournée	Pierre Blondel	Jean-Baptiste Francfort	Barthélémy Nioclas Debroy
March 11, 1766	Simon Tripperet	Clement Bernard	Etienne Sejournée	Pierre Blondel	Jean-Baptiste Francfort	Barthélémy Nicolas Debroy
March 31, 1767	Simon Tripperet	Clement Bernard	Etienne Sejournée	Pierre Blondel	Jean-Baptiste Francfort	Berthélémy Nicolas Debroy
March 15, 1768	Simon Tripperet	Clement Bernard	Etienne Sejournée	Pierre Blondel	Jean-Baptiste Francfort	Barthélémy Nicolas Debroy
March 7, 1769	Jean-Baptiste Guillain	Clement Bernard	Etienne Sejournée	François Couart	Jean-Baptiste Francfort	Claude Daix

(continued)

Table 3 Guild Officer Elections 1708–1775, Chambre de Procureur du Roi, Parc Civil, the Chatêlet–continued

Date	Syndic	Fb St. Germain	St. Martin	Marais/ St Paul	Montagne Ste-Geneviève	Port de Paris
March 27, 1770	Jean-Baptiste Guillain	François Barré	Pierre Ortillon	François Couart	Jean-Baptiste Francfort	Claude Daix
March 12, 1771	Jean-Baptiste Guillain	François Barré	Pierre Ortillon	François Couart	Paul Felix Vollée	Claude Daix
March 31, 1772	Jean-Baptiste Guillain	François Barré	Pierre Ortillon	François Couart	Paul Felix Vollée	Claude Daix
March 23, 1773	Jean-Baptiste Guillain	François Barré	Pierre Ortillon	François Couart	Paul Felix Vollée	Claude Daix
March 15, 1774	Jean-Baptiste Guillain	Alexandre Frère	Pierre Ortillon	François Couart	Paul Felix Vollée	Claude Daix
March 28, 1775	François Couart	Alexandre Frère	Pierre Ortillon	Jean-Baptiste Maindorge	Nicolas Delihue	Claude Daix

Source: AN Y 9383–88 and Y 9323–32

Table 4 Master Butcher Fortunes (in *livres*)

	Average	Mean
Assets	39,151 L	108,565 L
Liabilities	9,621 L	36,035 L
Net Worth	29,530 L	72,530 L

Source: AN Minutier Centrale, After-death Inventories

Exhibit 1 Records of La Maison de Sainte Pélagie

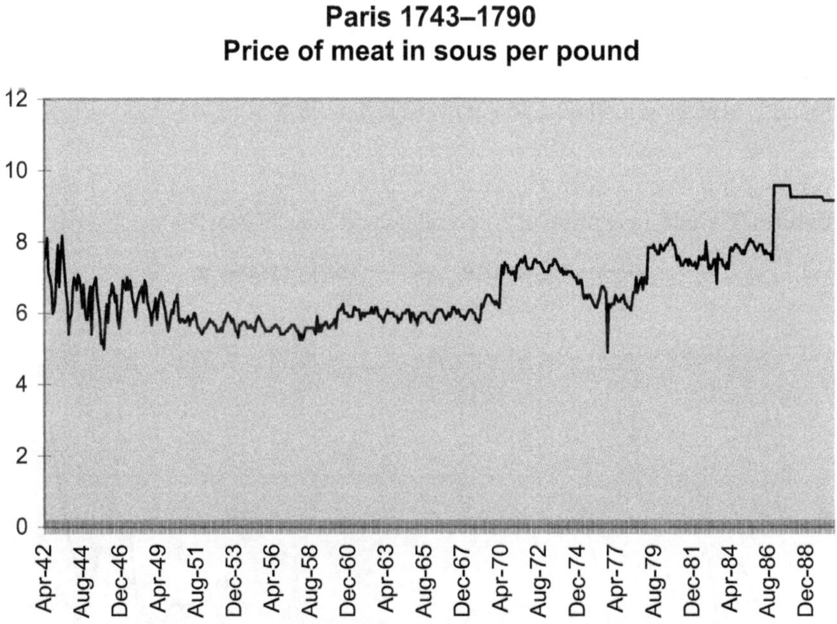

Source: Archives de l'Assistance Publique, Fonds Marcel Fosseyeux, FSS 105 (Hôpital General), liasse 3, 1741–90.

Exhibit 2 Guild Receptions across the Eighteenth Century

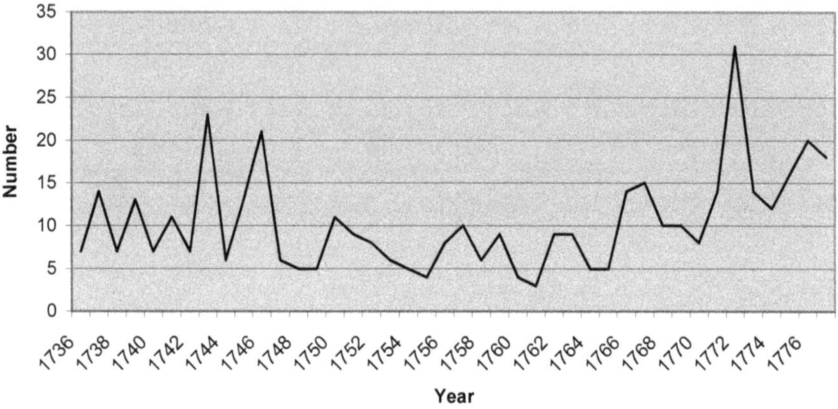

Source: Archives of the Procurator at the Châtelet, AN Y 9323–32.

Exhibit 3 Guild Reception of Apprentices and Sons of Masters

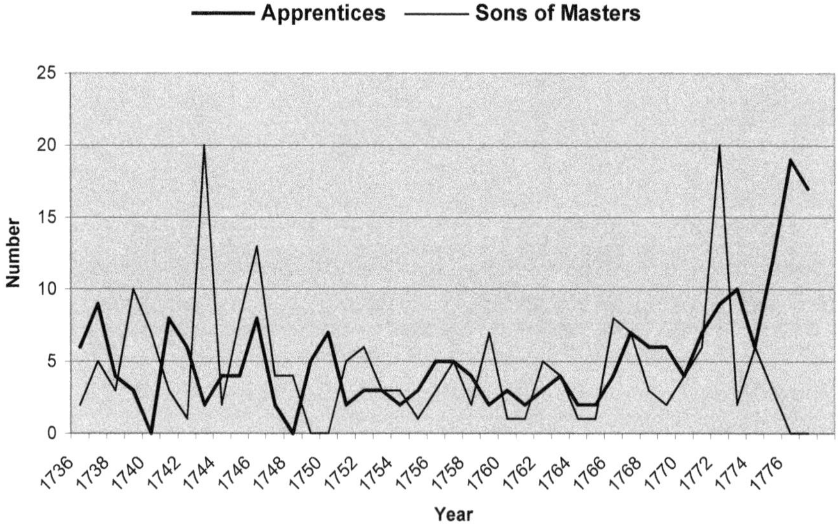

Source: Archives of the Procurator at the Châtelet, AN Y 9323–32.

Notes

INTRODUCTION

1. Letter dated September 1774, Anne-Robert-Jacques Turgot, *Oeuvres de Turgot* (Paris: F. Alcan, 1913–23), 4:200; Archives Nationales de France (hereafter ANF) F11 265.

2. The treatise presented to the National Assembly by the Parisian districts concerned "four objects of first necessity of existence," specifically wheat, butcher's meat, firewood, and wine. Chantrelle de Beaumont, *Traité importante sur les quatre objets de première nécessité de l'existence, présenté à l'Assemblée nationale le 24 Octobre 1790* (Paris: De l'Imp. de la veuve Delaguette, 1790[?]).

3. The statistics on cattle entries in 1637 are modest estimates. See Bibliothèque Nationale de France (hereafter BNF) Collection Joly de Fleury, ms. 1428, fols. 1–14, published in Arthur-Michel de Boislisle, ed., *Mémoire de la généralité de Paris* (Paris: n.p., 1881), 658–59. Thanks to the work of Bernard Garnier, the data on eighteenth-century entries are much more accurate. Garnier, "Des boeufs pour Paris, Commercialisation et élevage en Basse-Normandie (1700–1900)," *Annales de Bretagne et des Pays de l'Ouest* 106:1 (Jan–March 1999): 101–120; Garnier, "Les marchés aux bestiaux. Paris et sa banlieue," *Cahiers d'histoire* 42:3–4 (1997): 575–609.

4. Garnier calculates the annual per capita consumption, based upon livestock entering the city, at 52 kilograms at the mid-seventeenth century, to the 62 kilograms at the end of the eighteenth century. The rate of growth (*le taux de croissance*) for meat went from 0.45 in the period 1635–1700, to a negative growth rate of 2.40 during the years 1700–1711, then advanced consistently from 0.57 (1711–1819) to 1.10 (1819–1843), finally exploding at 2.27 (1843–1882) to the period when the average annual meat ration reached 77 kilograms in 1891. Garnier, "Les marchés aux bestiaux. Paris et sa banlieue," 597.

5. The current bibliography on the Parisian meat trade is limited to nineteenth-century studies with the notable exception of Reynald Abad, *Le grand marché: L'approvisionnement alimentaire de Paris sous l'Ancien Régime* (Paris: Fayard, 2002) and the collection of essays presented at a conference in 1993 organized by le Centre d'Histoire Moderne, A. Blanchard, Henri Michel, et Elie Pélaquier, eds., *De l'herbe à table: La viande dans la France méridionale à l'époque moderne, Actes du colloque organisé par le Centre d'Histoire Moderne en 1993* (Montpellier: Université Paul-Valéry Monpellier III, 1994).

CHAPTER 1

1. Sources on the women's march to Versailles can be found in Laura Mason and Tracey Rizzo, eds., *The French Revolution: A Document Collection* (Boston: Houghton Mifflin Co., 1999), 83–87. The phrase, "la viande de boucherie est la nourriture la plus ordinaire après le pain," appears in several eighteenth-century dictionaries including Diderot and d'Alembert's *Encyclopédie ou dictionnaire raisonné des sciences des arts et métiers* (Paris: Chez Durand, 1751), 2:350–52; the subsequent *Encyclopédie méthodique des arts et métiers méchaniques* (Paris: Chez Panckoucke, 1783), 26:229 draws directly from the original *Encyclopédie* entry, attributed to Jean-Baptiste-René Robinet.

2. For discussions of this earlier period of plentiful meat see Louis Stouff, *Ravitaillement et alimentation en Provence aux XIVe et XVe siècles* (Paris: Mouton, 1970), 169–94. Emmanuel Le Roy Ladurie finds a similar case in Languedoc, where in his study of population, monetary, and food crises, he traces moments of extreme dearth and famine in the mid-fourteenth century up until 1470 followed by a period of abundance. See *Les Paysans du Languedoc* (Paris: S.E.V.P.E.N., 1966), 267. Bernard Chevalier makes the same case for Tours in 1487, "Alimentation et niveau de vie à Tours à la fin du XVe siècle," *Bulletin philologique et historique jusqu'à 1610 du comité . . .* (1958), 143–57. Fernand Braudel speaks of a "carnivorous Europe," with tables piled high in pyramids of meat, a period that existed until 1580 in some parts of Europe. "Consumption of meat on this scale does not seem to have been a luxury reserved to the very rich in the fifteenth and sixteenth centuries." Braudel, *The Structure of Everyday Life: The Limits of the Possible,* trans. Sian Reynolds (New York: Harper & Row Publishers, 1981), 1:190.

3. Historians have pointed to the observations of contemporaries such as Marshall Vauban, whose 1696 reports on one of the poorest regions of France, the Nivernais, painted a miserable picture of daily life: "The general run of people seldom drink [wine], eat meat not three times a year, and use little salt . . . So it is no cause for surprise if people who are so ill-nourished have so little energy." Vauban, "Description géographique de l'Election de Verzelay . . ." as cited in Pierre Goubert, *The Ancien Regime: French Society, 1600–1750,* trans. Steve Cox (New York: Harper and Row, 1969), 118. See also Georges Lefebvre, *Etudes orléanaises* (Paris, 1962), I:218. C. E. Labrousse, *Esquisse du mouvement de prix et des revenus en France au XVIIIe siècle* (Paris: Presses Universitaires de France, 1933).

4. Ernest Labrousse, *Esquisse du mouvement des prix et des revenus en France au XVIIIe siècle* (Paris: Librairie Dalloz, 1933); Jean Meuvret, *Le Problème des subsistances à l'époque Louis XIV: Le Commerce des grains et la conjoncture,* 2 vols. (Paris: Mouton, 1988); George Rudé, *The Crowd in the French Revolution* (London: Oxford University Press, 1959); Richard Cobb, *Terreur et subsistances* (Paris: Librairie Clavreuil, 1965); and Steven L. Kaplan, *Bread, Politics, and Political Economy in the Reign of Louis XV* (The Hague: Martinus Nijhoff, 1976).

5. Jean-Jacques Hémardinquer, "The Family Pig of the Ancien Régime: Myth or Fact?" in *Food and Drink in History,* vol. 5 of *Selections from the Annales:*

Economies, Sociétés, Civilisations, eds. Orest Ranum and Robert Forster, trans. Patricia M. Ranum (Baltimore: John Hopkins University Press, 1979), 50–85.

6. Garnier, "Les marchés aux bestiaux. Paris et sa banlieue," 597; Emmanuel Le Roy Ladurie, "Baroques et Lumières," in vol. 3 of *Histoire de la France urbaine* (Paris: Editions du Seuil, 1981).

7. Royal proclamation, "Portant Reglement sur les Estaux des Boucheries de Paris," announced in Paris March 13, 1719, published in 1720. BNF Collection Delamare, ms. fr. 21656, fols. 216–17.

8. "Toute viande outre le pain et le vin," translated in Latin as *opsonium.* Nicot, *Thresor de la langue francoyse* (Paris: n.p., 1606), 659.

9. Antoine Furetière, *Dictionnaire universel* (1690; repr. Paris, n.p., 1972), 4:54.

10. Mary Douglas, "Deciphering a Meal," *Daedelus* 101 (1972): 61–81.

11. See Madame Campan, *Mémoires* 3:7, as quoted in Alfred Franklin, "La Cuisine," in *La Vie privée d'autrefois. Arts et métiers, modes, moeurs, usages des Parisiens du XIIe au XVIIIe siècle* (Paris: Libraire Plon, 1888), 176–79.

12. The earliest evidence of a butcher guild appears in 1146 when Louis VII (r. 1137–1180) granted "master butchers" the task of providing meat and wine to the city's lepers. Even at this early date, the crown directed butchers in serving the public good. See Eugène D'Auriac, *Essai historique sur la boucherie de Paris* (Paris: Librairie de la société des gens de lettres, 1861), 8–10.

13. Steven Laurence Kaplan, "The State and the Problem of Dearth in Eighteenth-Century France: The Crisis of 1738–41 in Paris," *Food and Foodways* 4:2 (1990): 111–41.

14. The police commissaires, who were assigned to specific neighborhoods in Paris, worked under the lieutenant general of police, one of the king's highest officers. The lieutenant general's responsibilities as royal judge and administrator impinged on every aspect of city life since the creation of the post in 1667 including overseeing provisioning. The objectives of his office were carried down to the commissaires and inspectors who worked underneath him at the Châtelet. Alan Williams, *The Police of Paris, 1718–1789* (Baton Rouge: Louisiana State University Press, 1979), 7–9.

15. The notion of public good embodies much of the political discourse of kingship; its use marks the development of the modern state. For further discussion see James Collins, "La guerre de la ligue et le bien public," in *Le Traité de Vervins,* eds. Jean-François Labourdette, Jean-Pierre Poussou, and Marie-Catherine Vignal (Paris: Presses de l'Université de Paris-Sorbonne, 2000), 81–95.

16. Delamare, *Traité de la police,* 1:2.

17. Delamare, *Traité de la police,* 1:3.

18. Delamare, *Traité de la police,* 1:6.

19. Delamare, *Traité de la police,* 2:600.

20. Delamare, *Traité de la police,* 2:1129.

21. For an excellent discussion of the *Encyclopédie*'s view of the butcher as well as other artisans see Cynthia Koepp, "The Alphabetical Order: Work in

Diderot's *Encyclopédie,*" *Work in France: Representations, Meaning, Organization, and Practice,* ed. Steven L. Kaplan and Cynthia Koepp (Ithaca, NY: Cornell University Press, 1986), 229–57.

22. *Encyclopédie méthodique,* 26:229.

23. Jean Jacquart, "Immobilisme et catastrophes, 1560–1660" in *Histoire de la France rurale: L'âge classique des paysans, 1340–1789,* ed. Emmanuel Le Roy Ladurie (Paris: Editions du Seuil, 1975), 220. As long as the localized need to grow cereals existed, the margin of evolution for husbandry would remain restricted. The "agricultural revolution" involved a learning process forwarded by agronomists in the latter half of the eighteenth century. See George Grantham, "Diffusion of New Husbandry in Northern France, 1815–1840," *The Journal of Economic History* 38 (June 1978): 311–37.

24. Mauro Ambrosoli has recently addressed this subject in his work on the introduction of fodder crops into France, England, and Italy. Ambrosoli, *The Wild and the Sown. Botany and Agriculture in Western Europe, 1350–1850,* trans. Mary McCann Salvatorelli (Cambridge: Cambridge University Press, 1997).

25. Normandy accomplished this task with the extension of pastures for animal grazing and a growing number of agricultural workers who specialized in cattle feeding and trading. During the eighteenth century, farmers utilized as much as one-half to two-thirds of the arable land for this purpose, while evidence suggests that small merchants as well as wealthy farmers invested in the cattle trade as a means of gaining income. Reynald Abad, *Le grand marché,* 125. See also Marcel Duval, "L'élection de Carentan du milieu du XVIIe au milieu du XVIIIe. Etude d'histoire sociale," *A travers la Normandie des XVIIe et XVIIIe siècles,* eds. Michel Caillard et al. (Caen: Annales de Normandie, 1963), 155–235; Bernard Garnier, "La mise en herbe dans le pays d'Auge aux XVIIe et XVIIIe siècles," *Annales de Normandie* 25:3 (1975): 157–80.

26. Abad, *Le grand marché,* 164; Garnier, "Les marchés aux bestiaux"; Armand Husson, *Les consommations de Paris* (Paris: Librairie Hachette, 1875), 206–14; Marcel Lachiver, "L'approvisionnement de Paris en viande au XVIIIe siècle," in *La France d'ancien régime: Études réunis en l'honneur de Pierre Goubert,* ed. by Université de Haute-Bretagne-Rennes II Centre National des Lettres de l'Université de Paris X-Nanterre (Toulouse: Société de demographie historique: Privat,1984), 345–54.

27. According to a report to the procurator general, the butchers acknowledged ". . . une augmentation de leur débit d'une cinquième depuis quelques années." BNF Collection Joly de Fleury, ms. 460, fol. 191.

28. According to the official correspondence " . . . one fears for the shortage of meat in Paris this year, and even one would contemplate the loss of certain breeds throughout the kingdom." ANF G7 1668–70, fol. 161.

29. "Mémoire concernant l'approvisionnement de la viande pour Paris." 1724. ANF G7 1668–70, fol. 206.

30. BNF Collection Delamare, "Viande" vol. 1, ms. fr. 21653, fols. 4–9, 167–68.

31. These royal proclamations are renewed throughout the eighteenth century. See a collection of printed sources in ANF AB XIX/655/bis, "Bestiaux (1716–1782)."

32. Henri Martin, *Histoire de France* (Paris: Fume, 1855–60), 13:102–104.

33. The gross revenue was about 15 million livres in 1690, about 150 million in 1706, and about 200 million in the 1730s. Compared with other taxes on primary goods, such as the tax on salt (*gabelle*), this income is a small sum.

34. Gustave Bienaymé, "La fiscalité alimentaire et gastronomique à Paris," *Journal de la société de statistique de Paris,* 31st year (1890), 40–60.

35. Gustave Bienaymé and A. de Saint-Julien, *Histoire des droits d'entrée & d'octrois à Paris* (Paris: Paul Dupont, 1887), 42–43.

36. ANF G7 1178, Mémoire sur les droits d'aides, as cited by A.-M. de Boislille, *Mémoires des Intendants sur l'état des généralités dressés pour l'instruction du Duc de Bourgogne,* vol. 1 (Paris: Généralité de Paris, 1881), 492.

37. de Boislille, *Mémoires des Intendants sur l'état des généralités dressés pour l'instruction du Duc de Bourgogne,* 485. This figure does not include the revenue gathered from the sol pour livre in the veal market of Paris. The government converted this proportional tax to a fixed tax of 32 sols per head by *arrêt de conseil* dated March 26, 1697. Finally, this tax fell under the *Ferme des Aides* by royal declaration dated February 4, 1698.

38. Bienaymé and de Saint-Julien, *Histoire des droits d'entrée & d'octrois à Paris,* 32–33.

39. Bienaymé, "La fiscalité alimentaire et gastronomique à Paris," 40–60.

40. Thomas Brennan, *Burgundy to Champagne: The Wine Trade in Early Modern France* (Baltimore: The Johns Hopkins University Press, 1997), 71–72, 119–21.

41. Raymond de Roover, "The Concept of the Just Price: Theory and Economic Policy," *Journal of Economic History* 18 (1958): 418–34.

42. Delamare, *Traité de la police,* 2:1278.

43. For price comparisons of cereals to livestock over the long term, see Labrousse, *Esquisse du mouvement des prix et des revenus en France au XVIIIe siècle,* 291–306.

44. Sir William Mildmay, *The Police of France, or An account of the Laws and Regulations Established in that Kingdom, for the Preservation of Peace and the Preventing of Robberies* (London: Own & Harrison, 1763), 99.

45. See Police Ordinance, November 9, 1725, BNF Collection Delamare, ms. fr. 21657, fols. 76–77.

46. For example, in February 1789, the prévôté of Passy-lès-Paris, a suburb of Paris, responded to three butchers who raised their prices above the 8 sous mark with a heavy fine of 100 livres. AP Fichier Général, 4 AZ 1291, BNF ms. fr. 6687, as cited in Hippolite Monin, *L'Etat de Paris en 1789: Etudes et documents sur l'Ancien Régime à Paris* (Paris: D. Jouaust, 1889), 442.

47. Letter from de Sartine to butcher guild leaders dated May 10, 1766, ANF Y 11253. See also police ordinance for the butchers of Versailles dated March 18, 1758, AD Yvelines, 5E5 "Ordonnances de Police, 1711–1785."

48. In 1788, a shopper paid 2 sous for each beef's liver, 5 sous for the heart, and 9 sous a pound for prepared tripe. By definition, the basse viande also included beef tongue, veal's feet, and *tête de veau* as well as other lower-end cuts. Police Ordinance, BNF, ms. fr. 6687.

49. Taken from a published ordinance of 1770 that echoes earlier declarations dated 1741, 1762, and 1764. From H. Monin, *L'état de Paris en 1789,* 441.

50. As Ernest Labrousse shows, fluctuations in the price of fodder (straw and hay) had the greatest influence over the price of meat. A bad hay harvest drove up the price of the cattle's principle feed and forced farmers to sell off their livestock, thereby flooding the market with cheap cattle and, by extension, cheap meat. In theory, the quick sale of cattle brought on scarcity and consequently, a steep rise in meat prices. Yet while extreme fluctuations did occur in the cattle markets (owing in large part, to the variable size and weights of cattle, as well as the variable supply), such shifts do not appear in what few records or reports we have of the Paris meat markets. See Labrousse, *Esquisse du mouvement des prix et des revenus en France au XVIIIe siècle,* 291–306.

51. Mercier, *Tableau de Paris* (Amsterdam: n.p., 1783), 5:121–22.

52. See Brennan's introduction in *Burgundy to Champagne: The Wine Trade in Early Modern France,* xiv.

53. Delamare, *Traité de la police,* 2:1220–39.

54. Albert Hirschman, "Rival Interpretations of Market Society: Civilizing, Destructive or Feeble?" *Journal of Economic Literature* 20 (4):1463–84.

55. Delamare, *Traité de la Police,* 2:1278.

56. The mémoire–part official record, part propaganda tool–served to give voice to many sides of a case. They were published as sheets and broadsides and distributed throughout the capital. For further examination of the *causes célèbres* that found their way into public opinion see Sarah Maza, *Private Lives and Public Affairs the causes célèbres of Pre-Revolutionary France* (Berkeley: University of California Press, 1993).

57. Abbé Tessier, "Bêtes à cornes," *Encyclopédie méthodique. Agriculture* (Paris, 1787–1816), 185–87; M. De Francourt, "Observations sur la population des bestiaux et leurs différentes espèces," *Mémoires de la société royale d'agriculture de Paris* (1789).

58. ANF Y 13020, 1746–1747; ANF Y 15520, "Bulletins de fournitures faites au S. Danet par la Caisse de Poissy, pendant les années 1782 et suivantes jusques et compris d'année 1786."

59. BNF Collection Joly de Fleury, ms. 104, fols. 194–96.

60. See weights for cattle purchased by butchers Vincent Bignon (1753–58), Dautier (1767–69), and Etienne Baudet (1781) AP D5B6 *registers* 2695, 3739, and 636, respectively.

61. Costs given in a butcher guild mémoire dated 1717. BNF Factum 12367.

62. See letter written by the lieutenant general of police to the officers of the butcher guild following numerous complaints to commissaires by Parisians, ANF Y 11253, May 10, 1766; complaint made by a customer, Y 11936, January 2, 1754.

CHAPTER 2

1. ". . . qui ne convenoit point [à] la maison du d. S. Non." ANF Y 11936, January 2, 1754.

2. Several ordinances from 1704 to 1736 point to rulings that date as early as 1540, which are later written into the butcher guild statutes. See BNF Collection Delamare ms. fr. 21654, fol. 144, and ms. fr. 216757, fol. 286.

3. Commissaire Vincent Laurent imposed a stiff penalty (100 livre fine) on a butcher at the Beauvais butchery. Sentences de Police, ANF Y 9498, July 24, 1721 and April 5, 1726.

4. A concept forwarded by Michael Sonenscher who argues for the makeshift arrangements between artisans, as members of a "bazaar economy," who were compelled to enter into short-term arrangements. Michael Sonenscher, *Work and Wages: Natural Law, Politics and the Eighteenth-Century French Trades* (Cambridge: Cambridge University Press, 1989).

5. Butcher Pierre Barré, at the time of his death in October 1738, paid 1,550 livres in rent on two stalls, a house, and a stockyard; disbursed 1,341 livres yearly for his staff of six stall workers, a domestic, and a shepherd; and held outstanding debts of over 9,600 livres for cattle purchases. ANF ET/XCIX/460, October 6, 1738.

6. Edmond, *Le Paysan,* 1:13, as cited in R. C. Cobb, *The Police and the People: French Popular Protest, 1789–1820* (Oxford, UK: Clarendon Press, 1970), 293.

7. Historians Jean Louis Flandrin and Stephen Mennell have remarked how the consumption of beef and mutton experienced a kind of social diffusion from the Middle Ages into the eighteenth century, especially among wealthier nonnobles. The contrasting diets of status-minded townsmen can be seen in historical cookbooks, particularly the *Ménagier de Paris* (1493), that took many of the recipes and ingredients of the courtly cooks and adapted them to the tastes of urban households. Mennell, *All Manners of Food: Eating and Taste in England and France from the Middle Ages to the Present* (Oxford, UK: Basil Blackwell, 1985), 61. See also Jean-Louis Flandrin, "Distinction through Taste," in vol. 3 of *A History of Private Life: Passions of the Renaissance,* ed. Roger Chartier, trans. Arthur Goldhammer (Cambridge, MA: Belknap Press, 1989), 272–74.

In Flandrin's serial analysis of nearly all culinary texts, the percentage of meat dishes shows a marked increase from the medieval period through the latter half of the eighteenth century, a rise that moves from 20 percent to over 50 percent. It is important to note here that Flandrin excludes *Le ménagier de Paris* from his analysis as he considers it "un cas à part." As a cookbook for urban dwellers, its emphasis on butcher's meat as well as a variety of cuts of meat distinguishes it from the court cuisine of the middle ages. Flandrin, "Dietary Choices and Culinary Technique, 1500–1800," in *Food: A Culinary History from Antiquity to the Present,* 403–17.

8. See his article in the special publication of *Dix-Huitième Siècle* devoted to food and cuisine, "Cuisine et alimentation populaire à Paris," *Dix-Huitième Siècle* 15 (1983): 7–18.

9. Duby, *Hommes et Structures du Moyen Age* (Paris: Mouton, 1973).

10. In the Aude and Quercy regions during the Grand Siècle, notables known as "monsieurs" were recognized by their "ventres d'or." R. Chartier and H. Neveu, "La ville dominante et soumise," in *Histoire de la France urbaine: La ville classique,* ed. Georges Duby, vol. 3 (Paris: Editions Seuil, 1981).

11. Thorstein Veblen, *The Theory of the Leisure Class* (1899; repr., London: Allen & Unwin, 1959), 36.

12. Mercier, *Tableau de Paris,* 5:597–98.

13. Grimod de la Reynière, *Manuel des Amphytryons. Contenant un traité de la Dissection des viandes à table, la Nomenclature des Menus les plus nouveaux pour chaque saison, et des Elemens de Politesse gourmande* (Paris: Capelle et Renard, 1808).

14. de la Reynière, *Manuel des Amphytryons,* 21.

15. *Les Oeuvres complètes de Voltaire* (Oxford: The Voltaire Foundation, 1987), 33:129.

16. Evidence taken from butcher account books rarely specify cuts of meat other than the large portions such as the loin, the shoulder, the leg, and the rack. For a few examples, see Butcher Bontemps, AP D5B6, registers 183, 1624, 2754, 3335, 3893, 4106, 4464, and 4863; Butcher Hebert, AP D5B6, register 11159; Butcher Sagot, AP D5B6, register 3304.

17. These tightly enclosed meat lockers, about 3 by 5 meters in area, devoid of light and air, served to hang raw flesh and keep them from quick spoilage. See Alfred Morin, "Les Dernières 'chambres à chair' des bouchers Troyens d'autrefois," *Vieilles Enseignes Troyennes* (Paris: n.p., 1958).

18. ANF MC ET/XXVI/458, June 16, 1751.

19. ANF MC ET/XXVI/458, June 16, 1751.

20. ANF MC ET/XXVI/458, June 16, 1751.

21. AP D5B6 registers 34, 467, and 2164.

22. "Variétés gastronomiques" (Paris: Libriarie Plon, 1891), 264–65.

23. AP D5B6 registers 2695, 4125, 4794, and 4846.

24. See for example, AP D5B6 registers 34, 636, 756, 1528, 2695, 2729, 3409, and 3739.

25. This year reflects consistency and precedes more difficult years when Sagot suffered heavy losses. He declared business failure on September 10, 1770. AP D4B6 carton 39, dos. 2121; D5B6 register 2969.

26. Other nobles listed included "Monsieur le Premier," "Monseigneur le Prince de Soubise," and numerous counts, countesses, dukes, and duchesses, "Monsieur l'Abbé de la Ville," the archbishop of Reims, the bishop of Orleans, the pages of the small stables, and "the Mesdames of France." AP D5B6 registers 63, 249, 483, 1396, and 3198.

27. Flandrin, "Dietary Choices and Culinary Technique, 1500–1800," 403–17.

28. Mercier, *Tableau de Paris,* 5:288.

29. Butchers were known to add lesser cuts of meat to purchases at market, a practice that Parisians knew as *charge* (and in Toulouse as *surpoids*). Butchers would weigh the bones and basse boucherie together with finer cuts and price

them collectively. See the anonymous pamphlet "Observations sur l'Article XXI du Bail de la Vente Exclusive de la Viande, qui prouvent qu'il est avantageux au peuple de la ventre nette & sans charge ou surpoids" (Toulouse: de l'Imprimerie Me. Rayet, 1779).

30. Butcher Gabriel Sagot left detailed accounts of cuts that included many "pieces" of veal, beef, and mutton as well as a *tête d'aloyaux* (upper loin), *cuisse* (leg/thigh), *gigot* (leg), *carré* (rack), *poitrine* (brisket or flank), *charbonné* (sirloin of the lower loin), *culotte* (rump), and *tendons* (sinew or hamstring?), see AP D5B6 register 3304. Butcher Bontemps recorded his remains at the end of the day:

> Viande de reste du vendredi, 2 moutons et 1 demie, 1 train de charbonné, 1 pied de boeuf, 2 cuisses, 1 palleron, 3 pièces de boeuf, 1 colliers, 1 creux de veaux, 1 pied de boeuf émouché, 19 pièces de mouton, 5 pièces de veaux, 2 gît, 7 cotes de charbonnée, 36 gobbet, 1 fois de veau [September 20, 1768]. Viande de Reste: 1 mouton et demie, 1 gros de cuisse, 1 morceau de charbonné, 1 alloyau, 1 morceau de poitrine, 1 vaine [*sic*], 2 cartiers de mouton, 3 pièces de veaux, 3 pièces de mouton, 12 gobbets."

[circa March 29, 1771]; AP D5B6 4863. Other butchers recorded the weights for certain cuts such as a cuisse or leg of 54 pounds, an aloyau or sirloin of 7 to 8 pounds, a *paleron* [*sic*] of 29 pounds, a *poitrine* or brisket and flank of 29 pounds, a *queue* or oxtail of 3 pounds; AP D5B6 registers 1528, 1624, 1848, 2660, and 3904.

31. This includes all dictionaries of the mechanical arts, the eighteenth-century dictionaries of Savary, Diderot and d'Alembert, Trevoux, and Furetière.

32. One would assume that such legislation appeared long before in Paris, although such documents are yet to be found. Police ordinances throughout the eighteenth century acknowledge the distinction between haute and basse boucherie. Yet the 1779 Ordinance is the earliest piece of evidence I have found that codifies these two categories of meat as particular cuts. Nowhere in the butcher statutes are these categorical distinctions made nor are these cuts included in the butcher guild's masterpiece, a display of slaughtering and butchering technique required of all journeyman who sought mastership.

33. *Encyclopédie méthodique,* 26:237, defines it as "Morceau qui contient le premier & le second travers avec la joue."

34. Given the fact that many of these terms are no longer in use, and others do not correspond to American terms for cuts of meat (as our butchering techniques differ greatly from the French), the document presents many difficulties for the translator. The beef cuts, given as " . . . le collier coupé dans le joint de la trente jusqu'à la première côte de charbonné, les veines grasses, les flanchets y [*sic*] compris toutes côtes de poitrine, barbeaux de poitrine, trumeaux et autres petits coupons," are equivalent to the chuck end cut in the shoulder joint toward the brisket side and including the rib end and the shoulder clod, the flank including the brisket, the shanks, and other trimmings. For veal, the document specifies the "bout saigneux [*sic*], jarrets, manches d'épaules et autres petits coupons," which correspond to the brisket side of the chuck, the knuckle, the

foreshank, and other trimmings. The basse boucherie of mutton followed along the same lines with "bout saigneux [*sic*], morceau d'épaule et petits coupons." See Police Ordinance, September 24, 1779; BNF Fonds Le Senne 599 (14).

35. The origin of term "rejouissances" dates back to the legendary Henry IV, the good king of France who "put a chicken in every pot." The folklore surrounding his reign extended beyond the monarch's ability to feed his people poultry to include cheap cuts of butcher's meat. With the advice of the city leader Miron (who held the highest municipal office of *prévôt des marchands*), Henry set forth a decree that effectively required butchers to sell an array of meats at different prices. According to this legend, the people "rejoiced" upon hearing the king's stipulations for lesser cuts of meat at a cheaper price. See Ch. Rozan, *Petites ignorances de la conversations* (circa 1600) as cited in Emile Littré, *Dictionnaire de la langue française* (Paris: Hachette, 1958): 6:1168.

36. Sentence de Police, January 18, 1788, BNF, Fonds Le Senne, fol. 599 (16).

37. Menon identified the *poitrine* (breast) that included the brisket as "the most esteemed pieces, after the *culotte* (eye of the round)" in *La Cuisinière bourgeoise* (Paris: Chez P. Guillaume Cavelier, 1771), 51. This piece also appears as one of the cuts that the *bailliage* of Versailles identified as basse boucherie. Both the poitrine and the culotte came from areas of much used muscle (neck and hips), which give meat a tougher quality. Tougher muscles that are frequently used may contain more myoglobin, which imparts a deep red color. They are also flavorful, which may explain their popularity.

38. See BNF Collection Delamare, ms. fr. 21657, fols. 76, 77; BNF Joly de Fleury, ms. 309, fols. 26–34.

39. BNF Collection Joly de Fleury, ms. 77, fol. 289.

40. Please refer to note 46 in Chapter 1.

41. All prices drawn from 1788 Police Ordinance, BNF, ms. fr. 6687 in Monin, *L'Etat de Paris en 1789,* 442.

42. Taken from a published ordinance of 1770 that echoes earlier declarations dated 1741, 1762, and 1764. From Monin, *L'État de Paris en 1789,* 441.

43. Jean Vidalenc, "Une industrie alimentaire à Paris au XVIIIe siècle: la préparation et la vente des tripes et abats," *Mémoires de la Federation des sociétés historiques et archaeologiques de Paris et de l'Ile-de-France,* 1 (1949): 279–95; Jeffry Kaplow, *The Names of Kings: The Parisian Laboring Poor in the Eighteenth Century* (New York, Basic Books, 1972), 53–54.

44. Letter from de Sartine to butcher guild leaders dated May 10, 1766, ANF Y 11253. See also police ordinance for the butchers of Versailles dated March 18, 1758, AD Yvelines, 5E5 "Ordonnances de Police, 1711–1785."

45. Galen spoke of the curative powers derived from the essence (*suc*) of certain meats from which one made bouillon. See *Le Livre de C. Galen traictant des viandes qui engendrent bon & mauvais suc* (Paris, 1553), translated from the Latin, "de euchymia et cacochymia."

46. L. W. B. Brockliss and Colin Jones, *The Medical World of Early Modern France* (Oxford: Clarendon Press, 1997), 249. See also M. Dinges, "L'hôpital Saint André de Bordeaux au XVIIe siècle: Objectifs et réalisations de l'assistance

municipale," *Annales du Midi* 99 (1987): 323; and for the eighteenth century, Colin Jones and Michel Sonenscher, "The Social Functions of the Hospital in Eighteenth-Century France: The Case of the Hôtel-Dieu of Nimes," in *The Charitable Imperative: Hospitals and Nursing in Ancien Régime and Revolutionary France,* ed. Colin Jones, The Wellcome Institute Series in the History of Medicine (London: Routledge, 1989), 48–86, esp. 76–78.

47. Bouillion, a restorative and the signature dish of early restaurants, became the "fad diet" for those with delicate appetites. See Rebecca Spang, *The Invention of the Restaurant: Paris and Modern Gastronomic Culture* (Cambridge, MA: Harvard University Press, 2000).

48. Archives de l'Assistance Publique, Fonds Marcel Fosseyeux, FSS 105, 2e liasse.

49. Henri Sée, *Economic and Social Conditions in France during the Eighteenth Century,* trans. Edwin H. Zeydel (New York: F. S. Crofts, 1931), 214–15.

50. The statistics for Hôtel-Dieu meat provisions are remarkably complete for this period. See AAP, Fonds de l'Hotel Dieu, liasse 879, "Etats de recette et depense (XVIIe–XVIIIe)." The number of steer averaged 280 per year; veal, 945; mutton, 5,9341/2. My calculations on meat intake are based upon food yields from an average animal weight, drawn from Armond Husson, *Les consommations de Paris,* these are 600 pounds for cattle, 70 pounds for veal, and 40 pounds for mutton.

51. Pierre Bourdieu, in his study of taste and social distinction, measures patterns of food consumption to further his theory of cultural capital contingent with economic capital. In his book, *Distinction. A Social Critique of the Judgment of Taste,* trans. Richard Nice (Cambridge: Harvard University Press, 1984), 174–75, he argues against observers who tend to see the effect of income on eating habits, whereby the proportion of income spent on food diminishes as one rises in the social hierarchy. According to Bourdieu, "this cannot account for cases in which the same income is associated with totally different consumption patterns. Thus, foremen remain attached to 'popular' taste although they earn more than clerical and commercial employees, whose taste differ radically from that of manual workers and is closer to that of teachers." This is only one example where Bourdieu maps out the relationship between classes and tastes constituted in the *habitus,* which is the capacity to differentiate and appreciate the practices and products (or tastes) that the represented social world is generated by and constituted of.

52. Marvalene H. Hughes, "Soul, Black Women, and Food," in *Food and Culture: A Reader,* eds. Carole Counihan and Penny Van Esterik (London: Routledge Press, 1997), 272–80.

CHAPTER 3

1. Letter dated April 20, 1707, ANF G7 1725, fol. 161; Letter dated April 25, 1707, ANF G7 1725, fol. 162.

2. Kristof Glamann, "The Changing Patterns of Trade," in *The Cambridge Economic History,* eds. E. E. Rich and C. H. Wilson (Cambridge, UK: Cambridge University Press, 1977) V:185–290, esp. 232–40.

3. For further discussion see Jean Jacquart, *La crise rurale en Île-de-France, 1550–1670* (Paris: A. Colin, 1974), 327–29; Jean Meuvret, ed., "La vaine pâture et progrès agronomique avant la Révolution," in *Etudes d'histoire économique* (Paris: A. Colin, 1971), 193–96. E. L. Jones, "Agricultural Origins of Industry," *Past and Present* 40 (1968): 58–71.

4. BNF Joly de Fleury, vol. 286, fol. 312.

5. Delamare, *Traité de la police,* 2:1141.

6. BNF Factum, 17937. See also François Olivier-Martin, *La police économique de l'ancien régime* (Paris, Editions Loysel, 1988), 284–87.

7. This rule was also written into the butcher guild statutes (article xxvii of 1744, article xxiv of 1782). The fine imposed upon guild butchers who purchased elsewhere was only 100 livres that went into the guild treasury. BNF Collection Joly de Fleury, vol. 1741 (Paris, 1744); F 931 (Actes royaux, 1782).

8. These arguments fill royal edicts, declarations, and regulations dating from 1529–1730, BNF Delamare ms. fr. 21653, fols. 190–200, 254–93.

9. Merchant Butcher Georges Mergery employed a "shepherd" (*berger*) for 24 livres a month. ANF MC ET/LXIX/659, May 12, 1751. According to his afterdeath inventory, Merchant Butcher Thomas Barré employed Sr. Glovian as shepherd and owed him 82 livres, "for having driven to the fields the sheep that were in Fontenay and to have them delivered and other things contained in the mémoire." ANF MC ET/LXII/423, January 13, 1751.

10. Butchers drew up notarized provisioning contracts with their major clients such as tanners and noble and religious houses. Most often these contracts serve as receipts for payment of accounts past due. Rarely do we find butchers who sign on clientele at the beginning of the season, with the exception of tanners and other leather workers. See ANF MC ET/XXXVIII/388, March 31, 1751; ET/LC/302, May 10, 1751; ET/XVI/458, June 16, 1751; ET/XX/605, September 25, 1751; Archives Departmental Seine-et-Oise, D 466, 1686–1788.

11. This appears as a recent decision included in the newly written statutes dated 1744. This article (number 31), along with several others, is noted as part of a parlementary arrêt dated February 18, 1743. BNF Collection Joly de Fleury, vol. 1741.

12. In the 1751 letter entitled "Supplique des Jurés et Syndic Bouchers au Procureur General" the guild leaders report the numbers of cattle in fifty-three fairs and cattle markets throughout eight regions compared with previous years. Their predictions for a "dissette apparente" are confirmed with another letter from the lieutenant general of police dated March 28, 1751 BNF Joly de Fleury, vol. 286, fols. 312, 330.

13. BNF Collection Joly de Fleury, vols. 104, 310, 1430; Collection Delamare, vols. 21653–54.

14. Declaration du Roy, 1539, ANF AD XI 46.

15. The impassioned mémoire written in 1629 entitled, "Le Sold Pour Livre ou Moyens de Me. Jean Laurent Fermier du Bestail à pied fourché de Paris, & c. demandeur, déffendeur & appellant. Contre la Communauté des Bouchers dudit Paris, déffendeurs, & intimez. Et les Prevost des Marchands & Eschevins d'iceluy Paris; les habitans de Poissy & les Dames dudit lieu, opposans, demandeurs, & intervenants." BNF Factum, 17937.

16. Under Louis XIII, the royal administrators had decided to set limits to Paris, only to have them trampled in vain. Under Louis XIV, a further attempt was made to establish a perimeter, broad but firm and well beyond the *enceinte.* In the outlying fields of the city, along the main roads and paths, posts, wooden fences, and milestones marked the king's determination to contain the growth of Paris within reasonable limits. Daniel Roche, *The People of Paris: An Essay in Popular Culture in the 18th Century,* trans. Marie Evans (Berkeley: University of California Press, 1987), 17–21.

17. BNF Joly de Fleury, vol. 77, fol. 296.

18. The same report submitted to the parlement's procurator general, on June 16, 1730 included statistics on the market at Poissy, claiming 1,135 oxen and 6,300 sheep arrived at market. On the same day purchases for 280 oxen and 5,000 sheep entered the city "that had never entered the market." The report pointed to 18 merchant butchers, many from large family firms, who bought cattle outside Sceaux and Poissy. Such reports are rare finds in the archives, as the seventeenth and eighteenth century records of entries and exits kept by the accountants of the Caisse de Poissy were destroyed along with all the records of the General Farm. BNF Joly de Fleury, vol. 104, fols. 198–99.

19. BNF Joly de Fleury vol. 2542, fol. 198. In my own database of all 1751 and 1761 notarial records that concern butchers in Paris, the faubourgs, and the surrounding communities, I have counted over 500 butchers of whom as few as 131 and as many as 167 live and work outside the city. The high rate of business failures points to the fragility of these provincial meatcutters. Out of 111 who appeared before the Paris courts of consular jurisdiction to seek credit protection, 50 came from towns just outside the capital. Archives de Paris, Fonds des faillites, B4D6, April 6, 1740–March 16, 1790.

20. As specified in an observation of "all the courts" (presumably the parlement, the court at the Châtelet, and the Cour des Aides) made by in reference to arrêts dated 1743 and 1756, these "country butchers" who included farmers, proprietors, workers (*laboureurs*), and nourrisseurs were under no obligation to shop at the provisioning markets. Although a March 29, 1746 arrêt specifies that butchers in the towns of Paris, Chartres, Saint Germain, Nanterre, Argenteuil, Versailles, Clamart, Chatillon, "and other areas in the Paris environs" were held to the provisioning zone. BNF Le Senne 599, fol. 23; ANF AD XI 46, "Commerce et Industrie," fol. 35.

21. Arrêts de conseil, April 1, 1704; December 27, 1707; November 29, 1710; December 1, 1711; September 27, 1735; March 26, 1746; Police Ordinance March 7, 1731. See ANF AD XI 46, "Commerce et Industrie," fol. 35.

22. ANF AD XI 46, fols. 23, 38; BNF Collection Delamare, ms. fr. 21654, fols. 87, 88; ms. fr. 21656, fols. 216, 217; See also Delamare, *Traité de la police,* II:1173.

23. Arrêt du parlement, July 13, 1699, and Sentence de Police, January 14, 1701. BNF Collection Delamare, 21653, fols. 15–16.

24. "Arrêt du Parlement qui confirme une sentence de Police du Châtelet de Paris," September 4, 1673 BNF Collection Delamare 21653, fols. 15–16. See also the large collection of printed sources in ANF AD XI 46, "Commerce et Industrie."

25. The successful containment of the cattle disease of 1745 is reported in the collection of the lieutenant general of police. BNF Collection Delamare 21653, fols. 179–88.

26. Delamare, *Traité de la police,* 2:1173.

27. See in particular the section on markets and purchasing, articles xxiii–xxxi. BNF Collection Joly de Fleury, vol. 1741 (Paris, 1744).

28. Evidenced by the *taille* of 3,000 livres he paid in taxes and his seven plows (*charrues).*

29. BNF Fonds Le Senne, fol. 599 (22).

30. "Mémoire pour Bocquet, Fermier & Boucher à Sarcelles, sa femme, sa fille & ses deux Chartiers, ci-devant détenus ès prisons des grand & petit Châtelets, d'où ils ont été élargis en vertu d'Arrêt rendu sur le vû des charges & informations respectives, le 21 Octobre 1758, Intimés & Appellans contre les Sieurs Durivault & de Chestret, Fermier & Directeur de la Caisse de Poissy, Appellans; prenant le fait & cause de leurs Commis, Accusés." BNF Fonds Le Senne, fol. 599 (22).

31. Two oxen were taken from Merchant Butcher Vilvaudé who purchased them at the market in Nangis from the Count de Guerchy on December 20, 1757; a second seizure from Butcher Blanchard on March 6, 1758; and a third seizure from Butcher Courtois on April 15, 1758. BNF Fonds Le Senne, fol. 599 (22).

32. ANF G7 1668–70, fols. 101, 102, 106, 111. See also BNF Fonds Le Senne, fol. 599 (25).

33. This conclusion is based upon the number of creditors (averaging between twenty and thirty) cited in butcher business failures and afterdeath inventories.

34. See numerous repeated arrêts and royal declarations from as early as 1642 through 1701. BNF Collection Delamare 21653, fols. 151–68.

35. Details of the internal operations of the caisse remain lost to historians. Unfortunately, almost all of the documentation generated by the employees of the credit institution no longer exists. This fact limits the perspective of my study as most of my sources (police archives, bankruptcy records, printed mémoires of the butchers and cattle merchants, and the archives of the finance minister) come from outside the organization. Nevertheless, these sources do allow me to sketch out the political, economic, and personal interests surrounding the establishment of the Caisse de Poissy: the financiers behind it, the government who supported it (and fed off it), and the police who oversaw it.

36. "Mémoire pour Jean-Baptiste Hayon, adjudicataire par Arrêt du Conseil du 27 Septembre 1735, des droits qui se percoivent sur les Bestiaux dans les Marchés de Sceaux et de Poissy." signed, Monsieur Le Controlleur Général, Me. Puy de Rony, avocat (Paris: l'Imprimerie de Claude Simon, 1735) BNF Joly de Fleury, vol. 1430, fol. 11.

37. "Mémoire pour les Syndics, Jurés en Charge & les Maîtres de la Communauté des Marchands Bouchers [. . .]" (Paris: l'Imprimerie de la Veuve Delatour, 1735), BNF Joly de Fleury, vol. 1430, fol. 12.

38. Ibid.

39. BNF Joly de Fleury, vol. 1430, fol. 11.

40. Second interrogation, November 29, 1774. Chambre de Police, ANF Y9528.

41. Judgment, March 16, 1775. Chambre de Police, ANF Y9528.

CHAPTER 4

1. ANF Y 14942, July 23, 1729.

2. Ibid.

3. According to the Châtelet archives and the Delamare manuscripts, the number of official stalls registered with the police increased from 195 in 1674 to 237 in 1701 to 368 in 1782. This collection consists of annual rolls of the owners and renters of butcher stalls beginning in 1629. See "Baux des étaux," ANF Y 9502, 9503, 9503B; see also BNF Collection Delamare, ms. fr. 21656, fol. 159. Please refer to Table 1 in the Appendix for complete data.

4. Mercier, *Tableau de Paris,* 9:181.

5. Mercier, *Tableau de Paris,* 1:124–25. Le Puy, a chronicler of the sixteenth century, called them "men of blood [who are] easily brought to violence." E. Médicis, "Le Puy," *Chroniques,* ed. A. Chassaing (Paris: n.p., 1869): 1:213, as cited in P. S. Lewis, *La France à la Fin du Moyen Age,* trans. Claude Yelnick (Paris: Hachette, 1977). For an excellent discussion of the *Encyclopédie*'s view of the worker in this trade as well as others see Cynthia Koepp, "The Alphabetical Order: Work in Diderot's *Encyclopédie,*" in *Work in France,* 229–57.

6. Françoise Salvetti, *Le boucher, métiers d'hier et d'aujourd'hui* (Paris: Berger-Lavrault, 1980), 78–81; See also Paul Sebillot, *Légendes et curiosités des métiers* (1894–95; repr., Marseille: Laffitte Reprints, 1981), 97–128.

7. *Le louchébem.* For more detail on butcher expressions and turns of phrase, see Georges Chaudieu, *Le Langage des Bouchers. dont plus particulierement le langage employé a Paris, dans les abattoirs, dans les étaux et sur les marchés des viandes et du bétail* (Paris: École professionnelle de la Boucherie de Paris, 1951).

8. *Encyclopédie méthodique,* 26:233.

9. Many histories report butchers as the most active participants, if not the leaders, of urban revolts in cities such as Paris, Metz, and Lyon throughout the fifteenth century. See René Fédou, "A Popular Revolt in Lyons in the Fifteenth Century: The Rebeyne of 1436," in *The Recovery of France in the Fifteenth Century,*

ed. P. S. Lewis (London: Macmillan, 1971), 242–64; Philippe Wolff and Michel Mollat, *The Popular Revolutions of the Late Middle Ages,* trans. A. L. Lytton-Sells (London: Allen & Unwin, 1973), 230–34, 300. Yves-Marie Bercé in his *History of Peasant Revolts,* also attests to the widespread participation of butchers in peasant revolts from the late sixteenth into the seventeenth century. Bercé, *History of Peasant Revolts* (Ithaca, NY: Cornell University Press, 1990), 48, 61, 227–28, 329. Bercé also cites other trades such as tanners, cutters, and barbers, who participated in revolts alongside butchers.

10. Mary Douglas, *Purity and Danger: An Analysis of the Concepts of Pollution and Taboo* (1966; repr., London: Routledge, 1991).

11. Some detailed examples include the inventories of Merchant Butcher Thomas Barré ANF MC ET/LXII/423, January 13, 1751; Charles Denis Tripperet MC ET/LIV/819, November 21, 1743; and Pierre Barré MC ET/XCIX/460, October 6, 1738.

12. Marie Madeleine Gallier, married to Butcher Vincent Gosse, kept busy with two daughters, four sons, and five stall workers. Her eldest daughter Marie Françoise, married to Butcher Antoine François Adam, lived with the family in their three-story house and butcher shop on the rue des Boucheries. In addition, the household depended on Genevieve as their domestic servant as well as Delanelle, the former who received yearly wages and the second weekly. Even a small household such as Butcher Robert Lauverjat and his wife Elizabeth Drieux–who without children or live-in workers–employed a live-in cook while they kept two stalls running in the Saint Germain quarter. ANF ET/IV/561, May 12, 1749; ET/XLVII/134, May 27, 1751.

13. AP D5B6, registers 636, 1664, 2555, 4744.

14. Papiers du S. Antoine Danet, boucher à Paris, 1782–1790, ANF Y 15520, liasse 3.

15. Sources most commonly identified the journeyman butcher as either a garçon boucher or an *étalier boucher.* An apprentice who worked under a master for his *brevet,* the credentials needed before being able to be hired as a journeyman, could also be referred to as garçon of a certain master. Yet, not all apprentices were known as garçon bouchers. As in the rare example of Louis Alexandre LeGrand who identified himself as both a stall butcher (étalier) and an apprentice.

16. Butcher Antoine Rebourg had his two stall workers begin working on four steer and twelve to fifteen sheep at midnight after having finished their day of work at 9:30 P.M. ANF Y 14311, June 18, 1751; Arlette Farge, *Fragile Lives. Violence, Power, and Solidarity in Eighteenth-Century Paris* (Cambridge, MA: Harvard University Press, 1993), 17.

17. One should keep in mind that wine in this period did not have the same level of alcohol as it does today as it was watered down. Archives de l'Assistance Publique (AAP) Fonds de l'Hotel-Dieu, liasse 881, March 4, 1702.

18. ANF Y 12100, June 11, 1691; Y 15220, June 15, 1713.

19. ANF Y 15248, October 10, 1741.

20. ANF Y 14539, June 19, 1744.

21. ANF Y 14518, November 20, 1721.

22. This claim is based upon research in the X series of the Châtelet records for capital crimes and personal communication with historian Arlette Farge. For a more general discussion on violence and popular culture, see Farge, *Fragile Lives. Violence, Power, and Solidarity in Eighteenth-Century Paris.*

23. Arrest de la Cour de Parlement, September 2, 1785, BNF Joly de Fleury, ms. 556, fols. 254–55.

24. See letter from Commissaire Bonin, dated July 1, 1785, BNF Collection Joly de Fleury, ms. 556, fol. 237.

25. See report from Commissaire Baudelle, July 11, 1785, BNF Collection Joly de Fleury, ms. 556, fol. 240.

26. See letter to Procurator General dated June 28, 1785, BNF Collection Joly de Fleury, ms. 556, fols. 235–36.

27. For the complete dossier on boeufs échappés see BNF Collection Joly de Fleury, ms. 556, fols. 233–55. See also Arrest de la Cour de Parlement, Septem-ber 2, 1785, BNF Joly d Fleury, ms. 556, fols. 254–55.

28. ANF Y 14531.

29. ANF Y 14523, December 14, 1737.

30. ANF Y 15180, December 29, 1751.

31. Sentence du Police. BNF Collection Delamare, ms. 21655, fols. 356–57. This 1718 police sentence originates with an arrêt of 1363 and is restated through the sixteenth and seventeenth centuries.

32. The office was entitled *Entrepreneur de la Place aux Veaux* and created in 1718 by police sentence. BNF Collection Delamare, ms. 21655, fols. 356–57. According to Parisian historian Alan Williams, the allocation of funds to pay for garbage removal more than doubled between 1718 and 1789; the number of carts collecting refuse grew from 85 to 130; Williams, *The Police of Paris,* 269.

33. Williams, *The Police of Paris,* 270–71.

34. The Ponceau fountain provided water to the twenty-one stalls at Saint-Denis. Butchers who worked in the six stalls in the Boucherie Rouge, located in the Faubourg Saint Marcel, had access to water from the nearby Bièvre tributary that fed the Seine. The earliest butcheries that predate the Grande Boucherie, appeared in proximity to the riverbank, along the edge of the city island on rue Pierre-aux-boeufs next to the Nôtre-Dame Cathedral; others emerged along the fortified walls and bridge leading from the city island north, called the butchery of the gate at Grand-Pont or Porte de Paris.

35. The police archives of Châtelet contain several dozen proposals along with their opinion (*avis*) on whether or not to grant the new butcheries and stalls throughout Paris from 1755 to 1789. See "Avis du lieutenant general de police et du procureur du Roy au sujet des étabissements intéressants a la sureté et la salubrité de Paris," and "Avis sur l'éstablissment des étaux de boucherie," ANF Y9500. As Jean Michel Roy has shown, the government established a large number of these food markets in the periods 1630–1660 and 1750–1780 as "a public service." Roy, "Les marchés alimentaires parisiens du XIVe au XVIIIe siècle, textes et documents," *Mémoires de Paris et l'Ile-de-France* 44 (1992): 77–132.

36. Table 2 of the Appendix lists thirty-two butcheries, the dates of establishment, the number of stalls, and the locations.

37. The ubiquitous term "butchery" (*boucherie*), however, did not necessarily mean several stalls housed in a single building. Many, such as those on the rue Saint-Martin or the rue des Boucheries, consisted of a conglomeration of several free-standing stalls in a tight row along a busy street. Throughout this chapter, I have termed these meat markets along urban streets as "open markets."

38. Delamare's police treatise attests to this rationale: "In order to avoid these disadvantages that would occur we established other markets in the most convenient locations for the city." Delamare, *Traité de la police,* 4:327.

39. Two new meat markets that appear in the eighteenth century are the Marché d'Aguesseau with first six then later eight stalls, and the "new market" of Saint-Martin with first six then sixteen stalls. See Table 2 of the Appendix.

40. BNF ms. fr. 8110, fols. 415–16.

41. ANF Y 9500, February 22, 1788.

42. ANF Y 9500, December 20, 1776.

43. ANF Y 9500.

44. ANF Y 9500.

45. ANF Y 9502, 9503, 9503B.

46. ANF Y 15227, March 30, 1720; Y 15228, March 27, April 8, and November 3, 1721.

47. Arrêt de Conseil, April 1, 1704. Collection Delamare, ms. fr. 21653, fols. 32–33.

48. The problem of unincorporated meat sellers is a chronic one that appears in the public records along with discussions of the butchers' incorporation put forth by the parlement on May 4, 1540, BNF Joly de Fleury, ms. 1430, fol. 61. Royal legislation against these illegal merchants dates to 1675 with a parlementary arrêt against merchants on the rue l'Oursine in Faubourg Saint-Marcel who are fined 500 livres, BNF Collection Delamare, ms. fr. 1257, fols. 97–100. The attempt to extirpate individual meat sellers from Les Halles dates to as early as 1667 with a police sentence that puts six women in prison, BNF Collection Delamare, ms. fr. 21657, fols. 91–92. The legislation against the resale of meat also appears in the butcher statutes of 1744, article IX, BNF Joly de Fleury, ms. 1741.

49. According to Jacques Savary des Bruslons, the butcher guild never exceeded 240 master members, *Dictionnaire universel de commerce,* 6th ed. (Paris: La veuve Estienne, 1750). Other dictionaries give the same population livre: Alfred Franklin and Émile Levasseur, *Dictionnaire historique des arts, métiers et professions exercices dans Paris depuis le treizième siècle* (Paris: H. Welter, 1906); M. Pary, *Guide des corps des marchands et communautés des arts et métiers* (Paris: Chez la Veuve Duchesne, 1766), 267–70; Macquer, d'apres Barbier. *Dictionnaire portatif des arts et métiers* (Paris: Chez Lacombe, 1766), I:146.

50. According to the butcher guild statutes published in 1744, articles XV and XLI, BNF Joly de Fleury, ms. 1741.

51. A letter of remonstrance written by the butcher guild in the late 1760s claims a total of 307 Parisian butchers plus an additional 300 forain butchers. See BNF Collection Joly de Fleury, ms. 2542, fol. 198. In my own research of all notarial records for 1751 and 1761. I have counted over 500 butchers in Paris, the faubourgs, and the surrounding communities.

52. Royal legislation clearly outlawed such practices, yet arrests only occurred in cases where large quantities of meat were discovered. See parlementary arrêt against merchants on the rue l'Oursine in Faubourg Saint-Marcel who were fined 500 livres, BNF Collection Delamare ms. fr. 1257, fols. 97–100; and police sentence that puts six women in prison in 1667, BNF Collection Delamare, ms. fr. 21657, fols. 91–92.

53. A spate of these seizures took place in the winter of 1722–23 under Commissaire Blanchard, ANF Y 14519, November 22, 1722; Y 14519A, November 29, 1722; Y 14519B, December 1, 1722; Y 14519C, December 5, 1722; 14520, January 2, 1723.

54. Y 14519A, November 29, 1722.

55. Y 14519B, December 1, 1722.

56. Steven Kaplan, "Les Corporations, les 'faux ouvriers' et le faubourg Saint-Antoine au XVIIIe siècle," *Annales: Economies, Sociétés, Civilisations* 43:2 (Mars–Avril 1988): 353–78.

57. Some of the seizures located in the Châtelet archives, ANF Y 14519, November 29, December 1 and 5, 1722; Y 15235, January 20, 1729; Y 15236, February 14, 1729; Y 11932, February 26, 1750.

58. See September 1739 Police Sentence, ANF AD I 27 B; B. Lizet, *Le Cheval dans la vie quotidienne. Techniques et representations du cheval de travail dans l'Europe industrielle* (Paris: Berger-Levrault, 1982).

59. Bibliothèque de l'Arsenal, Archives de la Bastille (AB), ms. 10999, fols. 220–28.

60. Mercier, *Tableau de Paris,* 72–73.

61. Mercier, *Tableau de Paris,* 1:6–7.

62. According to Alan Williams, police procedures to repair or demolish hazardous buildings remained "ambiguous and complex," *The Police of Paris,* 245. A recent study provides a more thorough understanding of the institutional parameters of city planning. Fayçal El Ghoul gives evidence of how the police carried this out through on-site visits and the imposition of *procès-verbaux.* His examples are limited to buildings in imminent danger of collapse. Fayçal El Ghoul, *La Police parisienne dans la seconde moitié du XVIIIe siècle (1760–1785),* 2 vols. (Tunis: Université de Tunis, 1995), 1:266–68.

63. Parlementary legislation dates back to 1567 and continues throughout the following two centuries. See BNF Collection Delamare, ms. fr. 21655, "Viande: Volume III" on the published legal history of the slaughterhouse, esp. fols. 246–364. For a summary of the arrêts, see "Extraits des Arrets" ms. fr. 21655, fols. 268–69. See also the 1689–91 initiatives of the city office responsible for trade along the rivers, the Prévôt des marchands et échevins, BNF Collection Delamare, ms. fr. 21655, fol. 312–13.

64. BNF Collection Delamare, ms. fr. 21655, fols. 281–82.

65. BNF Collection Delamare, ms. fr. 21655, fols. 329–35.

66. See butcher guild mémoires that respond to each effort, BNF Collection Delamare, ms. fr. 21655, fols. 283–86, 315; BNF Factum, Fm-24962.

67. Delamare, *Traité de la police,* 2:1274.

68. On February 9, 1810, the Emperor Napoleon established five central slaughterhouses throughout the city known as the abattoirs du Roule, de Montmartre (also known as Rochechouart), de Popincourt (or Ménilmontant), Grenelle (or Invalides), and Villejuif (or Deux-Moulins). Eugène D'Auriac, *Essai historique sur la boucherie de Paris,* 111. The central slaughterhouse and railway at La Villette opened in 1867. J.-A. Dulaure, *Histoire physique, civile et morale de Paris depuis les premiers temps historiques jusqu'à nos jours,* 2nd ed. (Paris: Guillaume, 1824), 9:162; Maurice Agulhon, "Le sang des bêtes. Le problème de la protection des animaux en France au XIXème siècle," *Romanticisme* 31 (1981): 81–109.

CHAPTER 5

1. The event, described by Boucher d'Argis, appears in the first volume of *Variétés historiques, physiques et littéraires* (1752). According to his account, the ceremony took place in most of the major cities of the kingdom where they named it the *Boeuf villé,* after its urban setting. In Paris, the boeuf gras festival began and ended at the l'Apport-Paris butchery where guild butchers sacrificed the prize steer for the public. Napoleon reinstated the ceremony on February 23, 1805, apparently with great success, as the parade was adopted by the city police who oversaw it on a yearly basis. The tradition continued to be performed at the slaughterhouses of La Villette until 1952, when it was prohibited by law under the pretext of a traffic violation. Eugène d'Auriac, *Essai historique sur la boucherie de Paris,* 46–53.

2. As Victor Turner defines such rituals of status reversal: "if liminality is regarded as a time and place of withdrawal from normal modes of social action, it can be seen as potentially a period of scrutinization of the central values and axioms of the culture in which it occurs." *The Ritual Process* (Chicago: Aldine Publishing Co., 1969), 167.

3. Legal theorists and their exponents promoted the corporate system as deeply rooted in nature. As the magistrates of parlement intoned, "from the first [corporations] of all, which are empires, to the last, which are families." Remonstrances, March 2–4, 1776, in Flammermont, *Remontrances du Parlement de Paris,* 3:309, 321. For further discussion see Steven Laurence Kaplan, "Social Classification and Representation in the Corporate World of Eighteenth century France: Turgot's 'Carnival,'" in *Work in France,* 176–228.

4. René de Lespinasse, *Les métiers et corporations de la ville de Paris* (Paris: Imprimérie Nationale, 1886), 1:260–61. Delamare refers to the history of the guild "as old as the monarchy itself." *Traité de la police,* 2:1202.

5. The butchers marched alongside these most privileged guilds perhaps in appreciation for their support of the English-sided Burgundians during the period of civil unrest from 1410 to 1420. The Six Corps in the eighteenth century consisted of drapers, grocers, haberdashers, furriers, hosiers, and goldsmiths. Alfred Franklin, *Dictionnaire historique des arts, métiers et professions,* 645; Alfred Fierro, *Histoire et dictionnaire de Paris* (Paris: Editions Robert Laffont, 1996), 1154; *Journal d'un bourgeois de Paris,* ed. Tuetey, 276.

6. The second category was labeled as "the trades between the best and the mediocre." Among those listed in the butcher category are barbers, hatters, freshwater fishmongers, silk dyers, drapers, coppersmiths, and furriers. The fourth and fifth categories were considered "petits métiers" many of which were not sworn trades and therefore were outside the corporate structure. *Liste generale & roolles de tous les arts & mestiers qui sont en jurande & qui s'exercent tant en la ville & faux-bourgs de Paris, qu'es autres villes, fauxbourgs, bourgs, bourgades de ce Royaume. Distinguez en cinq rangs, selon la bonté & valleur d'iceux.* [BHVP, N.F. 35380, n.d., sixteenth century].

7. *Encyclopédie méthodique,* 26:229.

8. In March 1211, an agreement between the Montmartre abbey sisters (then owners) and the butchers of the Grande Boucherie confirmed the leases of twenty-five stalls at 50 livres a year in perpetuity. By May 1233, the butchers succeeded in obtaining the butcher hall of the Grand-Pont and the place Philippe Hermian from the powerful chevalier, Adam Harenc. Later in 1260, twenty butchers of the community signed a contract giving them "as much in their name as in the name of the community," a hall or group of houses in the "Parisian Butchery" with the stalls that they contained. BNF ms. fr. 11192, fol. 1; ANF L 1030, No. 9; S 4448, No. 18; Delamare, *Traité de la police,* 2:1207; Héron de Villefosse, "La Grande Boucherie de Paris," 45.

9. Alfred Fierro, *Histoire et dictionnaire de Paris,* 721.

10. Lespinasse, *Les métiers et corporations de la ville de Paris,* 1:260.

11. Alfred Coville, *Les Cabochiens et l'ordonnance de 1413* (Paris: Hachette, 1888); Philippe Wolff and Michel Mollat, *The Popular Revolutions of the Late Middle Ages,* trans. A. L. Lytton-Sells (London: Allen & Unwin, 1973); Ferdinand Seibt, "Cabochiens, Lollarden, Hussiten. Zur sogennaten Krise des Spätmittelalters im europäischen Vergleich," *Francia* 12 (1984): 209–21.

12. Lespinasse, *Les métiers et corporations de la ville de Paris,* 1:260.

13. See Durbec, "La Grande Boucherie de Paris, Notes historiques d'après des archives privées (XIIe–XVIIe siècle)." *Bulletin philologique et historique du Comité des Trauvaux historiques et scientifiques* (Paris: Imprimerie Nationale, 1957), 69–71.

14. See ANF Y 9502–04; Delamare, *Traité de la police,* 2:1214.

15. Lespinasse, *Les métiers et corporations de la ville de Paris,* 1:287–88.

16. See Durbec, "La Grande Boucherie de Paris," 81–86.

17. In the Paris Parlement records of 1706, the names of certain members of the Grande Boucherie appear along with other royal titles. See André Gravereau, *Histoire de la Caisse de Poissy* (Paris: Imprimerie Henri Maillet, 1953), 30.

18. Delamare, *Traité de la police,* 2:1217–18. Delamare cites four arrêts between 1465 and 1521 regarding butcher abuses at the Grande Boucherie.

19. One called the Beauvais butchery, located on rue Saint Honoré, was named after the provisioning center north of Paris. The second butchery located at the Petit Pont going from the city island to the left bank on rue de Bûcherie was also known as la Gloriette. The third butchery was named after the Saint Jean cemetery and was built as a covered market off the place de la Grève. Finally, on the right bank not far from where the Grande Boucherie stood was the Saint-Gervais butchery.

20. Delamare, *Traité de la police,* 2:1222.

21. The legal document also provides seigniorial privileges for the four families that include exemption from all taxation, immunity from fines, police regulations, and the right to rent their stalls to any person so long as he is a master butcher. Lespinasse, *Les métiers et corporations de la ville de Paris,* 1:287–88.

22. Two valuable documents provide significant details as to the social hierarchies of guild members. One lists the names of 230 master members according to the date of their induction into the guild. The list, however, does not make clear who the active guild members are. *Liste des maistres et marchands bouchers de Paris suivant l'ordre de leur reception* (Paris: Chez Louis Denis Delatour & Pierre Simon, 1724). The second, dated March 1747, gives the names of 187 guild members present for the election of guild officers. *Liste des maistres et mds bouchers de Paris pour l'election d'un sindic et de trois jurés elu le Mardy 14 Mars 1747.* ANF Y 9502.

23. See Chapter 6 for a discussion of guild reception of new masters.

24. ANF MC ET/CVIII/336, March 31, 1719.

25. Gail Bossenga, *The Politics of Privilege: Old Regime and Revolution in Lille* (Cambridge: Cambridge University Press, 1991).

26. ANF Y 9323–32, March 20, 1708–March 28, 1775.

27. The shortest time span as a master before taking office was four years, the longest thirty-two years. For the eight syndics, the average number of years as master before taking charge was twenty-five years, the mean twenty-six. ANF Y 9323–32, March 20, 1708–March 28, 1775.

28. Examples include Christophe Frère (elected syndic in 1708), Nicolas Berjonneau (syndic 1737–1743), Pierre Louis Vollée (syndic 1745–1749), and Vincent LeLievre (syndic 1749–1759). Louis Thibert, a member of the Grande Boucherie dynasty, received his mastership on May 7, 1717 and was elected as juré of the Porte de Paris district twenty years later. By 1743, he rose to the office of syndic. ANF Y 9326, March 30, 1745. For a full list of the guild officer elections, see Table 3 in the Appendix.

29. Articles II, III, and IV of the 1741 statutes clearly spell out the jurisdiction of butchers with their clientele. See BNF Collection Joly de Fleury, ms. 1741.

30. The battle over free negotiation ensued on both sides throughout the eighteenth century. See numerous *sentences* and arrêts in the BNF Collection Delamare 21657, fols. 114–81.

31. BNF Factum, Folio Fm 12368, 1–2.

32. Earlier royal declarations (1704, 1710) give the guild jurés the right to levy 10 sous a week on their stalls. See BNF Delamare, ms. fr. 21656, fols. 211–13. BNF Factum Folio Fm 12368, 12369.

33. BNF Joly de Fleury, ms. 104, fols. 201–10, 220–23.

34. ANF AB XIX 655 bis, fol. 10, "Arrêt du Conseil d'Etat du Roi portant réglement pour l'administration des deniers communs de la Communauté des Maitres & marchands Bouchers et pour la reddition des comptes de jurande" (Paris, 1749).

35. Their choice of Saint-Sacrement can be explained by the presence of the steer and lamb in the manger scene, bestowing a certain sacred quality to these farm animals most familiar to the butcher trade.

36. ANF MC ET/XLIV/429, October 12, 1758; ET/LIII/373, June 15, 1761.

37. This is taken from the accounts of the guild from 1689 to 1718 published by demand of the guild members who have accused the jurés of fraud. See BNF Factum, "Au Roy et a Nosseigneurs les Commissaires Généraux, deputez par Arrests du Conseil, pour examnier, revoir & juger les Comptes, Affaires & Dettes des Communautes de la Ville de Paris" (Paris: De l'Imprimerie de Jean Francois Knapen, 1716).

38. Jacques Ménétra, *Journal of My Life,* ed. Daniel Roche, trans. Arthur Goldhammer (New York: Columbia University Press, 1986), 297.

39. The cost of a butcher apprenticeship far exceeded that of other guilds which averaged only 40.8 livres. Similarly, most guilds accepted apprenticed masters at 20 years, much younger than the butcher guild. See Pary, *Guide des Corps des Marchands,* 17–18. See also Alfred Franklin, *Dictionnaire historique des arts, métiers et professions;* Pierre Thomas Nicolas Hurtaut, *Dictionnaire historique de la ville de Paris et ses environs* (Paris: Moutard, 1779), 1:653; Macquer, d'apres Barbier. *Dictionnaire portatif des arts et métiers* (Paris: Chez Lacombe, 1766), I:146; Steven Kaplan, "L'Apprentissage au XVIIIe siècle: Le cas de Paris," *Revue d'histoire moderne et contemporaine* 40:3 (July–September 1993): 436–79.

40. Diderot et al., *Encyclopédie,* 9:911; Simon Clicquot de Blervache, *Considérations sur le commerce* (Amsterdam: n.p., 1758), 18; Clicquot de Blervache, *Mémoire sur les corps de métier* (Le Haye: n.p., 1758), 13–23; M. J. Auffair, "Le Commerce abandonné à lui-même, ou Suppression des compagnies, sociétés et maîtrises," *Journal de commerce* (March 1761): 120–24.

41. Jules Flammeront, ed., *Remonstrances du parlement de Paris au XVIIIe siècle,* 3 vols. (Paris, 1888–98), 3:279, as cited in Cynthia Truant, *The Rites of Labor: Brotherhoods of Compagnonnage in Old and New Regime France* (Ithaca, NY: Cornell University Press, 1994), 118–19.

42. Truant, *Rites of Labor,* 119; Edgar Faure, *La disgrace de Turgot, 12 mai 1776* (Paris: Gallimard, 1961).

43. "Observations sur l'edit concernant la suppression des jurandes par les jurés, anciens bacheliers maitre queulx, cuisiniers, porte-chapes, & traiteurs de la ville & fauxbourgs, banlieue, prévôté & vicomté de Paris" (Paris: Imprimérie de Jorry, 1776).

44. *Mémoire à consulter pour les proprietaires, fermiers, nourrisseurs, & marchands de bétails de la province de Limousin contre la Caisse de Poissy* (Grenoble: n.p., 1770), 216–17, also reprinted in the *Ephémérides du Citoyen,* vols. 9 and 10 (Paris: Lacombe, 1770).

45. Published as *Lettres patentes du Roy* (June 1782) BNF Reserve F 931.

CHAPTER 6

1. ANF Y 14311, June 18, 1751.
2. ANF Y 14311, June 18, 1751.
3. ANF Y 14311, June 18, 1751.
4. ANF MC XXVII/259, July 28, 1751.
5. 1744 Statutes, Article XLVIII. François Isambert, *Recueil général des anciennes lois françaises depuis année 420 jusqu'à la Révolution* (Paris: Berlin-Le-Prieur, 1821–33), 25:139–41.
6. This figure is based upon the number of stalls registered at the Châtelet with two to three workers per stall. It does not include the many nonguild butchers as well as the country butchers or forain butchers who lived and practiced their trade just outside the city gates and in the small villages surrounding the capital. Contemporaries estimated this butcher population outside the guild to number anywhere from one hundred to two hundred. Jacques Savary des Bruslons, *Dictionnaire universel du commerce.*
7. BNF Collection Joly de Fleury ms. 1430, fol. 98.
8. Clare Crowston, *Fabricating Women: The Seamstresses of Old Regime France, 1675–1791* (Durham: Duke University Press, 2001); Steven Laurence Kaplan, *La fin des corporations* (Paris: Fayard, 2001); Michael Sonenscher, *Work and Wages: Natural Law, Politics, and the Eighteenth-Century Parisian Trades* (Cambridge: Cambridge University Press, 1989).
9. The butcher's price of mastership was only exceeded by two guilds of the prestigious Six Corps: the drapers and the grocers (*épiciers*). See Pary, *Guide des Corps des Marchands,* 17–18, 236, 267, 368, 373. See also "Corporations des Métiers de Paris–Bouchers." BNF Collection Joly de Fleury, ms. 1733, fol. 16.
10. Article XLIII, *Statuts et reglemens de la communauté des maitres & marchands bouchers de la ville & fauxbourgs de Paris.* Paris: Chez la Veuve Delatour, 1744. BNF Collection Joly de Fleury, ms. 1741.
11. "Corporations des Métiers de Paris–Bouchers." BNF Collection Joly de Fleury, vol. 1733, fol. 16.
12. ANF MC ET/LXVI/532, March 4, 1761. The price of mastership is noted in Philippe Macquer's *Dictionnaire portatif des arts et métiers, contenant en abrégé l'histoire, la description & la police des arts et métiers des fabriques et manufactures de France & des pays étrangers* (Yverdon, n.p., 1766–67), 1:208–9.
13. The statutes of 1782 would later stipulate three years' work in the profession for sons of butchers as well as for apprentices beginning at age fifteen. Articles XLVII and XLVIII, *Lettres patentes du roi servant de statuts & reglemens de la*

communauté des maîtres & marchands bouchers de la ville & fauxbourgs de Paris (Paris: P. G. Simon & N. H. Nyon, 1782). BNF Collection Joly de Fleury, ms. 550, fol. 46 and BNF Reserve, F 931.

14. Pary, *Guide des corps des marchands,* 18; Steven Kaplan, "L'Apprentissage au XVIIIe siècle: Le cas de Paris," *Revue d'histoire moderne et contemporaine* 40:3 (July–September 1993): 436–79.

15. ANF MC LXII 423, March 30, 1751.

16. Unfortunately, there are few surviving apprenticeship contracts before the dissolution of the guild in 1791. We do know the number of apprentices who entered the guild as masters from the records of the procurator at the Châtelet (see Exhibit 3 in the Appendix); however, masters were no longer required to register apprenticeship contracts during the eighteenth century. Other gaps in our knowledge remain. For example, it is impossible to know how many apprentices who, with their apprenticeship brevets, either failed to or chose not to attain letters of mastership.

17. Article XXXIX of the 1744 statutes and article XLVIII of the 1782 statutes both require the brevet to be registered with the guild. *Lettres patentes du Roi servant de statuts & reglemens de la communauté des maîtres & marchands bouchers de la ville & fauxbourgs de Paris;* BNF Collection Joly de Fleury, ms. 550, fol. 46 and BNF Reserve, F 931; Kaplan, "L'Apprentissage," 458.

18. Lespinasse, *Les Métiers et corporations de la Ville de Paris,* I:260–62; *Dictionnaire portatif des arts et métiers, contenant en abrégé l'histoire, la description & la police des arts et métiers des fabriques et manufactures de France & des pays étrangers,* 1:208–9.

19. This amount was fixed by Arrêt du Conseil on June 16, 1745. See BNF Collection Joly de Fleury, ms. 1733, "Corporations des Métiers de Paris" fol. 16, "Bouchers." In the royal review of the guild's accounts careful attention was made to ensure that all amounts collected by the guild officers for the reception of apprentices and masters be noted in their books, as spelled out in the May 22, 1749 Arrêt de Conseil, articles V and VI. See transcript in ANF V7, 423 and in printed form in AB XIX, 655 bis, fol. 10.

20. Nowhere in the contract does it state Louis Laurent Poupet's position as an apprentice. Rather Master Butcher Pierre Blondel agrees to take the boy on informally "en pension chez moi pour apprendre mon métier de Boucherie." ANF Y 13020.

21. Kaplan's study of Parisian apprenticeship contracts posits two-thirds of the candidates as Parisians, although their origins could well be rural. Nevertheless, within the food guilds, a great number of apprentices appear with agricultural backgrounds. Among the thirty-five apprenticeship contracts for Kaplan's Parisian bakers, at least ten and as many as twenty apprentices' fathers exercised a profession within the rural milieu. Kaplan, "L'Apprentissage," 453; Kaplan, *The Bakers of Paris,* 198. In a study of Dijon, Edward J. Shephard, Jr. has shown that many of the masters who entered guilds in the eighteenth century were from agricultural backgrounds. Of over 5,000 letters of mastership recorded, over half were born outside of Dijon, and 637 of these new masters identified

their fathers as ploughmen (laboureurs). Shephard, "Social and Geographic Mobility of the Guild Artisan," in *Work in France,* 118–19, 124.

22. ANF MC LXII 426, December 31, 1751; Y 9330.

23. Alfred Franklin, *La vie privée d'autrefois,* 93.

24. Jean Dubois, René Lagane, and Alain Lerond, *Dictionnaire du français classique* (Paris: Larousse, 1992), 253.

25. ANF Y 15220, June 15, 1713; Y 14518, November 20, 1721; Y 14519, April 22 and November 22, 1722; Y 14522, October 23, 1725; Y 14525, December 23, 1729; Y 11935, August 28, 1753; Y 11936, May 7, 1754.

26. ANF MC, ET/CX/376, March 12, 1751; ET/XLVII/134, May 27, 1751; ET/CVIII/454, November 9, 1742; ET/LXII/423, January 13, 1751; ET/XCI/924, October 14, 1755; ET/LXII/424, May 5, 1751; ET/CX/348; December 18, 1738; ET/CX/3761, March 23, 1751; ET/LXII/362, February 24, 1736; ET/XXVII/301, March 9, 1761; ET/XCVIII/513, March 17, 1751.

27. ANF Y 14527, November 28, 1731.

28. ANF MC ET/LXIV/373, December 3, 1761.

29. ANF Y 11936, May 7, 1754.

30. BNF Collection Joly de Fleury ms. 254, fol. 120–27, "Commutation de peine et extrait des charges resultantes de la procedure extraordinaire instruite par le Lt. Criminel du Châtelet à la requête du Procureur du Roi," September 1747.

31. The average amount of total wealth among the four garçons inventoried after their deaths was 191 livres. None of the men in these documents had children or any heirs making claims to the estate apart from the spouse. See probate records of garçons bouchers: ANF MC ET/LXIV/373, December 3, 1761; ET/VI/744, March 3, 1761; ET/XXVIII/376, December 22, 1761; ET/XCVIII/622, July 31, 1777.

32. ANF MC ET/VI/744, March 3, 1761.

33. ANF MC ET/LXXXII/396, June 25, 1761.

34. ANF MC ET/IV/635, July 28, 1761.

35. ANF MC ET/IX/561, May 12, 1749.

36. Kaplan, *The Bakers of Paris,* 236.

37. Benoit Garnot, *La maison, la table et l'habit* (Chartres: CDDP, 1989), 79. For further discussion of the cost of living under the Old Regime see *Historia* 36 (July–August, 1995): 46–47.

38. The average fortune of the afterdeath inventories of eleven étaliers inventoried is 850 livres. ANF MC ET/V/422, December 14, 1745; ET/XXIX/489, November 18, 1751; ET/XXVIII/371, December 23, 1760; ET/XC/405, January 27, 1761; ET/XXIV/773, February 4, 1761; ET/LXXXII/396, June 25, 1761; ET/XXXI/171, July 18, 1761; ET/IV/635, July 28, 1761; ET/XXXV/709, August 6, 1761; ET/LXXVII/280, November 4, 1761; ET/LVII/448, December 11, 1761.

39. ANF MC ET/IV/635, July 28, 1761.

40. ANF MC ET/LXXVII/280, November 4, 1761.

41. Daniel Roche speaks of the "chronic shortage of labor in the provinces." Roche, "Work, Fellowship, and Some Economic Realities," in *Work in France,* 60.

Historians who have studied the movement of journeymen and hiring practices in the provinces include Cynthia Truant, *The Rites of Labor,* 109–47; Michael Sonenscher, "Journeymen's Migrations and Workshop Organization in Eighteenth-Century France," in *Work in France,* 74–96.

42. This may be explained by the large number of children (ten to fifteen) in their households. Maurice Garden, *Lyon et les Lyonnais au XVIIIe siècle* (Paris: Société d'edition les belles-lettres, 1970), 324.

43. According to Jean-Claude Perrot's study of population figures, the most inclusive of which measure the growth in the number of marriages for this period. *Genèse d'une ville moderne: Caen au XVIIIe siècle* (Paris: Mouton, 1975), II:712. For a history of Caennais butchers see A. Gallier, *Histoire de la boucherie caennaise sous l'ancien régime* (Caen: Imprimerie Charles Valin, 1902), 155–56.

44. The three major sects of compagnonnage (Rite de Maître Jacques, Enfants du Père Soubise, and Enfants de Salomon) included lists with over thirty-two member trades and their dates of recognition (*reconnaissance*). Nowhere do these sources–nor in my research of the secondary literature written on the early practice of compagnonnages–make mention of butchers as participants.

45. BNF Collection Joly de Fleury ms. 1430, fol. 98. Sentence de Police, June 2, 1690.

46. BNF Collection Joly de Fleury ms. 1430, fol. 98. Sentence de Police, January 28, 1653.

47. In the years of active recruitment (1743, 1746, and 1772), the number of masterships jumped from twenty-five to thirty a year, sons of masters being the most numerous initiates. The years of retrenchment (1740 and 1748) show only sons of masters receiving their letters of mastership. In other years, the number of apprentices dropped when sons of butchers rose. The source for rates of mastership is contained in the *Chambre de Procureur du Roi,* the judicial branch of the king's courts at the Châtelet, ANF Y series. (Exhibit 3 of the Appendix shows the total number of recorded masterships from 1736 to 1777.)

48. 1744 Statutes, Article XLI, BNF Collection Joly de Fleury, ms. 1741.

49. Steven Kaplan's study of apprenticeship contracts puts the average cost of apprenticeship contracts for ninety-four guilds at 40.8 livres (well below the cost for butchers). The amounts varied enormously. The only guilds to surpass the butchers formed part of the illustrious Six Corps, for example the drapers (300 livres). Kaplan, "L'Apprentissage," 436–79.

50. Among the twenty-three letters of mastership awarded through these hospitals only two had completed a formal apprenticeship.

51. The estimated Jewish population of Paris during the eighteenth century was small: 500–700 persons. They were authorized to travel but forbidden to settle. Like other French Jews, they gained their citizenship along with Protestants during the French Revolution. See Jean Favier, *Paris: Deux mille ans d'histoire* (Paris: Fayard, 1997), 60. The importance of kosher butchers became more apparent in the nineteenth century with the growth of the Parisian Jewish population.

52. Article XLV, *Statuts et reglemens de la communauté des maitres & marchands bouchers de la ville & fauxbourgs de Paris*. Paris: chez la Veuve Delatour, 1744. BNF Collection Joly de Fleury, ms. 1741.

53. ANF Y 9377, January 18, 1729; 1762 Mémoire, BNF Collection Joly de Fleury, vol. 396, dos. 4541, fol. 169.

54. ANF Y 15230, September 6, 1723.

55. The police inspector writing his report to the lieutenant general at the Châtelet describes the actions of the garçons as speculators: "On voyoit aujour-d'huy une petite quantité de suif, que les garçons bouchers n'en tendoient pas le vendre aux termes de la soummission mais au contraire que la pluspart d'Entr'eux demandoient trois livres de la mesure que ceux qui laissoient le suif au meilleur marché le vendoient cinquante huit sols la mesure." ANF Y 11972, October 19, 1780.

56. ANF Y 11972, October 19, 1780; Y 14957, September 7, 1741; Y 11962.

CHAPTER 7

1. Vollée was the second son of Adrien Vollée, who died in 1707, a fairly successful merchant butcher with seven children–all affiliated with the butcher trade. Pierre Louis and his four brothers were merchant butchers in their own right. His two sisters were also married to guild butchers. Adrien Vollée's success is measured in terms of his long-established social standing. The Vollée family maintained the same residence off the Vieille Place des Veaux for at least four generations. His finances assessed at his death, however, provide a different measure of his business. According to the notarial record the senior Vollée's assets totaled over 10,000 livres, his liabilities stood at 3,800 livres. This net worth falls well below the mean of 29,530 livres (see Table 4 in Appendix). ANF MC ET/IV/336, March 14, 1707.

2. Already, his three sons worked in the trade as merchant butchers. The eldest, Christophe, made a fortunate alliance with Marie Anne Barré, daughter of one of the most prominent butcher families in Paris.

3. ANF MC ET/LXII/398, February 4, 1745.

4. ANF Y 14518, March 10, 1721.

5. Roderick Phillips's study of Rouen (population 85,000) cites evidence of only thirty-three petitions between 1780 and 1789, and only four appear to have succeeded. The comparative popularity of divorces after 1792, when divorce laws were written into the Civil Code, suggests that the rarity of separations reflected their failure to respond to the needs of women in particular. Roderick Phillips, *Untying the Knot. A Short History of Divorce* (Cambridge: Cambridge University Press, 1991), 54–55. Julie Hardwick speaks of the rarity of financial separations. She contends that "turning to a court for the resolution of household difficulties was an exceptional measure. The families whose personal affairs were laid out before the court were inevitably in crisis, and lawyers as well as plaintiffs and witnesses had roles to play in producing the narratives that emerge." See her article,

"Seeking Separations: Gender, Marriages, and Household Economies in Early Modern France," *French Historical Studies* 21:1 (Winter 1998): 157–80.

6. This argument is made by Sara Hanley in "Family and State in Early Modern France," *Connecting Spheres: Women in the Western World, 1500 to the Present,* ed. Marilyn J. Boxer and Jean H. Quataert (New York: Oxford University Press, 1987). See also Stephen Ozment, *When Fathers Ruled: Family Life in Reformation Europe* (Cambridge, MA: Harvard University Press, 1983).

7. ANF ET/XCIX/460, October 6, 1738.

8. Yoram Ben Porath, "The F-Connection: Families, Friends, and Firms and the Organization of Exchange," *Population and Development Review* 6:1 (March 1980): 1–30.

9. For Merchant Butcher Thomas Barré this amounted to 54 livres for School Master Montalon who boarded his two sons, another 150 livres for two other children, and 62 livres for the eldest daughter from his third marriage. Jean François Lardenois, also a guild butcher, included 150 livres a year as the cost for the care of his five children. By the time of his death, Nicolas Séjourné had amassed debts for his five children's education that amounted to 2,584 livres. AP D4B6, dos. 3679, August 30, 1776; ANF ET/LXII/423, January 13, 1751; ANF ET/XVIII/839, April 27, 1784.

10. AP D5B6, register 2728.

11. Archives de la Bastille, ms. 10321, May 13, 1727.

12. See Statute LIX in the 1744 publication of butcher guild statutes. BNF Joly de Fleury, ms. 1741. For further discussion of guild widows, see Janine M. Lanza, "Les veuves d'artisans dans le Paris du XVIIIe siècle," in *Veufs, veuves et veuvage dans la France d'ancien régime,* eds. Nicole Pellegrin and Colette H. Winn. (Paris: Éditions Champion, 2003).

13. These women came from well-established shops with wide commercial networks and credit obligations. ANF Y 9502, 9503, 9503B.

14. James Farr contends that at least 10 percent of the bakeries and butchers' shops were run by mistress widows in Nantes between 1620 and 1650, and nearly 20 percent of the bakeries in York between 1581 and 1600. James Farr, *Artisans in Europe, 1300–1914* (Cambridge: Cambridge University Press, 2000), 113.

15. ANF MC ET/LXXVI/242, August 6, 1728.

16. ANF MC ET/XCI/986, July 7, 1761.

17. The Paris seamstresses established an all-female guild in 1675. They made clothing exclusively for women and children under the age of eight, distinguishing themselves from the male tailors' guild. See Clare Crowston, *Fabricating Women.* The linen drapers, with statutes dating from the fifteenth century, were one of the oldest women's guilds in Paris and numbered about 800 mistresses who employed about 1,200 lingères. Farr, *Artisans in Europe, 1300–1914,* 112. See also Margaret Wensky, "Women's guilds in Cologne in the later Middle Ages," *The Journal of European Economic History* 11:3 (1982): 631–50.

18. Clare Crowston, "Engendering the Guilds: Seamstresses, Tailors and the Clash of Corporate Identities," *French Historical Studies* 23:2 (Spring 2000): 339–71.

19. See the case against three women butchers–Jasmin, Bilaire, and Saint Laurent–taken to the hospital and detention center Salpetrière in March 1728, Archives de la Bastille, ms. 10999, fols. 220–28.

20. See James B. Collins's discussion of urban women in "The Economic Role of Women in Seventeenth-Century France," *French Historical Studies* 16:2 (Autumn, 1989): 436–70.

21. This sampling is taken from sixty-six marriage contracts, including all the catalogued cases that reference butchers in 1751 and 1761, plus several other years in the eighteenth century where information on the bride's father could be drawn.

22. ANF MC ET/LXXXVI/692, November 9, 1761.

23. ANF MC ET/XLIII/429, September 11, 1761.

24. Mercier, *Ibid.*

25. ANF MC ET/LVI/87, September 2, 1761.

26. ANF MC ET/C/603, February 7, 1751.

27. Widow Butcher Troquet was survived by seven children, five whom are butchers, ANF ET/LIV/816, February 27, 1743; Master Butcher Jean Baptiste Aubert survived by five children, three of whom are butchers, ET/CXXI/423, September 4, 1770; Master Butcher Vincent Gosse survived by six children, ET/IV/561, May 12, 1749.

28. Barbara B. Diefendorf, "Women and Property in Ancien Régime France. Theory and Practice in Dauphiné and Paris," *Early Modern Conceptions of Property,* ed. by John Brewer and Susan Staves (London: Routledge Press, 1995), 176.

29. T. K. Ramsay, *Notes sur la coutume de Paris: indiquant les articles encore en force, avec tout le texte de la coutume, à l'exception des articles relatifs aux fiefs et censives, les titres du retrait lignager et de la garde noble et bourgeoise,* 2nd ed., Titre XI (Montreal: C. O. Beauchemin & Valois, 1864), 54.

30. ANF ET/LXI/454, April 23, 1752; ET/XCCI/423, September 4, 1770, date of marriage February 23, 1755; ANF Y11837, March 6, 1723; ET/livres/461, June 3, 1760, date of marriage July 20, 1752; XXVIII/320, February 25, 1751; ET/18/656, February 15, 1761; ET/CX/376, March 24, 1751.

31. Taken from the afterdeath inventory of Jean-François Barré, father of Louise Margueritte, ANF MC ET/LI/184, March 13, 1786. Their marriage is dated September 4, 1781, by Notary Houlet.

32. ANF MC ET/LXVI/532, March 4, 1761. The price of mastership is noted in *Dictionnaire portatif des arts et métiers, contenant en abrégé l'histoire, la description & la police des arts et métiers des fabriques et manufactures de France & des pays étrangers,* 1:208–209.

33. ANF MC ET/LXII/423, January 13, 1751.

34. ANF MC ET/CX/376, March 23, 1751.

35. The fortunes they inherited at the time of their husbands' deaths, at least for Marie Catherine Fleury, hardly outweighed all other interests. At the time of her marriage, she was left with owing 4,087 livres to her children. See the *transaction et obligation,* ANF MC ET/XVII/800, October 26, 1751; her marriage contract to Mergery, ET/LXIX/659, March 11, 1742.

36. ANF MC ET/CX/376, March 24, 1751. Her husband's afterdeath inventory (ET/CX/376, March 12, 1751) reveals much about how she assumes control over the business. Perhaps without any family support in the trade, the need for a male head of household became a priority.

37. ANF MC ET/LXIX/659, March 11, 1742, and Y 11837.

38. ANF Y 9503A, "Baux des étaux de boucherie," 1761.

39. ANF Y 14960, October 25, 1744.

40. ANF Y 14960, October 25, 1744.

41. ANF Y 15227, July 13, 1720.

42. See "Plainte et Information," ANF Y 15227, July 14, 1720, and July 19, 1720.

43. ANF MC XXVIII/320, February 25, 1751. See the subsequent contract attached to the marriage document cited herewith.

44. Eustache Aubert appears in the guild roll call dated March 14, 1747, as one of the junior members (modernes et jeunes). ANF Y 9502.

45. See his father's afterdeath inventory, ANF MC ET/CXXI/423, September 4, 1770.

46. ANF Y 14960, May 23, 1744.

47. ANF Y 14960, May 23, 1744.

48. ANF Y 14960, May 23, 1744.

49. ANF Y 14521, March 29, 1724.

50. ANF Y 14523, August 27 and September 2, 1726; Y 14524, January 5, 1727.

51. This ordonnance appears in an arrêt written by the lieutenant general of police, put forth by the Parlement of Paris on July 13, 1699. The text states, "Que les séparations de biens d'entre les Marchands Bouchers & leurs femmes, ne pourront préjudicier aux Marchands Forains, si elles ne sont publiques avant la vente; & pour cet effet, qu'elles seront inscriptes en un Tableau attaché à un poteau qui sera dressé dans le Marché de Sceaux." ANF G 7/1668–70, fol. 28 bis.

CHAPTER 8

1. ANF MC ET/LXII/423, January 13, 1751.

2. ANF MC ET/LXXXVIII/160, May 18, 1781.

3. This data comes from a survey of afterdeath inventories from the Minutier Central series of master butchers taken over the eighteenth century. Less than 10 percent of master butchers had a negative net worth, 25 percent between 10,001 and 20,000 livres, and another 25 percent from 20,001 to 60,000 livres.

4. Daniel Roche, *The People of Paris,* 77. Kaplan, *The Bakers of Paris,* 343.

5. Butchers, ranked in the first class according to their economic importance, also paid some of the highest dues among the guilds. See Pary, *Guide des corps des marchands et communautés des arts et métiers;* Alfred Franklin, *La vie privée d'autrefois,* 93, 281.

6. This was the cost charged to Jean Louis Savar when he purchased the business from his late aunt, Widow Butcher Boudin. ANF MC ET/LXII/465, November 12, 1761.

7. The inventory of Philippe Boursier assesses these tools at 49 livres. ANF MC ET/CX/376, March 12, 1751; for Pierre Feuchez, his set of tools used in the stall are valued at 48 livres. ANF MC ET/livres/461, June 3, 1760; the notaries for the inventory done at Pierre Carraque's home figure 100 livres. Claude Chevalier's personal knives are worth 30 livres. ANF MC ET/XXXVII/301, March 4, 1761.

8. ANF MC ET/XCIX/460 October 6, 1738; ET/XCI/986, July 7, 1761; ET/CX/376, March 12, 1751.

9. My research has uncovered 138 separate cases for 114 butchers during the eighteenth century. The court reviewed cases for other trades during this period that includes 1 roast meat seller, 16 pork butchers, 3 tanners, 28 leather dressers (*mégisseurs*), and 46 cattle merchants. The majority of butchers (81 of the 138 business failures) came from Paris. The remaining 57 came from butchers from the countryside just outside of Paris and the nearby city of Versailles. See Archives de Paris (AP), series D4B6.

10. More than a third of the inventories (36 percent) neglected to mention any accounts payable for business expenses, which signals a weakness in the reliability of the probate records. These inventories were not included in calculating the average liability.

11. AP D4B5, dos. 2121, September 10, 1770.

12. For example, Charles Denis Tripperet, a merchant butcher who held the greatest amount of commercial liability at the time of his death (72,070 livres) owed 31,822 livres for cattle purchases, had no outstanding loans to the Caisse de Poissy. Needless to say, Tripperet held outstanding balances for forty-six clients in the year of his death that totaled 74,763 livres, giving him a positive net worth. ANF MC ET/LIV/819, November 21, 1743.

13. ANF MC ET/XLVII/134, May 27, 1751.

14. For example, Thomas Barré owed his shepherd, Glovian, 82 livres "for having driven to the fields the sheep that were in Fontenay and to have them herded and other things contained in the mémoire" for the given season. ANF MC ET/LXII/423, January 13, 1751. Pierre Feuchez owed his domestic servant, Marguerite Buffon, her annual salary of 75 livres. Pierre Barré owed the six journeymen he employed to work at his two stalls and melting house the weekly wages they had earned until his death several months into the season. ANF MC ET/XCIX/460, October 6, 1738.

15. Butcher Jacques André Pinparey claimed losses of over 1,500 livres after an illness of nine months. AP D4B6 dos. 3040. Pierre Nicolas Blanvillain and his wife both suffered illnesses, Pierre a relapse that lasted over several months. In all they claimed losses of 6,000 livres in addition to their medical costs of 1,500 livres. AP D4B6 dos. 3950.

16. "Pour leur commerce de boucherie ainsy qu'ils le reconnoissent et en tout contente." ANF MC ET/XLIX/730, April, 7 1761.

17. At present, I have uncovered three: ANF MC ET/XXXVIII/390, August 13, 1751; ET/XVIII/657 March 6, 1761; ET/XLIX/730, April 7, 1761.

18. Philip T. Hoffman, Gilles Postel-Vinay, and Jean-Laurent Rosenthal, "Private Credit Markets in Paris, 1690–1840," *The Journal of Economic History* 52:2 (June 1992): 293–306.

19. ANF MC ET/LXXXIII/1007, July 23, 1751.

20. ANF MC ET/LXIV/370, February 18, 1761.

21. Mercier, *Tableau de Paris,* 1:345.

22. Mercier, *Tableau de Paris,* 1:346.

23. This comes from his book entitled "La Culture des apparences," more plainly translated into English as *The Culture of Clothing: Dress and Fashion in the Ancien Régime* (Cambridge: Cambridge University Press, 1994).

24. Mercier, *Ibid.*

25. ANF MC ET/livres/461, June 3, 1760.

26. See "Registres" AP D4B5.

27. ANF MC ET/LI/1184, March 13, 1786.

28. ANF MC ET/CXXI/423, September 4, 1770.

29. AP D4B6 carton 68, dos. 4464, May 2, 1778.

30. AP D4B6 carton 59, dos. 3811, September 20, 1776.

31. At the time of his death Tripperet had delivered 96,040 pounds of meat since Easter to forty-six clients. ANF MC ET/LIV/819, November 21, 1743.

32. ANF MC ET/LIV/819, November 21, 1743.

33. ANF MC ET/XVII/857, February 6, 1761.

34. ANF MC ET/LXII/423, January 13, 1751; ET/CX/376, March 12, 1751; ET/XVII/857, February 6, 1761; ET/LI/1184, March 13, 1786.

35. ANF MC ET/CX/376, March 13, 1751.

36. AP D4B6, carton 39, dos. 2121, December 10, 1770.

37. AP D4B6, carton 39, dos. 2121, December 10, 1770.

38. This is less than 1 percent of the amount. ANF MC ET/XVII/857, February 6, 1761.

39. ANF MC ET/LI/1184, March 13, 1786.

40. For further details, see Chapter 2. ANF MC ET/XXVI/458, June 16, 1751.

41. ANF MC ET/XLIV/429, October 12, 1758 and ET/LIII/373, June 15, 1761.

42. ANF MC ET/CXXI/423, September 4, 1770.

43. ANF MC ET/XC/405, January 9, 1761.

44. The only exception comes from the inventory of Georges Cousin who sold off his share of a house on rue Jean Beausire in which he owned a fraction along with his siblings. See ANF MC ET/CX/348, December 18, 1738.

45. His title read: "officier en charge de languayeur" a job that entailed inspecting the health of bovine and ovine species before slaughter. ANF MC ET/XCVIII/513, March 17, 1751.

46. ANF MC ET/LXXVII/235, March 24, 1751.

47. ANF MC ET/VI/711, December 30, 1749.

48. Among the thirty-four master butchers inventoried, only sixteen butchers fell into this category.

49. Butcher elder Nicolas Séjourné held rentes that brought 4,936 livres in interest per year. ANF MC ET/XVIII/802, August 12, 1779.

50. ANF MC ET/LIV/819, November 21, 1743.

51. ANF MC ET/XC/405, January 9, 1761.

CONCLUSION

1. Legal theorists and their exponents promoted the corporate system as deeply rooted in nature. "From the first [corporations] of all, which are empires, to the last, which are families," the magistrates of parlement intoned, "men have always united to protect themselves, commanded by superiors or watched over by parents who guarantee the general stability of ensuring the stability of their own groups." The principle of incorporation embraced all of France in a chain whose links led directly to the king. Remonstrances, March 2–4, 1776, in Flammermont, *Remonstrances du Parlement de Paris,* 3:309, 321.

2. Diderot et al., *Encyclopédie,* 9:911, 913 as cited in Kaplan, *The Bakers of Paris,* 656; see, for example, the edict of August 1776, BHVP; Clicquot de Blervache, *Considérations sur le commerce,* 18; Clicquot de Blervache, *Mémoire sur les corps de métier* (Le Haye: n.p., 1758), 13–23; M. J. Auffair, "Le Commerce abandonné à lui-même, ou Suppression des compagnies, sociétés et maîtrises," *Journal de Commerce* (March 1761): 120–24.

3. Jean-Sylvain Bailly, *Mémoires de Bailly,* eds. Berville and Barrière, 3 vols. (Paris: Baudouin Frères, 1822), 2:275–76. See also Kaplan, *La fin des corporations,* 364–71.

4. Kaplan, "Les Corporations, les 'faux ouvriers' et le faubourg Saint-Antoine, au XVIIIe siècle," *Annales: Economies, Sociétés, Civilisations* 43:2 (Mars–Avril 1988): 353–78.

5. Roger Price, *An Economic History of Modern France, 1730–1914* (New York: St. Martin's Press, 1975), 52–53; Jacques Risse, *Histoire de l'élévage français,* ed. Dominique Desjeux and Babacar Sali, Alternatives rurales (Paris: Editions l'Harmattan, 1994), 40–47.

6. George Grantham, "Diffusion of New Husbandry in Northern France, 1815–1840," 311–38.

7. This subject has been recently addressed by Mauro Ambrosoli in his work on the introduction of fodder crops into France, England, and Italy. The book retraces the historical origins in ancient and medieval botany that allowed for a transformation in land potential and farm productivity. Ambrosoli, *The Wild and the Sown. Botany and Agriculture in Western Europe, 1350–1850.*

8. ". . . une augmentation de leur débit d'un cinquième depuis quelques années." BNF Collection Joly de Fleury 460, fol. 191.

9. Daniel Roche, "Between a 'Moral Economy' and a 'Consumer Economy': Clothes and Their Function in the 17th and 18th Centuries," in *Luxury Trades and Consumeries in Ancien Régime Paris: Studies in the History of the Skilled Workforce,* ed. by Robert Fox and Anthony Turner (Aldershot, Hampshire: Ashgate Publishing, Ltd., 1998), 219–29.

Selected Bibliography

Abad, Reynald. *Le grand marché: L'approvisionnement alimentaire de Paris sous l'ancien régime*. Paris: Fayard, 2002.

Adams, Carol J. *The Sexual Politics of Meat: A Feminist-Vegetarian Critical Theory*. New York: Continuum, 1990.

Agulhon, Maurice. "Le sang des bêtes. Le problème de la protection des animaux en France au XIXème siècle." *Romanticisme* 31 (1981): 81–109.

Audoin-Rouzeau, Frédérique. "Eléments nouveaux de l'élevage aux temps modernes." *Cahiers d'histoire* 3–4 (1997): 481–509.

______. "Medieval and Early Modern Butchery: Evidence from the Monastery of La Charité-Sur-Loire (Nievre)." *Food and Foodways* 2 (1987): 31–48.

Bataille, Georges. *Death and Sensuality: A Study of Eroticism and the Taboo*. Salem, NH: Ayer Company Publishers, Inc., 1962.

Bergeron, Louis. "Approvisionnement et consommation à Paris sous le Premier Empire." *Mémoires de la Féderation des sociétés historiques et archeologique de Paris et Ile-de-France* 14 (1963): 197–232.

Bienaymé, Gustave. "La fiscalité alimentaire et gastronomique à Paris." *Journal de la société de statistique de Paris* 31 (1890): 40–60.

Bienaymé, Gustave, and A. de Saint-Julien. *Histoire des droits d'entrée & d'octrois à Paris*. Paris: Paul Dupont, 1887.

Bizet, Louis Charles. *Du commerce de la boucherie et de la charcuterie de Paris*. Paris: Chez Paul Dupont, 1847.

Black, Antony. *Guilds and Civil Society in European Political Thought from the Twelfth Century to the Present*. Ithaca, NY: Cornell University Press, 1984.

Blanchard, Anne, Henri Michel, and Elie Pélaquier, eds. *De l'herbe à table. La viande dans la France méridionale à l'époque moderne, Actes du colloque organisé par le Centre d'Histoire Moderne en 1993*. Montpellier: Université Paul-Valéry Monpellier III, 1994.

Blanchard, Ian. "The Continental European Cattle Trade, 1400–1600." *Economic History Review* 39, no. 3 (1986): 427–60.

Bourde, André J. *The Influence of England on the French Agronomes, 1750–1789*. Cambridge, UK: Cambridge University Press, 1953.

Bourgeon, Jean Louis. "Colbert et les corporations: L'exemple de Paris." *Un nouveau Colbert*. Edited by Roland Mousnier and Michel Antoine. 241–53. Paris: SEDES, 1985.

Braudel, Fernand. *The Structures of Everyday Life: the Limits of the Possible*. Trans. Sian Reynolds [1st US ed.] New York: Harper & Row, 1981.

Braudel, Fernand, and Ernest Labrousse. *Histoire économique et sociale de la France*. Paris: Presses Universitaires de France, 1970.

Brelot, Claude-Isabelle. "Noblesse et animal domestique au XIXe siècle." *Cahiers d'histoire* 3–4 (1997): 639–53.

Brennan, Thomas Edward. *Burgundy to Champagne: The Wine Trade in Early Modern France.* Baltimore: Johns Hopkins University Press, 1997.

______. *Public Drinking and Popular Culture in Eighteenth-Century Paris.* Princeton, NJ: Princeton University Press, 1988.

Brentano, Lujo. *On the History and Development of Gilds and the Origin of Trade-Unions.* New York: B. Franklin, 1969.

Brockliss, L. W. B., and Colin Jones. *The Medical World of Early Modern France.* Oxford: Clarendon Press, 1997.

Bruneel, C. "Sus au monopole des bouchers bruxellois: Le franc marché du vendredi (1771–1787)." *Bijdragen tot de Geschiedenis* 81 (1998): 115–24.

Butel, Paul. "L'économie française au XVIIIe siècle." In *Regards sur L'histoire.* Edited by André Corvisier. Paris: SEDES, 1993.

Campbell, Bruce M. S., and Mark Overton. "A New Perspective on Medieval and Early Modern Agriculture: Six Centuries of Norfolk Farming c. 1250–c. 1850." *Past and Present* 141 (1993): 38–105.

Camporesi, Piero. *Exotic Brew: The Art of Living in the Age of Enlightenment.* Translated by Christopher Woodall. Cambridge, MA: Polity Press, 1994.

______. *Juice of Life: The Symbolic and Magic Significance of Blood.* Translated by Robert R. Barr. New York: Continuum, 1995.

Certeau, Michel de, Pierre Mayol, and Luce Giard. *The Practice of Everyday Life.* Edited by Luce Giard. Minneapolis: University of Minnesota Press, 1998.

Chartier, Roger. *The Cultural Origins of the French Revolution, Bicentennial Reflections on the French Revolution.* Durham, NC: Duke University Press, 1991.

Chaudieu, Georges. *L'evolution corporative de la boucherie.* 2nd ed. Paris: Dunod, 1943.

Chave, René. *Histoire de la boucherie lyonnaise.* Lyon: Imprimerie Nouvelle Lyonnaise, 1952.

Conte, P., and C. Vallet, eds. *Le geste du boucher: Découpe et consommation de la viande de la préhistoire à nos jours.* Limoges: Archéa, 1993.

Coquery, Natacha. *L'hôtel aristocratique: Le marché du luxe à Paris au XVIIIe siècle.* Paris: Publications de la Sorbonne, 1998.

______. "Hôtel, luxe et société de cour: Le marché aristocratique parisien au XVIIIe siècle." *Histoire et mésure* 10, no. 3/4 (1995): 339–69.

Corbin, Alain. *The Foul and the Fragrant: Odor and the French Social Imagination.* Cambridge, MA: Harvard University Press, 1986.

Cornette, Joël. "Les objets de la vie quotidienne. Les inventaires après-décès." *Revue d'histoire moderne et contemporaine* 36, Juillet–Septembre (1989): 464–86.

Couperie, Pierre. "Les marchés de pouvoirie: Viandes et poissons chez les grands au XVIIe siècle." *Annales: ESC* 19 (1964): 467–77.

Crowston, Clare Haru. *Fabricating Women: The Seamstresses of Old Regime France: 1675–1791.* Durham, NC: Duke University Press, 2001.

D'Auriac, Eugène. *Essai historique sur la boucherie de Paris.* Edited by E. Dentu. Paris: Librairie de la société des gens de lettres, 1861.

De Vries, Jan. *The Economy of Europe in an Age of Crisis, 1600–1750.* Cambridge, UK: Cambridge University Press, 1976.

Delahaye, B. *Le commerce de la boucherie à Eu du XIIe au XVIIIe siecle.* EU: Imprimérie du Messager Eudois, 1938.

Delor, Adrien. *La corporation des bouchers à Limoges.* Les Unions de la Paix Sociale; Union du Limousin ed. Limoges: Mme. Dumont, Mme Ducourtieux, 1877.

Desmaze, Charles Adrien. *Les métiers de Paris: D'après les ordonnances du Châtelet, avec les sceaux des artisans.* Genève: Slatkine-Megariotis Reprints, 1975.

Dinges, Martin. "L'hôpital Saint-André de Bordeaux au XVIIe siècle: Objectifs et réalisations de l'assistance municipale." *Annales du Midi* 99, no. 179 (1987): 303–30.

Douglas, Mary. *Food in the Social Order: Studies of Food and Festivities in Three American Communities.* New York: Russell Sage Foundation, 1984.

______. *How Institutions Think. The Frank W. Abrams Lectures.* Syracuse: Syracuse University Press, 1986.

______. *Purity and Danger: An Analysis of Concepts of Pollution and Taboo.* 1966. Reprint, London: Routledge, 1991.

Dulait, André. "Histoire de la boucherie à Bourges." Thèse de doctorat, Ecole Nationale Vétérinaire, 1965.

Duval, Michel. *Le régime seigneurial de la boucherie en Bretagne. Des origines à la fin du XVIe siècle.* Rennes: Imprimerie Bretonne, 1954.

El Ghoul, Fayçal. *La police parisienne dans la seconde moitié du XVIIIe siècle: 1760–1785.* Tunis: Université de Tunis Faculté des Sciences Humaines et Sociales, 1995.

Elias, Norbert. *The Court Society.* Oxford, UK: Blackwell Publishers, 1983.

______. *The History of Manners.* New York: Urizen Books, 1978.

Elias, Norbert, Johan Goudsblom, and Stephen Mennell. *The Norbert Elias Reader: A Biographical Selection.* Oxford, UK: Blackwell Publishers, 1998.

Epstein, Steven. *Wage Labor & Guilds in Medieval Europe.* Chapel Hill: University of North Carolina Press, 1991.

Erickson, Ken C. "Muscle Power and Meat: Rewriting a Story of Progress." In *The Story of Progress.* Edited by Gösta Arvastson and Mats Lindquist, 63–75. Stockholm: Studia Ethnologica Upsalieusia, 1996.

Fajans, Jane. "Exchanging Products: Producing Exchange," *Oceania Monographs* 43. Sydney: University of Sydney, 1993.

______. *They Make Themselves: Work and Play among the Baining of Papua New Guinea.* Chicago: University of Chicago Press, 1997.

Farge, Arlette. *Délinquance et criminalité: Le vol d'aliments à Paris au XVIIIe siècle.* Paris: Plon, 1974.

______. *Fragile Lives: Violence, Power and Solidarity in Eighteenth-Century Paris.* Cambridge, MA: Harvard University Press, 1993.

______. "Signe de vie, risque de mort. Essai sur le sang et la ville au XVIIIe siècle." *Urbi* 2 (1979): xv–xxii.

______. *Subversive Words: Public Opinion in Eighteenth-Century France.* University Park, PA: Pennsylvania State University Press, 1995.

Faure, Alain. *Paris Carême-Prenant. Du Carnaval à Paris aux XIXe siècle 1800–1914.* Paris: Hachette, 1978.

Faure, Edgar. *La disgrâce de Turgot, 12 Mai 1776.* Paris: Gallimard, 1961.

Faure, Olivier. "Le bétail dans la ville au XIXe siècle: Exclusion ou enfermement?" *Cahiers d'histoire* 3–4 (1997): 555–73.

Favier, René. "Taxation et libéralism. Les transformations du marché de la viande à Grenoble au XVIIIe siècle." *Histoire, économie, et société,* no. 4 (1994): 583–604.

Ferguson, James, and Akhil Gupta, ed. *Culture, Power, Place: Explorations in Critical Anthropology.* Durham, NC: Duke University Press, 1997.

Fiddes, Nick. *Meat, a Natural Symbol.* London: Routledge, 1991.

Fischler, Claude. *L'hommivore. Le goût, la cuisine et le corps.* Paris: Editions Odile Jacob, 1990.

Flandrin, Jean Louis. *Chronique de Platine: Pour une gastronomie historique.* Paris: O. Jacob, 1992.

______. *Families in Former Times: Kinship, Household, and Sexuality.* Cambridge, UK: Cambridge University Press, 1979.

______. "Mealtimes in France before the Nineteenth Century." *Food and Foodways* 6, no. 3–4 (1996): 261–82.

Flandrin, Jean-Louis, and Massimo Montanari, eds. *Food: A Culinary History from Antiquity to the Present.* New York: Columbia University Press, 1999.

Forster, Robert. "Obstacles to Agricultural Growth in Eighteenth-Century France." *The American Historical Review* 75, no. 6 (1970): 1600–1615.

Fosseyeux, Marcel. *L'Hôtel-Dieu de Paris au XVIIe et XVIIIe siècle.* Paris: Berger-Levrault et Cie, 1912.

Fox-Genovese, Elizabeth. *The Origins of Physiocracy: Economic Revolution and Social Order in Eighteenth Century France.* Ithaca, NY: Cornell University Press, 1976.

Franklin, Alfred, and Arlette Farge. *La vie privée d'autrefois.* Paris: Perrin, 1973.

Franklin, Alfred, and Émile Levasseur. *Dictionnaire historique des arts, métiers et professions exercés dans Paris depuis le treizième siècle.* Paris: H. Welter, 1906.

Gallier, Alfred. *Histoire de la boucherie caennaise sous l'ancien régime.* Caen: Imprimerie Charles Valin, 1902.

Garden, Maurice. "Bouchers et boucheries de Lyon au XVIIIe siècle." Paper presented at the Congrès National des Sociétés Savantes, Strasbourg, France 1967.

______. *Lyon et les Lyonnais au XVIIIe siècle.* Paris: Société d'edition les belles-lettres, 1970.

Garnier, Bernard. "L'approvisionnement de Paris en moutons, 1780–1820." *Annales de Normandie* 2, May (1990): 83–101.

______. "Les marchés aux bestiaux: Paris et sa banlieue." *Cahiers d'histoire* 3–4 (1997): 575–609.

______. "Viande et bêtes. Variations saisonnières de l'approvisionnement de Paris aux XVIIIe et XIXe siècles." In *La vie, la mort, la foi, le temps. Mélanges offert à Pierre Chaunu,* 147–70. Paris: Presses Universitaires de France, 1993.

Gascar, Pierre. *Les bêtes.* Paris: L'Imaginaire Gallimard, 1978.

______. *Les bouchers. Collection "La magie du métier."* Paris: Delpire, Editions Neuf, 1973.

Gay, M. "L'administration de la capitale entre 1770 et 1789: La tutelle de la royauté et ses limites." *Mémoires de la Fédération des sociétés historiques et archaeologiques de Paris et de l'Ile-de-France* 10 (1959): 181–233.

Geertz, Clifford. *The Interpretation of Cultures; Selected Essays.* New York: Basic Books, 1973.

Giffard, André Edmond Victor. *Droit romain et ancien droit français, les obligations.* 2nd ed. Paris: Dalloz, 1967.

Goubert, Pierre. *Beauvais et le Beauvaisis de 1600 à 1730.* Paris: SEVPEN, 1960.

______. *Louis XIV and Twenty Million Frenchmen.* [1st American ed.]. New York: Pantheon Books, 1970.

Granovetter, Mark. "Economic Action and Social Structure: The Problem of Embeddedness." *American Journal of Sociology* 91, no. 3 (1985): 481–510.

Grantham, George. "The Diffusion of New Husbandry in Northern France, 1815–1840." *The Journal of Economic History* 38, no. 2 (1978): 311–37.

Grassby, R. B. "Social Status and Commercial Enterprise under Louis XIV." *Economic History Review* 13, no. 1 (1960): 19–38.

Gravereau, Andre. *Histoire de la Caisse de Poissy.* Paris: Imprimerie Henri Maillet, 1953.

Grenier, Jean-Yves. "Consommation et marché au XVIIIe siecle." *Histoire et mésure* X, no. 3/4 (1995): 371–80.

______. *L'économie d'Ancien Régime: Un monde de l'échange et de l'incertitude.* Paris: A. Michel, 1996.

Gross, Charles. *The Gild Merchant; a Contribution to British Municipal History.* Oxford, UK: Oxford University Press, 1964.

Gudeman, Stephen. *Economics as Culture: Models and Metaphors of Livelihood.* London: Routledge & K. Paul, 1986.

Guenzi, Alberto, Paola Massa, and Fausto Piola Caselli. *Guilds, Markets, and Work Regulations in Italy, XVI–XIX Centuries.* Aldershot, Hampshire, UK: Ashgate, 1998.

Guigou, Jean-Louis. "Le sol et l'espace: des énigmes pour les économistes." *L'Espace géographique* 1 (1980): 17–28.

Gutmann, Myron P. *Toward the Modern Economy: Early Industry in Europe, 1500–1800.* Philadelphia: Temple University Press, 1988.

Hardwick, Julie. "Seeking Separations: Gender, Marriages, and Household Economies in Early Modern France." *French Historical Studies* 21, no. 1 (1998): 157–80.

Hauser, Henri. *Travailleurs et marchands dans l'ancienne France.* Paris: F. Alcan, 1920.

Hoffman, Philip T. *Growth in a Traditional Society: The French Countryside, 1450–1815.* Princeton: Princeton University Press, 1996.

Horowitz, Roger, Jeffrey M. Pilcher, and Sydney Watts. "Meat for the Multitudes: Market Culture in Paris, New York City, and Mexico City over the Long Nineteenth Century." *The American Historical Review* 100, no. 4 (October 2004): 1055–83.

Husson, Armand. *Les consommations de Paris.* Paris: Hachette, 1875.

Jamet, Jean. "Les bouchers du Châtelet à la fin du Moyen age (1420–1500)." Thèse de doctorat, Ecole Nationale Veterinaire à Alfort, 1966.

Jones, Colin. *The Charitable Imperative: Hospitals and Nursing in Ancien Régime and Revolutionary France.* London: Routledge, 1989.

Jones, E. L. "Agricultural Origins of Industry." *Past and Present* 40 (1968): 58–71.

Joubert, Laurent. *Popular Errors.* Tuscaloosa: University of Alabama Press, 1989.

Kaplan, Steven L. *The Bakers of Paris and the Bread Question, 1700–1775.* Durham, NC: Duke University Press, 1996.

______. *Bread, Politics, and Political Economy in the Reign of Louis XV.* The Hague: Martinus Nijhoff, 1976.

______. "Les corporations, les 'faux ouvriers' et le faubourg Saint-Antoine au XVIIIe siècle." *Annales: Economies, Sociétés, Civilisations* 43, no. 2 (1988): 353–78.

______. *Provisioning Paris: Merchants and Millers in the Grain and Flour Trade During the Eighteenth Century.* Ithaca, NY: Cornell University Press, 1984.

______. "The State and the Problem of Dearth in Eighteenth-Century France: The Crisis of 1738–41 in Paris." *Food and Foodways* 4, no. 2 (1990): 111–41.

Kaplan, Steven L., and Cynthia J. Koepp, eds. *Work in France: Representations, Meaning, Organization, and Practice.* Ithaca, NY: Cornell University Press, 1986.

Kaplow, Jeffry. *The Names of Kings: The Parisian Laboring Poor in the Eighteenth Century.* New York: Basic Books, 1972.

Koepp, Cynthia Joan. "The Order of Work: Ideas, Attitudes and Representations in Eighteenth-Century France." Ph.D. diss., Cornell University, 1992.

Kriedte, Peter. "The Origins, the Agrarian Context and the Conditions in the World Market." In *Industrialization before Industrialization: Rural Industry in the Genesis of Capitalism,* edited by Hans Medick, Peter Kreidte, and Jurgen Schlumbohm. Cambridge, UK: Cambridge University Press, 1981.

La Varenne, François Pierre de, Jean Louis Flandrin, Philip Hyman, and Mary Hyman. *Le cuisinier françois.* Paris: Montalba, 1983.

Labrousse, Ernest. *Esquisse du mouvement des prix et des revenus en France au XVIIIe siècle.* Paris: Librairie Dalloz, 1933.

Labrousse, Ernest, Pierre Léon, Pierre Goubert, Jean Bouvier, Charles Carrière, Paul Harsin. *Histoire economique et sociale de la France.* Vol. II. Paris: Presses Universitaires de France, 1970.

Lachiver, Marcel. "L'approvisionnement de Paris en viande au XVIIIe siècle." In *La France d'ancien regime.* Edited by Pierre Goubert. Toulouse: Editions Privat, 1984: 345–54.

Lanza, Janine Marie. "Family Making and Family Breaking: Widows in Early Modern France." Ph.D. diss., Cornell University, 1996.

Laslett, Peter. "The European Family and Early Industrialization." In *Europe and the Rise of Capitalism,* edited by John H. Hall, Jean Baechler, and Michael Mann. Oxford, UK: Blackwell Publishers, 1988: 234–41.

Lavergne, Léonce de. *La société d'agriculture de Paris.* Paris: n.p., 1859.

Le Charpentier, H. *Essai historique sur l'ancienne corporation des bouchers de Pontoise.* Pontoise: Imprimerie Amédée Paris, 1880.

Le Roy Ladurie, Emmanuel. *The Ancien Régime: A History of France, 1610–1774, A History of France.* Oxford, UK: Blackwell Publishers, 1996.

______. *Carnival in Romans.* New York: G. Braziller, 1979.

______. *Times of Feast, Times of Famine: A History of Climate since the Year 1000.* Garden City, NY: Doubleday, 1971.

Le Roy Ladurie, Emmanuel, and Joseph Goy. *Tithe and Agrarian History from the Fourteenth to the Nineteenth Centuries: An Essay in Comparative History.* Cambridge, UK: Cambridge University Press; Paris: Editions de la Maison des Sciences de l'Homme, 1982.

Lespinasse, René de. *Les métiers et corporations de la ville de Paris XIVe–XVIIIe siècle.* Paris: Impriměrie Nationale, 1886.

Levasseur, Emile. *Histoire des classes ouvrières et de l'industrie en France avant 1789.* Genève: Slatkine, 1981.

Luckett, Thomas Manley. "Credit and Commercial Society in France, 1740–1789." Ph.D. diss., Princeton University, 1992.

Lüdtke, Alf. *The History of Everyday Life: Reconstructing Historical Experiences and Ways of Life, Princeton Studies in Culture/Power/History.* Princeton: Princeton University Press, 1995.

Lüthy, Herbert. *La banque protestante en France de la Révocation de L'Édit de Nantes à la Révolution.* 2 vols. Paris: SEVPEN, 1959.

Lynn, John A. *Giant of the Grand Siècle: The French Army, 1610–1715.* Cambridge, UK: Cambridge University Press, 1997.

Mackenney, Richard. *Tradesmen and Traders: The World of the Guilds in Venice and Europe, c. 1250–c. 1650.* London: Croom Helm, 1987.

Maire, Catherine, and Société des Amis de Port-Royal (France). *Jansénisme et révolution: Actes du colloque de Versailles tenu au Palais des Congrès les 13 et 14 Octobre 1989, Chroniques De Port-Royal; No 39.* Paris: Chroniques de Port-Royal: Bibliothèque Mazarine, 1990.

Maire, Catherine-Laurence. *Les convulsionnaires de Saint-Médard: Miracles, convulsions et prophéties à Paris au XVIIIe siècle.* Paris: Julliard, 1985.

Margairaz, Dominique. *Foires et marchés dans la France préindustrielle. Studies in History and the Social Sciences,* 33. Paris: Ecole des Hautes Etudes en Sciences Sociales, 1988.

Marion, Rene S. "The Dames de la Halle: Community and Authority in Early Modern Paris." Ph.D. diss., Johns Hopkins University, 1994.

Martin Saint-Léon, Étienne. *Histoire des corporations de métiers.* New York: Arno Press, 1975.

Martin Saint-Léon, Étienne, and Émile Coornaert. *Histoire des corporations de métiers depuis leurs origines jusqu'à leur suppression en 1791.* 4th ed. Paris: Presses Universitaires de France, 1941.

Mauss, Marcel. *The Gift: The Form and Reason for Exchange in Archaic Societies.* London: Routledge, 1990.

McCollim, Gary Bruce. "The Formation of Fiscal Policy in the Reign of Louis XIV: The Example of Nicolas Desmaretz, Controller General of Finances (1708–1715)." Ph.D. diss., Ohio State University, 1979.

Medick, Hans. "The Proto-Industrial Family Economy." In *Industrialization before Industrialization: Rural Industry in the Genesis of Capitalism.* Edited by Hans Medick, Peter Kreidte, and Jurgen Schlumbohm. Cambridge, UK: Cambridge University Press, 1981.

Meek, Ronald L. *The Economics of Physiocracy: Essays and Translations.* Cambridge, MA: Harvard University Press, 1963.

Mendels, Franklin. "Proto-Industrialization: The First Phase of the Industrialization Process." *Journal of Economic History* 32 (1972): 241–61.

Ménétra, Jacques-Louis. *Journal of My Life.* Edited by Daniel Roche. Translated by Arthur Goldhammer. New York: Columbia University Press, 1986.

Menon. *La cuisinière bourgeoise: reproduction de l'edition de 1774.* n.p.: Temps Actuels, 1981.

Miller, Judith A. *Mastering the Market: The State and the Grain Trade in Northern France, 1700–1860.* Cambridge: Cambridge University Press, 1999.

Minard, Philippe. *La fortune du colbertisme: État et industrie dans la France des lumières.* Paris: Fayard, 1998.

Mokyr, Joel. "Demand vs. Supply in the Industrial Revolution." *Journal of Economic History* 37 (1977): 981–1005.

Montanari, Massimo. *The Culture of Food.* Oxford, UK: Blackwell Publishers, 1994.

Moriceau, Jean-Marc. *Les fermiers de l'Ile-de-France: L'ascension d'un patronat agricole (XVe–XVIIIe siècle).* Paris: Fayard, 1994.

______. "Un facteur de progrès agricole au centre du bassin parisien: l'équipement des grandes exploitations de L'ile-de-France du XVIe au début du XIXe siècle d'après les inventaires de fermiers." Paper presented at the actes du séminaire tenu dans le cadre du 9ème Congrès Internationale d'Histoire Economique de Berne, Louvain-la-Neuve, 1988.

Morière, Henri. *Le métier de boucher.* Paris: Librairie J-B Ballière et Fils, 1950.

Morin, Alfred. "Vieilles maisons, vieilles enseignes troyennes." In *Extrait De L'almanach De L'est-Eclair,* 2–4, 1958.

Muchembled, Robert. *L'invention de l'homme moderne: Culture et sensibilités en France du XVe au XVIIIe siècle.* Paris: Hachette, 1994.

______. *Popular Culture and Elite Culture in France, 1400–1750.* Baton Rouge: Louisiana State University Press, 1985.

Ogilvie, Sheilagh C. *State Corporatism and Proto-Industry: The Württemberg Black Forest, 1580–1797.* Cambridge, UK: Cambridge University Press, 1997.

Olivier-Martin, François. *L'organisation corporative de la France d'ancien régime.* Paris: Recueil Sirey, 1938.

Paillat, M., ed. *Le mangeur et l'animal. Mutations de l'élevage et de la consommation.* Paris: Autrement, 1997.

Parain, Charles. "The Evolution of Agricultural Technique." In *The Cambridge Economic History of Europe.* Cambridge, UK: Cambridge University Press, 1966: 170–79.

Pardailhé-Galabrun, Annik. *The Birth of Intimacy: Privacy and Domestic Life in Early Modern Paris.* Translated by Jocelyn Phelps. Philadelphia: University of Pennsylvania Press, 1988.

Paris le jour, Paris la nuit. Edited by Michel Delon and Daniel Baruch. Paris: R. Laffont, 1990.

Perjés, G. "Army Provisioning, Logistics and Strategy in the Second Half of the 17th Century." *Acta Historica Academiae Scientiarum Hungaricae* 16 (1970): 1–52.

Perrot, Jean-Claude. *Genèse d'une ville moderne: Caen au XVIIIe siècle.* Paris: Mouton, 1975.

______. *Une histoire intellectuelle de l'économie politique: XVIIe–XVIIIe siècle civilisations et sociétés* 85. Paris: Editions de l'École des Hautes Etudes en Sciences Sociales, 1992.

Philippe, Robert. "Une opération pilote: L'étude du ravitaillement de Paris au temps de Lavoisier." *Annales: Economie, Société, Civilisation* 16 (1961): 564–68.

Piuz, Anne-Marie. "Le marché du bétail et la consommation de la viande à Genève au XVIIIe siècle." *Annales: Economies, Sociétés, Civilisations,* Mai–Juin (1975): 575–83.

Postel-Vinay, Gilles. *La terre et l'argent: l'agriculture et le crédit en France du XVIIIe au début du XXe siècle, L'évolution de L'humanité.* Paris: A. Michel, 1998.

Pundt, Alfred G. "French Agriculture and the Industrial Crisis of 1788." *The Journal of Political Economy* 49, no. 6 (1941): 849–74.

Quesnay, François. *Tableau èconomique des physiocrates.* Paris: Calmann-Lévy, 1969.
Quinlan, Michael. *Hope Amidst Hard Times: Working Class Organisation in Tasmania 1830–1850.* Kensington, NSW, Australia: Industrial Relations Research Centre University of New South Wales, 1986.
Ramsay, T. K. *Notes sur la coutume de Paris: Indiquant les articles encore en force, avec tout le texte de la coutume, a l'exception des articles relatifs aux fiefs et censives, les titres du retrait lignager et de la garde noble et bourgeoise.* 2nd ed. Montréal: C. O. Beauchemin & Valois, 1864.
Ranum, Orest, and Robert Forster, ed. *Medicine and Society in France: Selections from the Annales: Economies, Sociétés, Civilisations.* Vol. 6. Baltimore: Johns Hopkins University Press, 1980.
Rappaport, Steve. *Worlds within Worlds: Structures of Life in Sixteenth-Century London.* Cambridge, UK: Cambridge University Press, 1989.
Revel, Jacques. *Un festin de paroles. Histoire littéraire de la sensibilité gastronomique de l'antiquité à nos jours.* 2nd ed. Paris: Hachette, 1982.
Rifkin, Jeremy. *Beyond Beef: The Rise and Fall of the Cattle Culture.* New York: Dutton, 1992.
Risse, Jacques. *Histoire de l'élévage français.* Edited by Dominique Desjeux and Babacar Sali. Alternatives rurales. Paris: Editions l'Harmattan, 1994.
Roche, Daniel. "Between a 'Moral Economy' and a 'Consumer Economy': Clothes and Their Function in the 17th and 18th Centuries." In *Luxury Trades and Consumeries in Ancien Régime Paris: Studies in the History of the Skilled Workforce.* Edited by Robert Fox and Anthony Turner. Aldershot, Hampshire: Ashgate Publishing Ltd., 1998: 219–29.
______. "Cuisine et alimentation populaire à Paris." *Dix-Huitième Siècle* 15, no. révue annuelle (1983): 7–18.
______. *France in the Enlightenment.* Cambridge, MA: Harvard University Press, 1998.
______. *Histoire des choses banales. Naissance de la Consommation dans les Sociétés Traditionnelles (XVIIe–XIXe siècle).* Paris: Fayard, 1997.
______. *The People of Paris: An Essay in Popular Culture in the 18th Century.* Translated by Marie Evans. Berkeley: University of California Press, 1987.
Roover, Raymond de. "The Concept of the Just Price: Theory and Economic Policy." *Journal of Economic History* 18 (1958): 418–34.
Roy, Jean-Michel. "Les marchés alimentaires parisiens du XIVe au XVIIIe siècle: textes et documents." *Mémoires de Paris et L'Ile-de-France* 44 (1992): 77–132.
Salvetti, Francoise. *Le boucher, métiers d'hier et d'aujourd'hui.* Paris: Berger-Levrault, 1980.
______. *Rue des bouchers: Les métiers de la viande à travers les ages.* 2nd ed. Paris: Editions Hermé, 1986.
Segurel, Marie-Claude. "Les bouchers bordelais dans la deuxième moitié du 18ème siècle." T.E.R., Université de Bordeaux III, 1971.
Servais, P. "Ustensiles de cuisine et vaisselle dans les campagnes du pays de Herve aux XVIIe et XVIIIe siècles." Paper presented at the Actes du séminaire tenu dans le cadre du 9ème Congrès Internationale d'Histoire Economique de Berne, Louvain-la-Neuve, 1988.
Shepherd, Robert Perry. *Turgot and the Six Edicts.* [1st AMS ed.] New York: AMS Press, 1970.

Smail, Daniel Lord. "Démanteler le patrimoine. Les femmes et les biens dans la marseille médiévale." *Annales: Histoire et Sciences Sociales* 2, no. mars–avril (1997): 343–68.

Spang, Rebecca Lee. *The Invention of the Restaurant: Paris and Modern Gastronomic Culture.* Cambridge, MA: Harvard University Press, 2000.

Spencer, Colin. *The Heretic's Feast: A History of Vegetarianism.* London: Fourth Estate, 1993.

Super, John C., and Thomas C. Wright. *Food, Politics, and Society in Latin America.* Lincoln: University of Nebraska Press, 1985.

Thompson, E. P. "The Moral Economy of the English Crown in the Eighteenth Century." *Past and Present* 50 (1971): 76–136.

Thrupp, Sylvia. "The Gilds." In *Economic Organization and Policies in the Middle Ages.* Edited by E. E. Rich, M. M. Postan, and Edward Miller. Cambridge, UK: Cambridge University Press, 1963.

Truant, Cynthia Maria. *The Rites of Labor: Brotherhoods of Compagnonnage in Old and New Regime France.* Ithaca, NY: Cornell University Press, 1994.

Veblen, Thorstein. *The Theory of the Leisure Class.* Boston: Houghton Mifflin, 1973.

Vial, Robert. *Moeurs, santé et maladies en 1789.* Paris: Londreys, 1989.

Vialles, Noélie. "Etude anthropologique des abbatoirs des pays de l'Adour." Recherche financée par la mission du Patrimoine ethnologique, 1986.

______. "Le sang et la chair. Les abattoirs des pays de l'adour." In *Collection: Ethnologie de la France.* Paris: Editions de la Maison des sciences de l'homme, 1987.

Vidalenc, Jean. "L'approvisionnement de Paris en viande sous l'ancien régime." *Révue d'histoire économique et sociale* 30, no. 2 (1952): 116–32.

______. "Une industrie alimentaire à Paris au XVIIIe siècle: la préparation et la vente des tripes et abats." *Mémoires de la Fédération des sociétés historiques et archaeologiques de Paris et de l'Ile-de-France* 1 (1949): 279–95.

Vigarello, Georges. *Concepts of Cleanliness: Changing Attitudes in France since the Middle Ages.* Translated by Jean Birrell. Cambridge, UK: Cambridge University Press, 1988.

Vincent, Jean-Christophe. "La mise à mort des animaux de boucherie: un révélateur des sensibilités à l'égard des bêtes à l'époque contemporaine." *Cahiers d'histoire* 3–4 (1997): 613–37.

Warde, Alan. *Consumption, Food, and Taste: Culinary Antinomies and Commodity Culture.* London: Sage Publications, 1997.

Watts, Sydney. "Boucherie et hygiène à Paris au XVIIIe siècle." *Revue d'histoire moderne et contemporaine* 51, no. 3 (July–Sept. 2004): 77–103.

Weise, Heinz. "Die Fleischversorgung der Nordwesteuropäischen Grossstädte vom XV. bis XIX. Jahrhundert unter Besonderer Berücksichtigung des Interterritorialen Rinderhandels." *Jahrbücher für Nationalökonomie une Statistik* 179 (1966): 125–39.

Weulersse, Georges. *La physiocratie sous les Ministères de Turgot et de Necker (1774–1781).* Paris: Presses Universitaires de France, 1950.

______. *Le mouvement physiocratique en France (De 1756 À 1770).* Paris: F. Alcan, 1910.

Weulersse, Georges, and Corinne Beutler. *La physiocratie à l'aube de la révolution, 1781–1792.* Paris: Editions de l'Ecole des Hautes Études en Sciences Sociales, 1985.

Williams, Alan. *The Police of Paris, 1718–1789.* Baton Rouge: Louisiana State University Press, 1979.

Wood, Roy C. *The Sociology of the Meal.* Edinburgh: Edinburgh University Press Ltd., 1995.

Woolf, S. J. *Domestic Strategies: Work and Family in France and Italy, 1600–1800.* Cambridge, UK: Cambridge University Press; Paris: Editions de la Maison des Sciences de l'Homme, 1991.

Young, Arthur. *Voyages en France dans les années 1787, 1788, 1789.* Paris: Union générale d'éditions, 1988.

Zeller, Olivier. "L'animal dans la Ville d'ancien régime: Quelques réflexions." *Cahiers d'histoire* 3–4 (1997): 543–54.

Index

www.ingramcontent.com/pod-product-compliance
Lightning Source LLC
Chambersburg PA
CBHW071248180926
51613CB00002B/168
* 9 7 8 1 5 8 0 4 6 2 1 1 2 *